Sidney
Crosby

Sidney Crosby

Taking the Game by Storm

Gare Joyce

Fitzhenry & Whiteside

Sidney Crosby: Taking The Game By Storm
Copyright © 2005 Gare Joyce

Fitzhenry and Whiteside Limited
195 Allstate Parkway
Markham, Ontario L3R 4T8

In the United States:
311 Washington Street,
Brighton, Massachusetts 02135

www.fitzhenry.ca godwit@fitzhenry.ca

Fitzhenry & Whiteside acknowledges with thanks the Canada Council for the Arts, and the
Ontario Arts Council for their support of our publishing program. We acknowledge the financial
support of the Government of Canada through the Book Publishing Industry Development
Program (BPIDP) for our publishing activities.

ONTARIO ARTS COUNCIL
CONSEIL DES ARTS DE L'ONTARIO

Canada Council Conseil des Arts
for the Arts du Canada

Library and Archives Canada Cataloguing in Publication

Joyce, Gare
Sidney Crosby : taking the game by storm / Gare Joyce.
ISBN 1-55041-253-1
1. Crosby, Sidney, 1987- 2. Hockey players—Canada—Biography.
I. Title.
GV848.5.C76J69 2005   796.962'092   C2005-903960-4

United States Cataloguing-in-Publication Data

Joyce, Gare.
Sidney Crosby : taking the game by storm / Gare Joyce
[256] p. : cm.
ISBN 1-55041-253-1
1. Crosby, Sidney, 1987-. 2. Hockey players—Canada—Biography. I. Title.
796.962/092 22   GV848.5C76J69 2005

Cover and interior design by Karen Petherick, Intuitive Design International Ltd.
All insert photographs courtesy of Dan Hamilton / Vantage Point
Printed and bound in Canada

3 5 7 9 10 8 6 4

Play it like you live.
Clarence "Gatemouth" Brown

We'd tell him we'll draft a fat kid in the second round.
— A National Hockey League general manager, when asked what he'd do if Sidney Crosby was a cannibal.

In the spring of 2003 I convinced Derek Finkle of *Toro Magazine* to send me to the Czech Republic to cover the exploits of soon-to-be 16-year-old Sidney Crosby. His faith in the story was the seed of this book.

Some months later I convinced Mark Giles at *ESPN The Magazine* of the merits of the hockey wunderkind and he dispatched me to Rimouski, Quebec, which was delightful, not daunting, and to Grand Forks, North Dakota, which was delightful, and bone chilling. That helped this book take root.

Other material in this book—its soil, water and sunlight—came together in researching stories about Sidney Crosby for other publications, among them *espn.com, The Christian Science Monitor* and *Maclean's.* I'd like to thank Sherry Skalko, Dave Hauck and James Deacon for their interest and support.

I'd also like to thank the many people who helped me in various and sundry ways: junior hockey's top photographer Dan Hamilton, the most dangerous driver not on the NASCAR circuit; Mark LaChappelle, the dean of Quebec's junior hockey reporters; my cohorts at *ESPN The Magazine,* E.J. Hradek and Lindsay Berra; Brad Pascall, Scott Salmond and Bob Nicholson of Hockey Canada; Aaron Wherry of the Canadian Hockey League and Yannick Dumais of the Oceanic for saving me spots in sold-out arenas; Bobby Smith, these days the owner and proprietor of the Halifax Mooseheads; the fraternity of NHL scouts, notably Mike Sands, Daniel Doré, Craig Button, Tod Button, Bob Atrill, Ted Hampson, Lorne Davis, Barry Trapp and Tim Bernhardt among others.

Thanks are also extended to my editor at Fitzhenry & Whiteside, Richard Dionne, for his confidence in this book.

I'd like to thank my partner Susan Bourette and my daughters Ellen and Laura for their patience and tolerance and time that I'll set about making up.

"He can stay on the third floor with the kids ..."

On a steamy afternoon in July 2005 in New York, the National Hockey League announced that the Board of Governors had ratified a collective agreement with the NHL Players Association, thereby ending the longest labour standoff in the history of North American professional sport. The 600-page collective agreement was supposed to assure the viability of franchises, no small concern after three teams listed toward bankruptcy in recent seasons. It was also drawn up to give teams in small markets a chance to compete against the established revenue giants.

At the same time, the league also announced a radical overhaul of the rules of play with the expressed intent of injecting offence and entertainment into a game that had seen scoring plummet for more than a decade. As scoring plunged so too did the league's cachet. Ten years ago the NHL hoped to rival the NBA for U.S. profile. By 2004 the NHL was getting lapped by NASCAR and competed with arena football for media attention. The game needed big fixes and league bosses thought they had them. And the rewritten rulebook was supposed to make for quick strikes and constant action, quelling criticism that NHL hockey was trench warfare, chess on ice.

SIDNEY CROSBY

The stakes were almost beyond comprehension—league revenues were set at just under two billion dollars, with billions more invested in franchises; hundreds of players' jobs were saved along with thousands more associated with the game. These were landmark developments, historic events.

But on this day, the collective agreement and rule changes were not the biggest news in sports. Or even in hockey.

No, incredibly, the foundation of the industry and the look of the game took a back seat to one player, still a boy, age 17, who sat in a living room in Cole Harbour, Nova Scotia. With a black baseball cap pulled low to eyebrow level and a t-shirt bearing the logo of Reebok's new line of hockey equipment, Sidney Crosby impassively watched news coverage of the NHL press conferences. Every few minutes he was able to watch himself watching the news coverage, because a camera crew had joined the Crosby family in their living room. He did his best to pretend that he didn't notice the camera when it zoomed in on him. He did his best to appear like he didn't mind the intrusion. He did his best and he almost pulled it off.

It's not fair to say that the NHL's announcements were glossed over by the sports networks and reporters covering the press conference, because really it was a case of making official what everyone knew was coming. Everyone knew the league governors were delighted with their deal. That news emerged over the previous days. Everyone knew the league had been brainstorming and experimenting with rule changes. That had been in the works for months.

Sidney Crosby, though, had put the game on notice three years ago. Ever since, the buzz about him grew louder and louder. The Canadian media started tracking Crosby at age 14, when he was the star of the nation's top tournament for midget-aged players. The U.S. media picked up the chase back in the fall of 2003, when he was playing junior hockey in small-town Quebec and turning into something more than an overnight sensation, something like an instant legend. And over the course of the 2004–05 season, when NHL arenas remained locked and dark, when the labour impasse became sport's longest-running staring contest, Crosby wasn't just the biggest news in junior hockey, but for long stretches the *only* news in hockey. By the time he wound up his career in the Quebec junior league, Sidney Crosby was undoubtedly the most famous teenager in the history of the game. He was first touted as the next great player. If that pressure wasn't great enough, he was by July of 2005 being touted as the boy who could save a deeply troubled league.

There was one simple reason that Crosby eclipsed the new collective agreement and the rewritten rules of play: though he was certain to play in the new NHL that fall, nobody knew where. What's more, every team in the league had a chance of landing the greatest hockey prospect in a generation. In other years, only the also-rans with the worst regular-season records had a shot at landing the first overall selection in the entry draft—a lottery of the teams that had missed the playoffs was used to set the draft order. But because of the lost NHL season, because the new economics of the league made all results from previous seasons almost moot and because of intense lobbying by owners and general managers, a league-wide lottery would be staged. Behind closed doors and under the watchful eye of witnesses from an accounting firm, a bingo-hall tumbler churned ping-pong balls with team logos. The league's usual powerhouses had a ball each, its mediocrities two each, and its four worst non-contenders three each. The first pick in the draft would go to the team whose ball rolled down the chute first. Nothing ordained. Nothing planned. Just chance. Dumb luck.

In a conference room at the Sheraton in New York, representatives from the NHL's 30 teams gathered for the announcement of the draft order, a countdown from the 30th pick overall to the first. The bingo tumbler had done its work. This was the official announcement. The suspense in the room in New York was crushing; and in Halifax equally so. When their teams' slots were announced from 30th to 3rd, hard-assed executives and general managers tried not to look disappointed. Most failed. All had entertained thoughts of what Crosby could do for their teams on the ice and in the marketplace. And when the New York Rangers were called at No. 15, no doubt some league executives' hearts sank as their dreams of rolling Crosby down Madison Avenue evaporated.

In the end it came down to two teams.

The Mighty Ducks of Anaheim well represented the NHL in

transition—they had a new owner, a new general manager, no coach under contract and a team name change in the works. The Mighty Ducks had been for sale for two full years and former owner, Disney, had been willing to listen to offers before that. They routinely missed the playoffs, but only had two balls in the lottery tumbler because they had not only made the playoffs in 2003, but had also come within one win of a Stanley Cup championship.

The Pittsburgh Penguins well represented the NHL in crisis—they had won Stanley Cups, gone through bankruptcy, and emerged with an owner who had been its largest creditor, and also, its playing legend. The Pens had also been crippled financially by the league's oldest and most outdated arena. In fact, rumours circulated for years that the team was relocating, most often with Portland the destination. The Penguins had three balls in the tumbler, thus making them about a 15-to-1 shot to come away with the top pick at the start of the day.

When at last Commissioner Gary Bettman opened the envelope and announced that Pittsburgh had won the right to draft first overall, Penguins governor Ken Sawyer looked happy enough to cry. Sawyer shook hands with Anaheim's general manager, Brian Burke, and was then rushed in front of television cameras where he was almost too excited to speak. He did confirm the obvious, that his team would select Crosby and wasn't about to entertain offers for the Penguins' first overall pick.

The franchise's owner, the team's captain and the league's only active member of the Hall of Fame, Mario Lemieux, wasn't in attendance in New York, nor was he even watching the lottery announcement on television—he was taking his daughter to a doctor's appointment. He got news of the Penguins' good fortune over a cellphone. The call came from his close friend from Quebec junior hockey days, Pat Brisson, an IMG agent and Sidney Crosby's representative.

Mario Lemieux was arguably the most talented player who had ever laced on skates, yet he often seemed embarrassed about showing enthusiasm for the game. His family, golf, his wine cellar: he could show enthusiasm for these things. But the game that he could dominate at will: at times he seemed to disdain it. When Pittsburgh drafted the Montreal native first overall at the Forum in 1984, he listened to the applause from the stands, but refused to come down to the stage to put on the Penguins' sweater as tradition warranted. "They don't want me badly enough," he said.

For many years it seemed he was hostile on his worst days, ambivalent on his best. When he battled back injuries and had beaten Hodgkin's disease, he stayed away from the arena for months at a time. When he retired from the game in 1997, he maintained that he was fed up with being mugged on the ice, but seemed just as tired of the media inconveniencing him. And he also seemed intent on staying away from the arena until the Penguins franchise—which still owed him millions in deferred salary—filed for bankruptcy protection in the summer of 1999. The then-retired star came up with a reorganization plan that made him owner, chairman of the board, CEO and president.

Only when he returned to the game in December of 2000 did Lemieux adopt a positive outlook, though skeptics said the new attitude was a by-product of his ownership interest in the franchise. And even after he led Canadian teams to victories at the Olympics in 2002 and the World Cup in the fall of 2004, his willingness to play on at age 40 and beyond was an open question. His absence from the 2005 draft lottery suggested he might be prepared to divest himself of the Penguins' franchise altogether and look at life after hockey.

And yet you could hear the joy in Mario Lemieux's voice when his call was patched into the televised broadcast of the draft. He seemed positively boyish in his enthusiasm for the game, for the team and, yes, for Crosby. It was fairer to describe this enthusiasm as new, rather than renewed. There was no question about Lemieux wanting Crosby bad enough.

Lemieux was asked if his future teammate faced more pressure as a first overall pick today than he did back in 1984. It sure looked that way from the images broadcast out of the Crosby home while the commissioner read out the results of the lottery. "There's always a lot of pressure on the first pick, but he's always (put) pressure on himself," Lemieux said. "He's used to it. It's part of the game. He's been able to take his game to another level when he's had to."

Lemieux could have made an appeal for patience with Crosby. He could have pointed out that other great young talents needed time to mature and develop—whole seasons' worth of dues-paying and hard work. But no, Lemieux didn't do anything to ease the pressure that Crosby was going to feel as the first pick in the draft and a boy trying to compete with the best players in the world. No, he seemed set on compounding it. Lemieux had scored his first NHL goal with his first shot on his first shift in his first game. He seemed to be expecting Crosby to deliver bigger things even faster.

First Lemieux predicted that the Penguins had "a chance to win right away" with the addition of Crosby. It seemed like a bold call. After all, the 2003–2004 Penguins had won only 23 of 82 games, scoring a league-worst 190 times and giving up 303 goals.

Then Lemieux upped the ante, floating out his hope that Crosby might just be the catalyst to prompt the city of Pittsburgh to build the Pens a new arena, like it did for the Steelers and the Pirates. "This changes the whole thing. (He'll) be able to help us get a new building—that's always been my goal."

Lemieux also suggested that the new NHL was tailor-made for both Crosby's skills and his own—"the stretch pass is going to be part of the game ... we'll have a few set plays." The greatest talent to come along in the '80s meeting up with the shining prospect of the new millennium. Lemieux finding Crosby with long, searching passes—and vice versa. It was the stuff to give opposing coaches and players nightmares.

Lemieux made it clear that he hadn't forgotten that it was a 17-year-old he was talking about and not a 30-year-old All-Star with Hall of Fame credentials—a kid who had yet to play in an NHL arena, a kid who had never visited Pittsburgh or a lot of other cities on the NHL circuit. Sure, there'd be an orientation period—he talked about the rookie Crosby staying at his house— "he can stay on the third floor with the kids ... there's plenty of room."

If it had been tough for Crosby to be billed as the game's next great player, it was going to be tougher still to arrive in a town where he was going to be expected to save the franchise and get an arena built. But then again, he had put a smile on Mario's face. Anything was possible.

That was a central theme in Sidney Crosby's life story to this point:

he made anything possible. Moreover, he never seemed disheartened by long odds and daunting challenges. He was a little ball of positive energy.

At some points Crosby's career ran a course similar to Lemieux's—playing in the Quebec junior league, running up mind-boggling scoring numbers and establishing himself as the pre-eminent young talent in the game. At other points Crosby's life intersected with Lemieux's—whether it was his father playing in the Quebec league or his meeting and working out with Lemieux in California a year earlier.

Yet Crosby's personality was the perfect counterpoint to Lemieux's as a young man. Crosby's love of the game was plain to see. His desire to play bordered on obsession. Their differences hadn't escaped Lemieux's notice. When he was asked about Crosby after their first meeting the year before, Lemieux said he was "a nice kid," but joked that he "likes to talk about hockey too much."

When the phenom finally spoke after the draft tension had broken, he tried to apply the brakes to the runaway hype. "First thing, I have to make the team," he said.

False modesty? Perhaps. Then again, Crosby had always made a point of not only knowing his place in the game but also accepting it. A rookie's job is to first win a spot in the line-up and that's how he was going to approach it. He wasn't going to get ahead of himself—and he certainly wasn't going to be seen as a kid with an ego. He tried not to make waves wherever he went. He would never be the one to say that a team didn't want him enough.

If winning a spot on the roster was truly going to be an issue, then all those general managers wouldn't have been wishing on stars and saying little prayers in the days leading up to the lottery. Draft choices, even first-rounders, even first overalls, are about risk and chance; the lottery offered all the suspense that there'd ever be with Sidney Crosby. And when Sidney Crosby was the lead story on the sportscasts that night and in the sports pages the next day, it was the star's name playing above the title of the movie. And also, thankfully, the human element of the game was trumping the league's business and politics for the first time in for too long.

"I'm telling you he's the best player
you'll see all year."

Breclav, Czech Republic
August 12, 2003

Hockey scouts are supposed to be skeptics. They're supposed to be the
game's doubters. You might think that their key role is to find talent.
That's the lesser half of their job description as they see it. More than
anything, scouts are not supposed to get fooled. They're not supposed to
waste time, money and draft picks on kids who can't play. The worst
thing you can say about a scout is he got carried away in his enthusiasm
about a player—that he saw talent that just wasn't there. That's why
scouts tend to be definitive in their evaluations of those who won't make
the pro ranks and conservative about prospects who seem like lead-pipe
cinches to everyone else in the stands.

In fact, most scouts talk guardedly about their finds even after
they've emerged as stars. I once talked to a scout who had done a work-
up for Dallas on Jarome Iginla, whom the Stars had drafted before trading
to Calgary for Joe Nieuwendyk. "Iginla's been a pretty good player so
far," he said, which sounded like faint praise given the fact that Iginla had

just led the league in goal scoring. The scout wasn't defending his team's trade of Iginla. No, the Stars came out of the trade with a Conn Smythe Trophy winner and a Stanley Cup. It's an extreme example to prove a point: a scout considers it unprofessional to get ahead of himself and Iginla had led the league in goals *once*. Let the fans buy his sweaters and wear them to the rink. Let the agents talk him up as a star. Scouts want evidence. They want proof.

That's why I was surprised by Tim Burke's enthusiasm about Sidney Crosby, a centre on the Canadian under-18 team. I was sitting in front of Burke, a Boston-based scout with the San Jose Sharks, on a Czech Airlines flight from Frankfurt to Prague. I was fighting jet lag and neck spasms, twisting around to listen to an NHL scout rhapsodizing about a kid who had celebrated his 16th birthday just a week before, a kid who had yet to play a game in the major junior ranks. I had expected griping and grousing about this midsummer scouting assignment session. After all, Burke is an avid golfer, a two handicap, and Breclav and Piestany, the sites of the summer under-18 World Cup hockey tournament, left a lot to be desired for scouts who tried to squeeze in rounds between games. The best Burke could find was a *12-hole* course near Breclav. But he wasn't complaining. "I'd pay to see this Crosby kid play," he told me. "I think that's true of anybody in our business. Yeah, we're supposed to be skeptical about players we evaluate. But I think we love the game more than anybody else. What's more, we respect the game and want the best for it. So it's not just that this kid can be good in the NHL. He will be and that's something you can only say about a handful of players over the years. Thing is, he can be good for the NHL."

A 16-year-old who will be good for the NHL: that's a heck of a limb for a fan or a journalist to crawl out on, never mind a scout.

I had just sold a magazine story on Crosby and hadn't gone quite so far as Burke in the pitch to my editor. The one thing I did seize on was something Wayne Gretzky said a couple of weeks before. The Great One suggested his own records might one day be threatened by Crosby, then all of 15. And though Crosby did not yet have a driver's licence, NHL scouts and junior coaches talked about his play in national midget-age tourneys and at the Canada Winter Games like fans would reminisce about classic games in Stanley Cups past. "It's one thing to be talented enough to earn a legend's respect," I told my editor. "It's another thing to be burdened by that much expectation and hype." I stopped short of the guaranteed-star line and way short of the boy-saviour stuff. In fact, I'd loaded an escape clause in there: "If he doesn't make it, it's because he has been saddled with all this baggage."

Still, I had worried about booking a flight to Prague. I feared I had oversold my story, that I had cooked the intelligence like a press-row version of George Tenet. When I heard Crosby had been invited to the tryouts and training camp for the Canadian under-18 squad, I called up Brad Pascall, Hockey Canada's public relations man. I asked if there was any chance Crosby wouldn't make the cut. After all, the Canadian team had never taken an underage player to the summer under-18s. Not Joe Thornton nor Vincent Lecavalier, both of whom would go on to play for the under-20 team at age 17 before being drafted first overall in their NHL draft years. Not more recent junior phenoms, such as Jay Bouwmeester, who at age 16 was already more physically gifted than the older defencemen selected instead. And not Jason Spezza, who at age 15 had not only managed to put in a full season in the Ontario Hockey League, but also a couple of games with the Canadian national men's team as well.

The other members of the Canadian team going to this tournament in Breclav were, in the parlance of scouts, 86s, players born in 1986. All but three of the 86s were eligible for the 2004 draft.* Crosby, however, was the team's only 87, which made him eligible for the 2005 draft. In fact, had he been born five weeks later than his August 7 birthday, he would have fallen into the "late birthday" category, which would have pushed ahead his year of eligibility to 2006.

Taking Crosby to the summer under-18s, then, would have constituted a break from tradition. Pascall assured me I was taking no risk buying my ticket ahead of time. "I'd be shocked if he didn't go to the tournament and play on the first line," he said.

When Burke and I cleared Czech customs we met up with the Sharks' Czech scout, who was going to drive us three hours, directly to a game

---

* Mike Blunden of the Erie Otters, Alex Bourret of Sherbrooke and Wacey Rabbit of Saskatoon were born after September 15th, 1986 and were thus eligible for the 2005 draft as late '86 birthdays.

between Switzerland and Canada in Breclav, out near the Slovak border. Burke picked up where he left off on the flight. "I'm telling you he's the best player you'll see all year. Nothing you'll see over here (in Europe) will measure up. You hear what this kid did yesterday. His first game in the tournament, youngest kid on the team, he scores in regulation, then scores the winner in the shootout. Everything you could ask for. And what's really great is the fact that this kid looks after himself on the ice. He fights his own battles. He doesn't just take it. He dishes it out. He's fearless out there."

The Sharks' man in the Czech Republic looked puzzled but he didn't argue the point or pooh-pooh it. For this I was thankful, because he was doing about 170 kph and jockeying around tractor-trailers on what seemed the Czech version of the Autobahn. He told us it was going to be "life or death" to catch the Switzerland-Canada game and not for a second, not until the arena was in sight, did I doubt him.

When we pulled into the parking lot, the Canadian team was just finishing its pre-game warm-up. The players were assembled in a circle and were working to keep a volleyball in the air: a game of hot potato. Any player who let it drop had to take a lap of the parking lot and then head into the dressing room. There was plenty of reason to dog it, to fake it, to let the ball drop and get into the dressing room and the cool of the arena as soon as possible. Europe was in the throes of the worst heat wave in recorded history. Thousands were succumbing across the continent. The temperature in Breclav was 42°C and it was even hotter for the players with the heat reflecting off the blacktop. Inside the arena it was about 16°C and rising, not ideal for ice-making, but a lot more comfortable than out in the parking lot.

The scouts went into the cool arena. I lingered outside, hoping to locate the *wunderkind*. He was easy to pick out. He was the only one taking the drill seriously, maybe a little too seriously.

If someone had told you that one player in the circle was younger than the rest, more than a year younger than most, Crosby would have been the easy choice. It wasn't simply that he didn't have a fuzzy beard, like many did. Nor was it the fact that he didn't have any tattoos, like some. Nor that he was, at five-foot-nine (maybe a half-inch taller than that), shorter than virtually all his teammates. Nor that his body was struggling to take on muscle. Though he had the basic hockey-player trademarks—massive thighs and a bowlegged walk—he looked like a lot of kids in any high school weight room who had pushed iron to thicken arms and chest and back but were still waiting for results.

No, the tipoff was how Crosby was so wrapped up in this volleyball warm-up. He seemed utterly lost in it. He played with such childlike wonder and seriousness. While others were trying to beat the heat, it seemed he'd have stayed out in the sun all day. Others were thinking about the game against the Swiss, which presented the Canadians with a chance to clinch a berth in the semi-finals. For Crosby this little volleyball contest was the only game in the world. It wasn't just that he made me feel old. He made his 17-year-old teammates feel old.

Crosby watched the flight of the volleyball as it bounced up from one set of hands to another. His mouth was open. He was not self-conscious in the least. Bombs could have dropped and he wouldn't have noticed. His entire world was not hockey, not this tournament, but the game that was in front of him at that very moment.

One by one the other players were eliminated. A couple of times it looked like Crosby was in trouble. At least once it looked like he might dive across the parking lot and risk road rash just to dig out the ball. I saw the team doctor grimace. It would have made a helluva headline—*Star junior collides with parked car*. It came down to the last two players, Crosby and Jean-Michel Rizk, a kid from Saginaw of the Ontario league. They traded sets, endlessly, with all the raw drama of a game of Pong. Finally Rizk dinked the ball to Crosby who was looking for another high, skyward set. He turned to Rizk with a momentarily plaintive look familiar to anyone who has ever spent time on a playground—raised eyebrows and gaping mouth, the unspoken universal expression of "No fair." Crosby's straggling teammates gave it a big "Aww!" And coach Bob Lowes clipped, "That's you Sidney. Take a lap."

Crosby looked sheepish for a second but then rolled his eyes and laughed. He jogged a lap and made his way into the dressing room.

What to make of the whole scene?

Initially I thought of a great athlete's ability to be in touch with his inner child. The very best athletes don't feel the least bit goofy about caring so much about childhood games, mostly because they don't see them as childhood games. Every time Michael Jordan touched a basketball he was sticking it to the coach who cut him from his high school team. Every time Muhammad Ali laced on his gloves he was somehow transported back to the time when he joined a boxing gym because his bicycle had been stolen. Every time Wayne Gretzky touched a puck the arena transformed into that backyard rink flooded by his father. Athletic genius issues from that boyhood ability to believe, for that moment, nothing else matters. For the very best this belief, this ability spills over to other things. For Jordan, he was no less as obsessively competitive on the golf course or in a casino as he was on the court. He was just a lot less successful. Likewise was Gretzky so competitive playing baseball or basketball or lacrosse growing up.

Sidney Crosby wasn't necessarily an athletic genius because he was so intensely focused on this game of hot potato. That alone didn't qualify him. Maybe it put him on the short list. Of course, the easy explanation is that he cared too much or lacked any sense of proportion.

Only afterward, on further review, did I appreciate that he had done something childlike followed by something wise beyond his years. The game offered one example of Crosby's competitive streak but the aftermath showed a gift for managing relationships, something a manager or CEO could go to school on. Crosby had pushed and pushed during this volleyball game but never protested when he was finally knocked out. By shrugging it off he just blended in with the rest of his teammates and alienated no one, which might be for the most heralded athletes the toughest play of all. When he was at last eliminated, he sucked it up, forced a smile and defused any hard feelings. It was potentially a difficult situation. As a first-liner—if he was leading off in a shootout he was certainly on the Canadian first line—Crosby was getting more ice time than older teammates who had played in the Canadian Hockey League, the top junior loop. A lot less than that has caused resentment in the ranks of a team. And yet somehow these players, who had already paid dues in the CHL, who had given up a month of their summers, who were hoping to attract the attention of NHL scouts, didn't seem at all bothered by Crosby's presence.*

All of this wouldn't have mattered if Sidney Crosby didn't have game, but a couple of minutes after the anthems it was clear that he had great gobs of skill. His skating was as good as any other player's in the game. The same with his shot. On both counts he rated top marks. And he played not with total effort so much as with a sense of desperation, like a kid on the cut line. What raised Crosby's game was stuff that's impossible to quantify or teach. Like Gretzky he seemed to be wired differently, owning hands that felt everything, eyes that saw things on the ice that everyone else missed. He made difficult plays look as effortless as breathing. No matter how a player drifted or wired a pass, he adjusted intuitively, taking it cleanly and in stride. He didn't have awkward moments. He never fought the puck.

Bob Lowes, who had coached the Regina Pats the previous season, had him out on the first line and first power play. Crosby found ways to snake around big Swiss defencemen on the rush and duck under them on the cycle. He played beside a big winger named Wojtek Wolski and found ways to deliver him the puck in traffic, through tangles of skates and sticks, when defenders were looking the other way. As Wolski would say afterward, "I never have played with someone who does the things that he does. He forces you not to take your attention off the puck for a second. It could be coming anytime."

Despite Crosby's extraordinary play, the Swiss hung around. They were like a lot of recent teams coming out of Switzerland. The guys wearing the white cross were big, could skate and liked physical play. They were just sort of clunky, lacking any feel or intuition. Though Swiss teams fared well in international age-group play in recent years, they found a way to lose to Canada every time. For years this lifetime losing streak and resultant defeatism were matters for gallows humour among

* The Canadian Hockey League (CHL) is the body that governs the three Canadian major junior hockey leagues: the 21-team Western Hockey League (WHL, often called "the Dub"), the 20-team Ontario Hockey League (OHL, or the "O"), and the Quebec Major Junior Hockey League (QMJHL, or the "Q"), which expanded to 18 teams with the launch of expansion franchises in Saint John, New Brunswick, and St. John's, Newfoundland in fall 2005. CHL teams compete for the Memorial Cup, the national championship trophy. They can have two European players on their playing roster, along with three 20-year-old players (as at December 31 of the season in play).

Swiss hockey reporters—possibly among the Swiss hockey players themselves. But was this finally Switzerland's breakout? Meeting a Canadian team softened by a close game against Finland less than 24 hours earlier and perhaps further weakened by sunstroke from a pre-game parking-lot volleyball game?

The Swiss plan was a simple and brutal one: they chased Crosby and whenever they caught up to him, during play or after the whistle, they finished checks or cross-checked or slashed him. Crosby was Canada's best weapon but not a secret one, though this was his first trip to Europe and his debut on the international stage. He didn't seem to weary from running the gantlet but the ref didn't seem inclined to hand out any penalties either. To this extent, the plan did seem to be working out for Switzerland. The underdogs carried a 1–0 lead midway through the first period.

At this point came an incident that at first seemed to doom not just Canada's chances in this game and tournament, but possibly Sidney Crosby's prospective stardom. It started innocently enough. Crosby was skating near the boards at centre ice during the second period when play was whistled dead. At least three seconds after the whistle, a Swiss forward named Mathias Joggi delivered a vicious cross-check to Crosby's head.

I couldn't tell if it caught him on the side of the helmet or just below the hard plastic on his neck. Regardless, it was a one-shot kayo and he barely moved when he fell face down on the ice. It was a savage hit. In the small cluster of Canadian parents it was easy to pick out Crosby's. In facial features, the son borrows from both. His father Troy, a great big bear of a fellow, was in full throat—the Swiss player should get tossed out of the game. Meanwhile Sidney's mother Trina covered her mouth, horrified. The Canadian players swarmed the Swiss player, shoves gave way to punches and it looked like the attack might escalate into an international incident, the Swiss being at last dragged into a war.

For a moment I imagined I had come thousands of miles to catch a handful of shifts by a kid who might never play again, by a kid who might for the rest of his days be pushed around in a wheelchair. A story of triumph becomes tragedy. My heart sank. It sank as far as my knees. And if Crosby hadn't somehow managed to get back up on his skates with the help of a couple of teammates and the team doctor, I'm sure my heart would have filled up one of my sneakers.

Tim Burke said that Crosby was tough and that he fought his own battles, but few players get up from that kind of cheap shot. A few hardy souls would sit on the bench and try to shake out the cobwebs. Crosby, though, slammed his stick when he got back to the bench and, though woozy, started jawing. He made it clear to Lowes he wanted to get back into the game. As soon as possible.

And Crosby was back into the game a couple of minutes later. He missed a shift, maybe two, but that was it. Events weren't lifted straight from the inspirational storybook. He didn't immediately score. But what he did do was in its own way no less impressive. Crosby started hitting Swiss players at every opportunity. More than scoring to exact some sort of payback, he sent them a message: he couldn't be intimidated.

Canada carried a 2–1 lead into the third period, though Crosby didn't figure into the scoring. Five minutes into the final frame the Swiss tied the game. It wasn't the worst 45 minutes in Canadian hockey history but neither did it suggest the dawn of a new era.

It was at this point Crosby took over.

On his very next shift he scored a goal that could have appeared on a Hall of Fame highlight reel if only there had been a video of the Switzerland game. Crosby had the puck on the boards on the left wing and his teammates were in the middle of a line change. Three defenders stood between him and the goaltender. It seemed like the most harmless of offensive forays. Then Crosby just took off on a pure solo effort, a gambit that you'd see in a shinny game at a neighbourhood rink. He went through one defenceman, then another, spun off a backchecking forward and at last completed a wide, sweeping deke of the Swiss goaltender. He raised his stick in the air and spun a couple of more times and the first body to touch him was one of his own celebrating teammates. It was a small wonder.

The Swiss came right back. With Crosby off the ice, the Swiss got a puck past lanky Canadian goaltender Devan Dubnyk on their very next shot to tie the game at three. It could have been a spirit-busting turn of events for Canada. The old rule in hockey is not to give up a goal in the last minute of a period or on the shift after scoring—either is enough to suck the oxygen out of an arena.

So when Crosby came over the boards on the next shift he entered the fray at a critical juncture. For almost the full duration of the shift Canada controlled the puck in the Swiss end. And Crosby did the heavy lifting on the cycle before setting up Wolski for a couple of chances. Ultimately, Crosby cleaned up a rebound to put the Canadians back in front 4–3. And the old rule in hockey is doubly true twice over—if you think it's bad conceding a goal on the shift after scoring, it's nothing compared to having that get-back goal just as quickly nullified.

To say the Swiss played the rest of the game in a fog is true in every sense of the word. By this point a fog had engulfed both teams in the rapidly warming arena. And in the next couple of minutes, the Swiss conceded a goal to Fred Cabana of the Halifax Mooseheads and then to Wolski, again set up by Crosby. The Swiss were done. For Crosby it was two goals and an assist in three consecutive shifts, an absolute tour de force. Tim Burke had set the bar impossibly high and Crosby cleared it. He didn't just show extraordinary skill, he showed it at the time of greatest need. "When he needs to, he can get it done," Burke had said.

Further, Crosby displayed a nasty streak that was absent from the play of Wayne Gretzky and Mario Lemieux. It only started with his willingness to finish every hit on the forecheck. It carried through his refusal to dive and writhe with every hook and slash. And it shone most brightly when he skated back into the fray after the cheap shot and started running the biggest Swiss players he could find. Burke compared it to Theo Fleury's cold, hard style. It was all of that and more. It was a toughness that hockey fans hadn't seen in the greatest players since Bobby Orr and Gordie Howe walked away from the game more than a generation ago.

Crosby's play in Breclav wasn't without precedent, mind you. Crosby had done all this before and more. He had done it in age-group play out in Halifax. He had done it at the Canadian midget championships. At the Canada Winter Games. At Shattuck-St. Mary's in Minnesota, where he spent a year. At workouts at the IMG camp. This display against the Swiss was extraordinary in only one sense—it was one of the last few times that Sidney Crosby aired out his considerable gifts in front of such a small albeit select crowd. There couldn't have been one hundred people in the arena. It was tantamount to a pre-opening movie screening for critics. Within a month or so, he'd play to arenas with thousands of fans and nary an empty seat. Within a few months he'd be on the media radar, on the front page of newspapers across Canada, featured in U.S. magazines, the subject of a documentary that aired on CBC. To an extent, the genie was already out of the bottle. Crosby's hockey card from Shattuck (yes, it's a big high school hockey program that issues its own hockey cards) was already fetching $11 U.S. on the internet.

"Maybe it wasn't talent he gave me . . ."

Sidney Crosby was supposed to be the next Wayne Gretzky. So said Wayne Gretzky. To begin to tell the story of Sidney Crosby, you need to go back to the last reel of the Gretzky saga. To know where Crosby is supposed to pick up, go back to where Gretzky left off.

Today, Gretzky's retirement from the NHL seems like a long time ago, a hockey generation ago. It was in fact the spring of 1999. A lot of hockey has been played since then—although one NHL season less than originally anticipated—yet Gretzky is still on the scene. In fact, he never really left us. He went from the ranks of on-ice wonder to the ranks of ownership, becoming a partner with the Phoenix Coyotes. He went from starring in international play to managing the Canadian team to gold medals at the Olympics in 2002 and the World Cup in 2004. And though rumours of a comeback circulated for a time, he put on skates only a few times in his first five years removed from the ice, most memorably in the 2003 "Heritage Classic" between old-time Oilers and alumni of les Canadiens at Commonwealth Stadium. By 2005 the rumours of a comeback were transformed—he would be back with the players on the bench, but now as a coach of the Coyotes, ostensibly to sell tickets.

So much of Gretzky's life after the game has made news and so much about his retirement has been forgotten.

Ottawa, Ontario
April 15, 1999

Gretzky didn't so much announce his retirement back in April 1999; he fairly shocked the hockey world when he started talking about it in the last week of the regular season. He certainly caught the Rangers' general manager, Neil Smith, off guard. Earlier in the month Smith told reporters that Gretzky's retirement was only "50-50" when it was, in fact, a *fait accompli*. But then Gretzky didn't give the league or anybody else much notice. He didn't give the networks enough lead time to put together the polished career retrospectives. And there wasn't a farewell tour per se. There was no glitzy packaging of his final appearances in Toronto, where he had always managed to light up the Leafs; or Montreal, where his Oilers had first skated into prominence with a playoff upset in the early '80s; or Detroit, where his boyhood hero Gordie Howe had starred. Instead, Gretzky's last games in those cities just seemed like his last games there until the next season. In fact, his retirement didn't even float weightlessly about the hockey world as speculation until the second last Saturday of the season when, on *Hockey Night in Canada*, New York Rangers' broadcaster John Davidson said he had it on good authority that Gretzky would be retiring at season's end. Davidson described it as an "80 percent" likelihood, which gave him an escape hatch should Gretzky have had a change of heart. Still, Davidson's uncertain revelation was more than enough to become the talk of hockey the moment it hit the airwaves.

It was a remarkable turn of events. Gretzky not only managed to scoop his long-time pals and trusted confederates in the press. He managed to scoop himself. For several months Gretzky had been a "columnist" for the *National Post*. The editors of the newly launched broadsheet had hoped, in vain as it turned out, to attract attention to the paper by recruiting hockey's most famous name to their sports section. There was but one problem with this line of thinking: throughout his long career, Gretzky was usually the most cautious and least opinionated quote in the business. So, in his *Post* column, he came out for, well, fatherhood, the flag, love of the game and anything else that could fill the space without whipping up controversy. Improbably, news of his retirement was news to the *Post* and Gretzky's ghost writers. It was just the type of exclusive that the *Post* thought it was buying for $200,000 a year, but it proved even too hot for Gretzky himself to touch.

With the Rangers out of the playoff hunt, that meant Gretzky was going to be done after a game in Ottawa and a regular-season finale at Madison Square Garden against Pittsburgh.

I worked Gretzky's second last NHL game for an Ottawa newspaper. The game was fittingly played in the nation's capital because it was one part an exercise in nostalgia, one part state funeral. Every hockey journalist with a national reputation booked a seat on the Corel Centre's press row. And Stanley Cup finals have drawn smaller gangs from the fourth estate.

Over the course of the preceding days several thousands of gallons of ink were spilled on recollections of Gretzky's greatest moments. Some of the memory-stoking was dedicated to familiar images: Gretzky working his magic from his office behind the net, picking out open teammates or working a wrap-around; Gretzky crossing the blueline and then pulling up, allowing teammates to skate into the picture before dishing the puck out to them or artfully using them as decoys. Some of the remembrances focused on golden moments: Gretzky's unselfish assist on Mario Lemieux's winning goal in overtime of the final at the 1987 Canada Cup; Gretzky racking up 50 goals in 39 games to obliterate the records of Rocket Richard and Mike Bossy.

There was also some ink spilled about Gretzky's retirement marking a time of transition for the NHL. To be sure, Gretzky wasn't leaving the league at one of its high points—like its glorious media honeymoon back in 1994, when *Sports Illustrated* declared the NHL was "hot" and the NBA was "not." But he was leaving it when there were teams just getting comfortable with new buildings, when the operating buzzwords were "luxury boxes" and "revenue streams," when price tags for expansion franchises shot through the roof.

The weeklong Gretzky sendoff put on the back burner a hot topic of discussion that had been boiling over for more than a year, namely Canada's sorry fortunes in international hockey. It had started back in 1996 when the U.S. team beat Canada in the final of the World Cup of Hockey. It gained momentum when the Canadian under-20 squad, the dominant crew in the early- and mid-'90s, finished eighth at the 1998 World Junior tournament, losing to a Kazakhstan team that iced players wearing mismatched skates. And when the Canadian Olympic team returned from the 1998 Winter Games in Nagano without a medal, the collective results amounted to a national crisis.

These shocking defeats set off widespread soul-searching and finger-pointing. Hockey Canada staged summit meetings to look at player development at home and in the European nations that were lapping our best. Many lamented the fact that Canada had not turned out a player to rival Gretzky or Mario Lemieux in a generation. Sure, the pipeline still pumped out good players, very good players, but not anyone who *inspired*, not anyone who possessed anything resembling genius. The conferences were staged, the white papers drafted. Yet there were no answers. Or possibly too many answers. Too little coaching, some said. Over-coaching, said others. Too many games, not enough practices. And defenders of the status quo noted that grassroots hockey wasn't so very different when Orr and Gretzky and Lemieux had come along.

The Corel Centre was akin to the set of *This is Your Life*. Walter Gretzky flew in with a bunch of his friends from Brantford. Hundreds made their way from across the continent. And the fans were decked out in replica Gretzky sweaters from his stints with the Rangers, the St. Louis Blues, the Los Angeles Kings, the Edmonton Oilers and various Team Canadas. There were not, however, any replicas from the Indianapolis Racers, the Soo Greyhounds, the Peterborough Petes (a two-game stint as an underager), nor, for that matter, the Nadrofsky Steelers, the team he had scored hundreds of goals for as a boy out in Brantford.

It would have been wholly impolite to write about the state of Gretzky's game at the end of his career, the erosion of his formerly nonpareil skills. The Rangers and the Senators played to a 2–2 tie and Gretzky managed to pick up a point, but these are just meaningless and misleading notes in the record book. There was an immense difference in talent between the teams and throughout the game the ice seemed tilted in the Senators' favour. Some accounts from that game unnecessarily pad Gretzky's legend. "He seemed to be the one most enjoying a game too many others have come to see as work," Roy MacGregor wrote in the *National Post*. "His passes—the on-ice signature that defied forgery— were still so perfect, still so inspired, creative and surprising ..." Were it only so. That night Gretzky was the oldest player on the ice and you could have guessed it without a program or without ever having seen a game. The leading scorer in NHL history looked frail. He looked shaky and uncertain on his skates, almost jittery. Once he had an uncanny pre- science, arriving in the right place just ahead of the puck. But by the time of this second last game—that was gone. Though the fans were chanting "one more year," he struggled just to stay up with play. It seemed like he had already retired and was going through the motions—something he had never been accused of before, something wholly understandable given the hubbub around the occasion. If another player in his late 30s had been struggling like Gretzky was, the media and fans wouldn't have been lamenting his retirement. They'd have been calling for it. And if he had truly been undecided about bidding farewell, then he might have been soul searching out there against the Senators. It might have been his own variation on Pierre Trudeau's walk in the snow.

In retrospect, you might ask why more people hadn't seen his retire- ment coming. After all, through to Game 80 of the 1998–99 campaign, Gretzky, who had once scored 92 goals in a season, had scored but 9 times. This would have shown a lack of production from even a checking- line player, never mind a first-liner and first option on the power play.

Yet, while his greatest days were long behind, Gretzky was not so very far removed from being an elite player. When Bobby Clarke, the gen- eral manager of the Canadian team at the 1998 Nagano Olympics, was second-guessed about the inclusion of Gretzky on the roster, he brusquely pointed out that Gretzky had led the NHL in scoring after the Olympics through the end of the regular season. "If anyone should have been tired after the Olympics it should have been him and clearly he had a lot of game left," Clarke said. "The Rangers missed the playoffs (in '98) but it wasn't his fault."

In just one season something had gone out of Gretzky. It's tempting to put it down to heartbreak after coach Marc Crawford passed over Gretzky for the shootout against the Czechs in Nagano. Or to point to a mediocre supporting cast in New York. Or to a body failing, to injuries and aging.

It's most tempting, though, to put it down to an advanced case of celebrity fatigue. Simply, Wayne Gretzky got tired of being Wayne Gretzky. I talked to him at length a dozen or so times over the previous five years and he always seemed to be fighting a been-there-done-that weariness. (I'm presuming it wasn't all due to me.) When hundreds of sportswriters and various hangers-on descended on Ottawa for Gretzky's penultimate game, he could scarcely have looked less comfortable. It was understandable. All the tributes had the aspect of eulogies and thus placed Gretzky in the unenviable position of eavesdropping at his own wake. The sportswriters seemed to cling to fond memories more than he did. Their eyes seemed damper than his.

Perhaps the best description of Gretzky's career-long burden came from Kevin Lowe, Gretzky's former teammate with the Oilers and the Rangers. "He wasn't just playing hockey all these years," Lowe told Cam Cole of the *National Post*. "He was talking hockey with the media, every day, every city, nonstop. He's basically been the NHL's marketing department for 20 years."

That fatigue was obvious when Gretzky walked up to the stage set up in a conference room at the Corel Centre that night. He was tired of answering personal questions, tired of having his every word and action scrutinized. He was almost certainly of that mind before he signed as a free agent with the Rangers. His ennui reached critical condition when the New York media trained its klieg lights on him, after the Rangers ceased to be a playoff contender. Winning had mitigated the intrusions. The thrill of competition had made it all worthwhile. Without winning, he couldn't rationalize carrying on.

"All indications are pointing in that direction," Gretzky said when his retirement was broached by one of the couple of hundred accredited media and well-connected rubberneckers who crowded into the conference room. "It's not one hundred percent. When I make a decision it will be one hundred percent. This is not a weak decision. I really feel right. I didn't want to put the team through any disruption during the playoff drive." And Gretzky continued, saying that if he did go through with retirement, "the next time you see me skating, it'll be with my kids."

"I've never considered myself bigger than any person I ever played with," he said. It was a remarkable notion: the famous name in possession of just about every meaningful scoring record in NHL history saw himself as just one of the boys. And even if he couldn't convince the public of the idea, he aimed to have his teammates think of him that way.

And in that press conference he waxed philosophically about his talents, about the idea that God had gifted him with genius. This was something out of the ordinary for Gretzky. "I was lucky enough to be gifted," he said. "Maybe it wasn't talent He gave me. Maybe it was passion."

Again, Gretzky, seemingly not an introspective sort, offered up a telling self-assessment. Would there have been genius without the passion? Some would say, not altogether fairly, that this was the difference between Gretzky (the passionate one) and Lemieux (the seemingly reluctant superstar).

What is now clear in hindsight (but was not widely noted at the time), is the fact that Gretzky's retirement marked a breach in a chain of succession. This chain dated back to the '40s. There had been Richard but when he left the game, Howe and Beliveau were there to carry on. Before they were gone there was Hull and later Orr. Potvin and Lafleur skated into the picture and Clarke too. And then came Gretzky and not long after Mario Lemieux. But in the spring of 1999, Lemieux was retired. Eric Lindros was not living up to his early promise. There were players for fans to admire: Ray Bourque, Joe Sakic, Peter Forsberg, Brett Hull and Steve Yzerman among others. They were easy to respect, but none transcended. None crossed over. There were other sublimely skilled players, including Pavel Bure, Alexander Mogilny, Sergei Fedorov and Jaromir Jagr, but they didn't inspire. It wasn't simply that they were European so much as they were remote, less inclined to engage the public and the media. Though they were capable of great moments in a game, they were often less than great game in and game out. And the difference between their best seasons and their worst was far greater than anything in

Gretzky's run through championships and trophies. No, Gretzky's retirement left a void in the league. There were players who possessed character or skill or some combination of both, but none possessed genius like Gretzky. Or for that matter, like Richard or Howe or Orr or Lemieux. None was on the scene.

In the last week of Gretzky's career few sportswriters, commentators or players played up this vacuum, but even though no one spoke of it, the result was clearly understood. No one was nominating any active NHLer to skate into the breach. No one was calling Mario Lemieux out of retirement to save the game. The presumption was simple: *We'll never see his likes again.*

This was the consensus in the media and with the public even though history shows that great players give way to other great players. The one lesson from the past is, *There's always someone in the pipeline, just not necessarily in plain sight.* Gretzky was a case in point. When Gordie Howe skated off the ice with the Detroit Red Wings for the last time and into retirement (albeit, a retirement, like Lemieux's, that wouldn't take), Wayne Gretzky was a scrawny kid who scored hundreds of goals in Brantford's youth leagues and had once posed for a photograph with Howe. When Bobby Orr's knees were deteriorating and his game was winding down too soon in the mid-'70s, Gretzky was making his mark with the Seneca Nats as a 14- and 15-year-old.

At that game in Ottawa I thought back to a time when Gretzky was in the pipeline, back to my university days in Ottawa, to buying a ticket to see Gretzky play at the old Civic Centre as a junior with the Sault Ste. Marie Greyhounds.

In the late '70s the Ottawa 67's were a junior hockey powerhouse. In the spring of '77 they went all the way to the Memorial Cup championship game, only to lose to the New Westminster Bruins. The next season, the 67's ran away with the regular-season title in the Ontario Hockey Association* and they looked like a sure bet to come away with

* The Ontario Hockey Association (OHA) was the precursor to the present-day Ontario Hockey League (OHL).

a national championship. They had lost defenceman Doug Wilson to the NHL but were otherwise loaded. And they had Bobby Smith, a rangy 20-year-old centre who was ranked the best player in junior hockey, a lock to the first pick overall in the 1978 NHL draft. That season Smith racked up 192 points, three points a game. He was a player who dominated in what you might describe the usual way—he played the same game that everyone else did, just with more size, more strength, more speed. Smith was better, though not different. He was a conventional star, right down to that most conventional name.

But in the OHA playoffs in April of 1978, the 67's met up with the Soo Greyhounds, a team that finished far back in Ottawa's wake during the regular season. The Greyhounds had fired their coach, Muzz MacPherson, during the season. They had brought in a long-haired 27-year-old coach, Paul Theriault, who by his appearance and his idiosyncracies might have passed for a disciple of Charles Manson. They had a couple of decent talents who would go on to NHL careers, among them defenceman Craig Hartsburg and goaltender Greg Millen. And they had a 16-year-old kid whom they had selected with the third overall pick in the OHA draft, a scrawny 150-pounder named Wayne Gretzky.*

Gretzky didn't exactly sneak up on Smith and the 67's in the playoffs. He had finished as a runner-up to Smith in the league scoring race. He scored 70 goals and 112 assists, setting an Ontario league rookie scoring record that still stands. Gretzky had made the Greyhounds into the biggest attraction in the OHA that season—the Soo arena had sold out all year long and road games had often drawn a couple of thousand over average attendance.

Gretzky had also already gained unprecedented national media attention for the OHA—newspaper outlets and magazines cast regular glances Gretzky's way. The stories inevitably remarked on his politeness, his slightness, his blond hair and the media savvy that he had developed since giving his first interviews at ages 9 and 10. They noted that Walter Gretzky had sent a letter to the Greyhounds, advising them that he wouldn't let his son play for a junior team located too far from Brantford.

* Tom McCarthy was selected first overall by Oshawa, Steve Peters was selected second by Niagara Falls.

And the reports noted that the Greyhounds rolled the dice in the draft and convinced the Gretzkys to send Wayne to the Soo. They also reported on rumours. One had him playing in the Swedish pro league instead of returning to junior, which was, he said, a misreading of his desire to train in Sweden over the summer—to improve on his skating, which he saw as a soft spot in his game. Another report turned out to be on the money: the idea that he wasn't going to wait until age 20 to be drafted into the NHL and intended to follow other underage players to the World Hockey Association.

Even international media found their way to the Soo. *Sports Illustrated* dispatched a reporter, E.M. Swift, a fellow on the debut assignment of a long and distinguished career. Swift fairly placed Gretzky in a category of wunderkind alongside two contemporaries, the Triple Crown jockey Steve Cauthen and Olympic gymnast Nadia Comaneci—"one of those rare youths who leapfrogs the stage where they speak of potential, whose talent is already front and centre." Swift's article provides great insight into the character of Gretzky at 16. He was by turns self-deprecating (describing his speed as "brutal") and self-confident (proclaiming that "from the redline to their net I play a solid game compared to anyone in the NHL"). He had a clear idea of his game (describing his style as "different from anyone else's") and his limitations (admitting he was scared of players who were "out to get me out of the game"). And he was gullible enough to fall for a prank phone call from a team member posing as Prime Minister Pierre Trudeau's secretary, yet self-possessed enough to beg off the prime minister's invitation to lunch because of a prior engagement, a team meal.

Despite Gretzky's incredible numbers and his emerging celebrity, some scouts thought his game wouldn't work at the NHL level, that he'd get knocked into next week the first time a pro defenceman ever labelled him. The idea that he'd find time and space against the pros was anathema. There was no split opinion on Bobby Smith. The scouts were sold on him. He was everything they looked for in a prospect. Many reserved judgment on Gretzky. Some gave him no shot.

The stage seemed set for one outcome: the clock striking midnight for a junior-hockey Cinderella. Gretzky, of course, turned expectations inside out. In those days, the Ontario league's playoffs weren't best-of-seven series, but rather eight-point series, no overtimes. Not much of a difference on the face of it. But the 67's-Greyhounds series was one of those rare matchups that came down to an eighth game.

I took in a lot of 67's games that season and I saw a couple of games in that series. Some of my memory banks are a little foggy—I'm not sure which of the earlier games in that series I caught, though I'm sure it wasn't Game 1, which the 67's won as expected 13–3. But I do remember seeing the seventh game. A win in Game 7 would have moved the 67's into the next round.

That night Gretzky put the Greyhounds on his narrow shoulders. He dictated play in a 6–3 win, undressing defencemen as he rushed by them, setting up in his office behind Ottawa goaltender Jay O'Connor. He was, as he had advertised himself, playing a game "different from anyone else's." He created chances all night long and I was probably like a lot of people in attendance—I had to remind myself that he was dominating play not just against a great team but against players two, three and even four years older than him. And I thought that I'd likely never see anything quite like it again.

Proving that the hockey world is a small one, Greg Millen, the Soo's goaltender during that 1978 Ontario league series, was working as the colour commentator for the Senators' TV broadcast when Gretzky played his second-last NHL game in Ottawa. The conventional wisdom has always been that Canadian junior hockey provides the best apprenticeship available to an aspiring pro player. But Millen pointed out that Gretzky thrived despite a less than ideal situation in Sault Ste. Marie. According to reports published back at the time, Craig Hartsburg, the Soo captain and the established star from the previous season, didn't say a word to Gretzky all winter long. That said, it's hard to imagine that Hartsburg as captain didn't wield influence in the dressing room. And E.M. Swift's *Sports Illustrated* story alluded to several hazing incidents— maybe standard stuff for first-year players, even superstars, but it does seem that Gretzky was subjected to more than his share.

Additionally coach Muzz MacPherson was fired during the season. Millen explained, "For two weeks we went without a coach. I had to run practice for a while. At one point the players broke into a meeting of the team executives and said that they weren't going to play if Muzz wasn't put back in. The league almost lost a team right there." And though the team eventually landed a coach, Paul Theriault preached defensive hockey when everybody else in the league opted for firewagon hockey— he didn't necessarily want to turn Gretzky into Bob Gainey but neither did he seem to fully appreciate the talent he had on hand. Theriault ended up benching Gretzky when the Greyhounds played Kingston in the opening round of the playoffs.

Yet despite the jealousies, absence of guidance, debatable strategies bordering on incompetence, Gretzky survived and transcended, which suggests that genius finds a way to prevail.

The 67's at last vanquished the stubborn Greyhounds in the eighth game back in the Soo. Gretzky couldn't quite push his team past Ottawa. Bobby Smith moved on to the pros. After the Minnesota North Stars selected him with the first overall pick in the draft, the 67's made a little noise in the press about trading for Gretzky. Wishful thinking. Though he had told Swift he was figuring on playing one more year in the Soo, Gretzky really had nothing more to prove. He was ready for the next stage. The NHL however, was still operating with a 20-year age minimum for its draft; but the World Hockey Association played fast and loose. The WHA had previously signed a bunch of 18-year-olds, Wayne Dillon, Ken Linseman and John Tonelli among them. Gretzky was only 17 when his first agent, Gus Badali, negotiated his jump to the WHA. Within a year the WHA would be folded into the NHL and Gretzky started writing his legend in good—the first pages of which were the stuff that played out in minor hockey and OHA rinks across Ontario.

When Gretzky retired, it might have been reasonable to expect a star to emerge from those shaken out of the junior ranks in the mid- or late-'90s. That is, it might have been reasonable to expect that Gretzky's successor was a fair way up the pipeline—after all, Gretzky wasn't out of his teens when Gordie Howe retired for the second and last time, but he was already in the NHL.

On this count, though, there was no immediate successor, either.

You would have looked to a player in his first couple of years in the pros, someone barely out of his teens—a player who dominated junior hockey and made a seamless transition into the pros. The likeliest candidates would have been the two players who were selected with the top picks in the 1997 and 1998 drafts, Joe Thornton and Vincent Lecavalier. These players weren't just the top 18-year-olds coming out of their respective years. They were the consensus No. 1's, the obvious picks.

I saw both as juniors, Thornton with Gretzky's former team, the Soo Greyhounds, Lecavalier with Sidney Crosby's future team, the Rimouski Oceanic.

Thornton was like Lindros, a big man who had a small man's feet. You expect a big man to be able to skate swiftly when he finally unfurls his long limbs and gathers speed. Thornton lived up to those expectations but, like Lindros, he also had the quick acceleration and could dance in traffic, darting in and out of close quarters. He also possessed feral intensity on the ice that was like Mark Messier's or Howe's. One night in Kingston I saw Thornton put on a display that I'd rank with the best of them. He scored a couple of goals, racked up at least a couple of assists, scored a unanimous decision over Kingston's tough guy and, with the ref's back turned, landed a right hook to the head of an opponent who reached from the bench to hold him behind the play.

Lecavalier was an entirely different package. He was as tall as Thornton but less physically mature, lacking the burst and high gear. Though less physically overpowering Lecavalier was more creative with the puck. His game evoked Jean Béliveau, imperious and dignified. He was so rangy that defenders seemed yards away from the puck when he went wide. Another Béliveau-esque quality: he was a serious-minded kid, who seemed to measure every word and do nothing of waste off ice.

Together, Thornton and Lecavalier were signs of a healthy Canadian game. Many hockey men and commentators were sure that European methods of skill development were eclipsing the Canadian approach but the two best players in these two draft classes were graduates of the grassroots Canadian game.

It was all heartening—until you looked closely at the picture.

Going into their draft year, both had put up great numbers in junior but nothing like Gretzky's.

At 18 neither was a patch on the player Gretzky had been at that age. Thornton could not even earn a regular spot in the Boston Bruins' line-up. And he wasn't the best 18-year-old rookie in Boston. That honour belonged to Sergei Samsonov. Over the course of his rookie NHL season, Thornton scored but three goals. Lecavalier fared somewhat better on the brutal Tampa Bay Lightning—13 goals, 15 assists. Lecavalier's worst struggles would lie a season or two ahead. The truth of the matter is, the sum of Thornton's and Lecavalier's rookie years was a fraction of Gretzky's year as an 18-year-old NHLer. In fact, as an 18-year-old, all Gretzky did was tie for the league lead in points scored (he lost the Art Ross to Marcel Dionne because the L.A. Kings' centre had managed two more goals over the course of the season).

Maybe officials at Hockey Canada could lay plans to turn out very good players, players like Thornton and Lecavalier, players who would be stars in the NHL, players who would represent Canada in international play. But when it came to genius, to transcendent talent, like Orr, like Gretzky, like Lemieux, it seemed all of Hockey Canada's white papers and coaching clinics were for not. You might even have presumed that all their programs might encumber or stifle real genius if it happened along.

After his last game in Canada, Gretzky's thoughts turned back to his days with the Soo Greyhounds, to that series against the 67's. He wasn't offering up an answer to a question from the floor. No, under the spotlights, with cameras rolling, he turned back the clock of his own accord.

"We were making 21 bucks a week and I was just as happy as I am today," he said.

The weekly pay Gretzky mentioned didn't quite jibe with the

number cited in *Sports Illustrated* back in 1978. E.M. Swift referred to a $75-a-week pay scale. No matter.

Here, Gretzky was offering up the idea that his season in the Soo, his stint in junior, was one of the best times of his life. There was no material gain, no championship. There was some significant sacrifice. But there was some return on his talent, or, as he would have had it, passion. There wouldn't be career-defining moments in junior but there were plenty that foreshadowed the great stuff to come—and plenty that would serve as the measure for his would-be successors and inheritors.

— T H R E E —

"Every hour that he wasn't sleeping or in school
he'd be doing something with hockey in it."

Canadian hockey officials didn't know but could only hope that
Gretzky's successor was out there. They couldn't have known that his
successor was just 11 years old.

The week before Gretzky's retirement made headlines across Canada
and the U.S., Sidney Crosby made it into the Halifax *Daily News* sports
section, page 54. It wasn't a profile or a splashy feature. In fact, it was a
footnote at the bottom of a roundup of local news on minor hockey.
Crosby's name had appeared in scoring summaries a few times over the
previous couple of years. This, however, was the first time his name broke
out of the small type.

> Last weekend at Charlottetown, Cole Harbour captured
> the Atlantic Peewee championship, defeating Fredericton
> 6–3 in the final. Tim Spidel—the tournament MVP—
> scored three goals for Cole Harbour. Sidney Crosby, Joe
> Sanford, and Andrew Newton had one each.

Passing mention perhaps*, but Crosby was already well known in
minor-hockey circles in Halifax. He was also well known in the sports

* see page 28

department of *The Daily News*. The sports editor at the time, Carl Fleming, coached against Crosby's first rep team, the Cole Harbour Novice C's, back in the winter of '93–'94.

"It was one of Sidney's first years in the game," Fleming explained. "He would have been six. He was so much tinier than the rest of the players who were two or three years older than him. It's not a situation that you'd want to put most kids in, but there was no problem for Sidney … no risk that he was going to get hurt or discouraged. Even at that stage he was capable of doing some amazing things on the ice. He could do things with the puck that the older boys just weren't capable of. I didn't really take note of his name at the time—one of my players came up to me a few years after and told me that the Crosby kid setting all the scoring records in peewee was that same little kid who played against our team before. It made sense that he'd developed into this amazing talent because he'd shown a lot back in that first year."

Ed Spidel's son Tim played with Crosby for several years coming up through minor hockey and, as noted in the clipping from *The Daily News*, occasionally stole the spotlight from the phenom. "Both Tim and Sidney were on the small side," he said. "But they both had amazing skills. Tim's game was all speed. Sidney had the puck skills and awareness on the ice—the ability to read situations. When they played together, it was really an amazing thing to watch. It's what you really wanted to see—the way the game should be played—when you went to a rink on a Saturday morning."

And yet many in minor-hockey circles in Halifax decried the lack of

---

* In contrast, Wayne Gretzky's arrival got a much splashier treatment, almost certainly because of his proximity to the national media hub in Toronto. Back in October, 1971, John Iaboni of the *Toronto Telegram* profiled the 10-year-old Gretzky, then property of the Nadrofsky Steelers. That story, with a photo of the blond, 70-pound waif, took up the top half of the paper's minor hockey page. Gretzky was quoted as saying: "Gordie Howe is my kind of player. He had so many tricks around the net no wonder he scored so many goals. I'd like to be just like him. And if I couldn't play hockey I'd like to play baseball with the Oakland Athletics and Vida Blue." Iaboni seized on what was an issue for the young Gretzky and the Steelers, namely the tons of ice time he was getting. The Steelers coach defended the strategy, but even Walter Gretzky expressed concern. "To be very honest, I don't like seeing him on the ice all the time," Gretzky's father said. "I'll leave it (to the coach). Wayne has always been a good skater, although he's never had the size. As long as he likes the sport, I won't complain." Iaboni's account of the young phenom was placed, prophetically, beside "Bobby Orr's hockey tips," a regular advice section for young players. On this occasion Orr's advice was "no socks—just bare feet for a snug fit."

support top young players received. It wasn't a line of discussion about Crosby in particular but rather about the significant handicap that the best players in every class had to work under.

"A lot of people thought that the shortage of ice time, teams only getting a practice or two in a week, put our players and teams at a disadvantage compared to what you'd see in programs across Canada," Fleming said. "Then you factor in the idea that hockey's very much a seasonal thing here—which is to say that a lot of young players here just don't have the access to summer hockey schools or ice out of season that players in other parts of the country do. The players, these young boys and girls, were not necessarily being well-served.

"In a lot of other places in this country, players had advantages over our players here in Halifax. The top minor-hockey programs in Ontario or the West or in Montreal have resources that just aren't available to our players (in Halifax). And the fact is, in a lot of other places in this province, young players have advantages. It's not a surprise that, say, Al MacInnis is a Nova Scotian, but comes from a smaller centre where he can get lots more practice time than in Halifax, where ice time is limited and playing outside isn't an option often because of inclement weather. So it isn't just that Nova Scotia and Atlantic Canada were the unlikeliest places in Canada to develop a good professional player, never mind an amazing talent like Sidney. It's more than that. Out here, Halifax is the most unlikely place in the most unlikely region."

Sidney Crosby's former minor hockey teammate was aware of the disparity. "When we would go out of town for tournaments," Tim Spidel explained, "we'd talk to players from other cities at our hotel and we were always amazed to hear how much ice time and practice time these other teams were getting. We were really lucky to get a third practice in a week every once and a while. Usually it was just two. These other kids had practices or games every day. Sometimes, they said, they were practicing in the morning and having a game later. Plus, they were skating through the summer. We were playing baseball or doing something else. You know, we didn't even really think about (skating during the summer). And the thing was it was like that not just when we were seven, eight and nine years old. Right into bantam and midget, that was the usual thing—two practices a week. Which makes it all the more amazing that Sidney became as good as he did. Everyone talks about how some kids don't have a chance to develop into players, but I always wonder how much better Sidney might have been if he had been growing up somewhere with a great hockey program, lots of practice time and all that other stuff."

The same debate in Halifax was playing out across Canada: in the effort to find ice time and coaching for all who want to play, do we punish the very best by limiting what we do for them? Should we dedicate the lion's share of resources to the most promising among them? The former seems to be the democratic approach but its inefficiencies are plain—if your child were gifted it would be easy to feel poorly served. The latter lays out a harsh, outcomes-based approach like you'd find at the national ballet school—all well and good until it's your child who falls one place short of making it into the program.

And yet several years after Fleming first saw Crosby, the boy was excelling. Scoring goals by the hundreds. Leading Halifax teams to unprecedented victories in regional and national play. How had that little kid from the Cole Harbour Novice C's broken through?

⚓

I witnessed the disadvantages that Carl Fleming and Tim Spidel described. I saw them play out over two thousand kilometres away from Halifax in Northern Ontario. Eight months after Sidney Crosby's name appeared in that write-up about the Cole Harbour peewee's championship in the Atlantic, I ventured up to Timmins for the World Under-17 Challenge. Though billed as a "world" tournament, it was something less so. Hockey Canada invited everyone, and teams from Russia, the Czech Republic, the U.S., Finland and Germany were in the mix. But the Swedes didn't send a squad. Nor did Slovakia. And Canada made up half the field: going west to east, Team Pacific (comprising British Columbia and Alberta), Team West (Saskatchewan and Manitoba), Team Ontario, Team Quebec and finally, last and least, Team Atlantic.

The Russian team won, led by a player of already exquisite skill and only a couple of years away from NHL stardom, Ilya Kovalchuk. The core of that Russian team would go on to win the world junior title in Halifax three years later. In the final at the under-17s, Russia shut out Team Ontario, which featured a bunch of players in their first year with Ontario Hockey League clubs and already touted as high NHL draft picks, even future NHLers. A good number of them, including Steve Eminger, Brendan Bell, Carlo Colaiacovo, Derek Roy and Jay McClement would play on the Canadian team at the 2003 world junior tournament in Halifax.

Every team had a story. Team West had an Inuit kid, Jordin Tootoo, who over the course of a week became a folk hero with his fearless, punishing checking. Team Pacific had Dan Blackburn, a goaltender that some scouts ranked above Roberto Luongo at the same age.

I was fascinated by Team Atlantic. The kids from Down Home managed only one win—Germany's invitation to the tournament ranked a courtesy to Team Atlantic. The East Coast team managed to stay close in a couple of games in their group—though they never seemed in danger of winning. When the Atlantic boys finally went in against the strong Ontario squad, well, the final score, 11–2, was a fair measure of the difference not just between the teams, but between the sophistication of the hockey cultures that spawned them. In truth, the players on Team Atlantic just didn't have the same type of background as those on the other Canadian squads. They didn't come out of major junior. They came out of weak local Junior A programs, midget hockey in Newfoundland, stuff barely a step up from recreational hockey. Some might have held hopes of grabbing a hockey scholarship to a smaller U.S. college. But for most, this turn in Timmins was as close as they were ever going to get to the bright lights. And this isn't just how it played out in Timmins. This was a theme that ran through the history of Team Atlantic at the under-17 tournaments.

I sat at a couple of games with a bunch of the Atlantic players and they all seemed remarkably well-adjusted. In short, they appeared less like participants in the tournament than fans who had lucked into tickets. To a one they felt like they were held back by living and growing up in the Maritimes—that they just didn't have the numbers. Not enough good players to push each other. Not enough teams to compete against. Not enough top coaches to develop the top physical talents. Not enough money to get teams out to national tournaments, to gain exposure to what the game can be. When I suggested they weren't as disadvantaged as, say, Jordin Tootoo coming out of Rankin Inlet, they pointed out that Tootoo had shipped out of the Far North and moved to the near north, Edmonton, in his early teens, to play youth hockey before stepping up to junior.

These weren't just kids from Halifax, but they did represent the entire Atlantic region, and the culture of young players from there. "If you're still home at 15 or 16, then odds are you're not going anywhere," one of them told me. It sounded self-evident, a Newfieism you'd expect a character on *Codco* to spout, but there seemed to be an element of truth to it. These young men pointed to Atlantic-born players who made a mark in major junior, like Dan Cleary, a first-round pick of the Chicago Blackhawks. Cleary left Newfoundland a year before his junior career to get exposure and find out what it was going to take at the next level. To that point he hadn't played in a league that allowed body-checking. Same with fellow Newfoundlander Terry Ryan before him; Ryan had gone to B.C. to play in the Rocky Mountain League, one of the country's toughest Junior A leagues, at 15. In this way he set the table for playing in major junior and for being drafted in the first round by the Montreal Canadiens. The Atlantic players at this tournament were those who hadn't ventured off like Cleary and Ryan. They stayed home and against top international talents or the major junior players from Ontario and the like, they just felt out-matched—thrown in against players of another class.

One night, with Timmins buried under a couple of feet of fresh snow, I sat down with Team Atlantic's coaches. The minutes of the conversation might have been written on a long-lost cocktail napkin. But no matter, the significant points lingered in memory. The Atlantic coaches saw their invitation as symbolic. The World Under-17 Challenge were Canada's idea of a development program for the world junior team. Though one player from the Atlantic figures significantly in Canadian junior lore—Newfoundland's John Slaney, who scored a gold-medal-winning goal back in 1991—only occasionally did a player from the Maritimes make the national under-20 team. For that matter, even Quebec most years had a slim representation, a goaltender or two and a couple of players from the Q. No, the national under-20 program was dominated by the West and Ontario. Team Atlantic at the under-17s? Just filling out the field.

At that point in Timmins, Team Atlantic's coaches were waving the white flag. They couldn't see anyway to make their team competitive at this tournament—realistic perhaps, but too defeatist to be healthy for coaches. Likewise, they accorded their opponents respect, which would have been okay in small doses—these coaches, however, sounded too much impressed. Happy just to be there.

So how did Sidney Crosby transcend the limits of his hockey environment? And how did he not fall into that self-defeating mindset so evident on that Atlantic under-17 squad I met up with in Timmins? Doing forensic work on genius is a speculative exercise at best and often a fool's errand. You have to rely on anecdotes to divine method.

"I remember some of our players talking about it," Carl Fleming recalled. "We used to schedule practices at six or six-thirty a.m. Weekdays, weekends. Getting up that early tested the soul of a lot of our players, some good kids, some who have gone on to play in the Quebec league. Well, they would talk about getting to the arena and see Sidney Crosby working out with his father Troy before our practices—he was coming off before we were going on. This is when he was just a schoolboy—9, 10 or 11.

"I've come to know Sidney and Troy over the years," Fleming continued. "Troy was a goaltender in major juniors and was drafted by the Montreal Canadiens the same year they took Patrick Roy. So he had played at a high level and knew the game. Still, I'm convinced that this wasn't a case of Troy forcing his son to do something—to practice before dawn. I don't think that there was some sort of plan that Troy had for Sidney—nothing like that. I don't think that you could make a kid do something like getting up at dawn to practice if he didn't truly want to. Likewise, I don't think that a father would put himself through something like that unless he was sure that his son was benefiting from it and enjoying it. And if it was a case of a father dragging his son out in the morning and forcing him to do something he didn't want to, well, I think it would cause a lot of resentment later on and I can't see any evidence of that with Troy and Sidney. They really are very close. The only sense that I have is that Troy was prepared to go to practically any lengths for his son."

Tim Spidel, Sidney's friend and former winger from peewee, backed up Fleming's point about Troy supporting rather than pushing his son. "Maybe some people thought that Troy was pushing Sidney but I know that was never the case," Spidel said. "Sid always wanted to play. Always. Every hour that he wasn't sleeping or in school he'd be doing something with hockey in it. I'd go over to his house to hang out and we'd shoot pucks instead of playing Nintendo or watching TV. Or we'd go out and play road hockey. That's the thing with Sidney when we were coming up. I don't think that we ever looked at it like it was work or a grind—he just made a game of what we were doing. He 'played' hockey, like it was *play*, like it was something to have fun with. And I really think that we did and that's why we never got tired of it."

Spidel suggested that hockey was like a gathering storm for Crosby—what started out as an interest became a consuming interest. Consuming interest developed into an obsession. And the product of that obsession was a hockey prodigy.

"Early on Sidney had lots of success," Tim continued. "He played for winning teams. He scored goals. And I think that the success gave him momentum. He didn't care how much time he put in. People at school talked about it—you know, he's *always* playing hockey. There would be the normal school things that he'd miss because of hockey. But because it was sports, people didn't think it was geeky. And I think with Sidney, he always believed that no one cared as much about the game as he did. He believed—and I'm sure he was right—that he always came to the rink more ready to play than anybody else. He had confidence no matter who he was playing against. It didn't matter if they were older, or if they were from other teams and other provinces that had more ice time or whatever. No matter who he was playing against, they hadn't spent as much time practicing and working on their game as he had."

It's no great leap to find in Spidel's characterization of young Sidney Crosby certain threads that Wayne Gretzky spun to describe his own gifts. *I was lucky enough to be gifted. Maybe it wasn't talent He gave me. Maybe it was passion.*

Sidney Crosby's passion struck Rick Bowness the first time they met. Bowness, the coach of the Phoenix Coyotes and a Halifax resident in the off-season, came across Crosby back when he was first tearing up leagues as an eight- and nine-year-old. "It's a small city and a small hockey community. Everybody knows everybody. I've known Sidney and Troy for years. Sidney soaks up the game like a sponge. It's not just that he has an incredible work ethic. He wants to learn about things that can make him better. Some great players might be tough to coach or are even uncoachable …"

Here I had to resist interrupting and raising the name of his former protégé / bête noire with the Ottawa Senators, Alexei Yashin.

"… but Sidney was always prepared to take in whatever a coach or an instructor at hockey school had to offer—a coach's dream. He was just so positive about the game. Sure, there were a lot of other places where there was more support for talent. But that support is no substitute for will. And a will to succeed and to always improve was something that Sidney had early."

It was more than a will to succeed, though. That's just a polite way to express it. Though Crosby was passionate about the game, he was consumed by winning. Not just at hockey. Not just in sport. No, there was something deep-seated, almost needy, about his attitude toward victory and defeat.

"In the ordinary way of guys playing hockey, Sidney liked to win and just hated to lose," said Andrew Gordon, who played age-group hockey with Crosby. "He just took losses harder. He would just be ruined after a loss—nothing you could say could pick him up. He was way more than just competitive. It was more than the games we played. Sidney had a way of turning everything into a contest. Whether it was something on the ice during practice or playing shinny or road hockey or just playing around. Or if we were playing some other game. It didn't have to be a game, though. If we went for dinner, he'd want to bet on who could finish his meal first. And if he lost, the next thing you knew he'd be wanting to go again, double or nothing."

Gordon's words reminded me of an anecdote from Wayne Gretzky's youth. Years ago, I did a story on those who had fleeting associations with No. 99. One of them, a friend, Glenn Miller, hit a game-winning triple off the 12-year-old Gretzky who was pitching for Brantford at a Little League tournament. Miller talked about Gretzky, dejected and tearing up, taking his place at shortstop after being pulled from the mound. Given what Gordon said, it's easy to imagine Crosby reacting in much the same way.

Still, this ultra-competitive component of Crosby's character seems closer to Michael Jordan than to Wayne Gretzky. Consider what one NHL scout later said of Crosby: "It's clear that he holds himself to a very high standard. Talk to enough people and you find that it's a bigger picture than that. He has a history of making teams better than they should have been—even as a young kid. What we see wherever he goes is that he almost forces everyone around him to be better and do better and push harder. They say that the best players make other players better. With his will to compete, Crosby makes other players *make themselves better.*"

Just think of Jordan mercilessly goading Scottie Pippen, humiliating a generation of younger teammates, stepping on toes, pushing the envelope. And think of his competitive instinct overtaking him, whether it was running up gambling debts in the millions, undertaking a misbegotten baseball career or an even more misbegotten comeback with the Washington Wizards.

It's hard to fathom Jordan's or Gretzky's will to compete, harder still to trace it to its source. It might be a little easier with Sidney Crosby. After all, it's not a matter of decades. It's asking a high school student to go all the way back to the days of his childhood.

FOUR

"We taught him to be a good person ... "

For Wayne Gretzky it started with a backyard rink that his father Walter flooded. For hockey fans years later, after all the stories had been told and retold, it became easy to visualize that Gretzky family rink: a boy spending hours after school and at night toiling away on the ice, his father watching on, his little brothers putting on their skates. This kind of scene has played out across Canada for generations—but when genius on the scale of Wayne Gretzky emerged, the backyard rink became more than a local landmark. It became sacred ground. And those days and nights on the ice became something more than a family memory or neighbourhood lore. They became Canadian heritage moments.

For Sidney Crosby his development started out in a less likely venue, the basement of his grandmother's house. And it started with an object that has never before figured in Canadian hockey legend: a Whirlpool dryer. Young Crosby, when he was first big enough to hold a stick and raise a puck off the ice—or the floor—fired shots at a dryer in his grandmother's basement. And when he was ready to take aim at something other than inanimate objects, there was a ready and qualified candidate: Sidney's father Troy who had, after all, played goal for Verdun in the

Quebec major junior hockey league. But instead of Troy, Sidney's grand-mother filled the role of first goalie to be beaten by the youngster. "She was tough to beat," a straight-faced Sidney would tell me.

Over time he graduated to shooting on Troy in the basement. Troy mocked up a rink downstairs—painting the floor white complete with blue and red lines. Troy stepped aside when Sidney was nine. "He was killing me," Troy told *Sports Illustrated*. "I told him, 'You don't need a goaltender, just shoot at the net.'" While that might seem exaggerated—a former major junior goaltender getting worn out by a tyke—it's important to note that the longest shot in the basement was all of 20 feet and Troy did mention that his son had a predilection for taking full wind-up slapshots. In Troy's absence, the dryer kept on taking a beating. Covered in dents and black rubber streaks and with the nobs long gone, it still functions. Already the dryer has taken a prominent place in Crosby lore and in time it might make the strangest display at the Hockey Hall of Fame.

What can we read into Sidney Crosby's hundreds of hours of toil in the basement? It does seem central to recurring themes in his story.

First and most obviously, there is his work ethic, which is again a thread in common with Gretzky. As Tim Spidel said, he spent seemingly every waking hour away from school invested in the game, albeit with what might have been laborious practice sometimes morphing into another game, a challenge, with his friends. It was almost certainly no dif-ferent for Gretzky on the backyard rink, for Bobby Orr on the icy ponds in Parry Sound, or for Gordie Howe on the frozen sloughs of Saskatchewan.

Again, borrowing from the Gretzky story, Crosby benefited from the support of his family with his father playing the most prominent role. It dated from the moment Troy and Trina took him to a neighbourhood rink, before his third birthday, and put him on skates. It carried through to them taking Sidney to the arena for league games as a youngster. And even today, with Sidney finishing junior on the height of hockey stardom and on the cusp of much bigger things with Mario Lemieux and the Penguins, at the arena or at a product launch, you're likely to find Troy by his side, like Wayne Gretzky moved in tandem with Walter.

However, standing apart from the story of Gretzky or other stars who came along, is the quality of resourcefulness. With the support of his family, Sidney made the best of less than ideal situations and in fact didn't seem to realize he was missing out on anything. As Carl Fleming said, kids in Halifax don't have as much access to ice as those who grow up elsewhere in the country or in a lot of places around the world. A limited number of arenas means that ice time for team practice is hard to come by; inclement weather means that outdoor pads are often unplayable.

☺

From his first trips to the rink, from his first attempts to skate at age three, from his first season of organized hockey at age five, it was clear Sidney Crosby had something above the average aptitude for learning the game. It wasn't simply that he picked up skating more quickly than others his age or that he could raise the puck when others were sliding it along the ice. It wasn't just about acquiring skills. According to lore around Halifax rinks, his understanding of the game was intuitive, not learned—he knew before being told for instance that he should lead teammates with passes. As Troy told Shawna Richer of *The Globe and Mail*: "He was doing a lot of things naturally. Kids that age want to carry the puck from one end of the ice to the other to score. Even at six, Sidney was a natural passer. Stuff like that is not normal." He was like a musical prodigy in that his sense of the game seemed to reside within him. He never had to be told something twice and a great deal of the time he didn't need to be told anything at all.

And to a one, the coaches, players and officials who encountered him always came away impressed with his attitude. In Shawna Richer's story, Trina Crosby best summed up the values that she and Troy tried to instill in their son—apparently successfully. "We taught him to be a good person and treat others like he wanted to be treated," Trina said. "It wasn't complicated. We asked him to treat people with kindness and respect his elders. He's sensitive to other people. He's thoughtful."

It sounds so basic to good parenting that it's a wonder so many get it wrong.

Trina and Troy seemed to get everything right with their son and obviously made their relationship with Sidney their highest priority, likely because their own youths were marked by absent fathers. In Trina's case, her father died while still quite young. Troy's parents divorced and his father was largely absent, never seeing him play junior hockey. As Shawna Richer noted, both Trina and Troy were the youngest children in their families and both were "essentially raised by their mothers."

To this day many people in hockey are put off by Troy always being in the picture with Sidney. They see him as one wanting to bask in the reflected glow of his son. They see him not as a benign and sage advisor like Walter Gretzky, but rather like Carl Lindros, who, fairly or not, was viewed as a meddler, always looking to get special consideration for his son, Eric. Yet when Troy's own youth is taken into account, it's easy to explain why he is always by Sidney's side—because he understands what it's like to go it alone.

In fact Wayne Gretzky pointed to Sidney's relationship with his father as one of the reasons he's held up so well through all the attention, the good and the bad. "It helps to have that one person who you can always talk to," Gretzky told me. "When that one person has been with you all your life, at all the games, he can know you so well. I had that with my father and Sidney does too. I think that Troy is a great guy. And Sidney is just such a great young man, really well-grounded. He's been raised right."

Indeed, Trina Crosby seems to take more pride in the fact that Sidney hasn't been affected by the attention and acclaim than she does in all his successes. "He completely understands the concept of enjoying things while they're here because he knows they could be gone tomorrow," she explained. "It's neat for him to be a role model, and for kids to knock on our door at Halloween and say 'Is Sid home?' It's neat for us too, for the kids to look up to our child like that."

Those who knew him back in Cole Harbour vouch for Sidney's good character. "It's not that Sidney isn't capable of having fun or that he tries to be a goody-two-shoes or something," said Tim Spidel. "He just gets along with people. I've seen it so many times—him taking time to talk to little kids who come up to him or spending time with (his little sister)

Taylor. All the years we played together and hung out I never had a fight or an argument with him—and you just sort of expect that stuff. It's strange that we never did, but that's just the way he is or the way he carries himself." And that's the way he carried himself even through trying times.

☙

The adults in charge of the Cole Harbour Hockey Association were able to do what the boys on the ice couldn't: they stopped Crosby. They did this by ruling against him playing up. It's a cruel irony that the young man who has already done more than any other citizen to put Cole Harbour on the map faced so much opposition close to home.

When Sidney was 12 and already regarded as a prodigy, he played a game for the Cole Harbour Red Wings AAA bantam team in a tournament. "Playing up"—youngsters playing for teams in advanced age categories—is always a contentious issue. In most instances it's regarded as a regrettable and usually non-productive by-product of overly ambitious parents rather than an indicator of real talent. And this did seem to be "playing up" in the extreme. Sidney at 12 was put in against players as old as 15. In fairness, he had played up his entire young hockey life. However, by the time players reach their early teens, the issue is more troublesome—the over-reaching of parents can put their progeny at significant physical risk. The difference between a 6-year-old and a 9-year-old in a non-contact league is not so significant as that between a 12-year-old and a kid in high school in a league that allows body-checking.

Harry O'Donnell, the coach of the Cole Harbour Red Wings bantams, made the decision to play Crosby. The coach was suspended for a game. And in no uncertain terms he was told to cease and desist. "I knew that I would get spanked for it, but I didn't expect this," O'Donnell told reporter Chris Kallan of the Halifax *Daily News*. "I just wanted to put the best players on the ice ... that's the bottom line. They didn't agree with that."

And O'Donnell pleaded his case to the newspaper by invoking a familiar name. "What would have happened to Wayne Gretzky if they did that to him?" he asked.

The Cole Harbour Hockey Association wasn't moved by O'Donnell's arguments. The CHHA officials didn't buy the notion that an exception should be made for Crosby, even though he had led his Cole Harbour peewee team to an Atlantic championship the previous weekend. They didn't see a kid who had more than handled a season of play in a league that allowed contact. And they certainly didn't see a kid who had scored more than 200 points in 70 games against the best kids in his age group as the next Gretzky. All they saw was a jockey-sized five-foot-two squirt in against more than a few kids who would have stood better than six feet. It was here they saw the potential for disaster. And they didn't see it as any less of a risk despite Crosby having scored a goal and three assists in this single, lopsided victory for O'Donnell's bantam squad.

"They probably should have asked guys on the teams that played against Sidney if he could play up," said Chad Anderson, who played on several different squads that faced Crosby going back to novice hockey through bantam. "He was short but nobody would say that he was small. He was stronger than some of the biggest guys on the team—on his skates he was stronger than practically anyone. Nobody who played against him—no matter how big or how much older—thought that he was easy pickings or anything like that."

In other leagues kids played up and turned out to be a lot less than hockey prodigies. And in Cole Harbour other kids had played up before Crosby and few outside their families remember their names. According to *The Daily News*, several players played up from peewee to bantam the previous season, but Cole Harbour officials changed the rules—no doubt with the foreknowledge that Crosby was in the program and would be affected by the rule. In fact, some make the case it was a change in policy made with Crosby in mind, and it had to be hard for him not to take it personally.

"I think it's pretty cheap, because Brent Theriault (another peewee playing up) will be playing for the Halifax Hawks, and I can't play," a disappointed Crosby told *The Daily News*. "I wanted to finish my season this weekend playing in the Bantam Atlantics, but now I can't. It's just poltics, I guess.

"I played with those same guys most of last year. It was no big deal (playing with them in bantam). It wasn't that hard. After the first period, I was pretty well used to it."

Troy Crosby appealed to the Cole Harbour officials but couldn't sway them. He couldn't even get a meeting with them. "It was just a flat no," he said. "That was their position. That was it. We want what's best for his development. Everyone should be challenged to play at his best, otherwise it's just a waste of time."

Who's to say who's right?

In retrospect, it's easy to ridicule the Cole Harbour Hockey Association for its inflexibility—for its unwillingness to bend rules and give an inch to so spectacular a talent as Sidney Crosby. In the story that played out in Cole Harbour, the CHHA is the equivalent of the high school coach in Wilmington, North Carolina, who achieved a level of infamy for cutting a Grade 11 student named Michael Jordan.

On the other hand, given all that Sidney Crosby would go on to achieve, he doesn't seem particularly damaged by the Cole Harbour Hockey Association's decision. Yes, he was disappointed at the time, but it's hard to make a case that it adversely affected his development in the long run.

Andrew Gordon is uniquely positioned to judge the issue of playing up—moreover, the issue of Sidney Crosby playing up in Cole Harbour. He was more than just a contemporary of Crosby's; Gordon was caught up in the controversy.

"I ended up getting my spot on a team because they had to send Sidney back down," Gordon explained. "I was the player who was cut and that they had to bring back. I wanted to play but I didn't think for a second that I deserved to ahead of Sidney. And to be honest I felt bad about it. I would have liked to see what Sidney could have done. They should have let him play, no question. Obviously he wasn't just a talented player but a very, very special player who could have handled playing up. There's no sense having a rule that you apply across the board without ever looking at the individual player.

"A lot of other guys would have been sour in (Sidney's) situation. A lot of guys would have made something personal out of it. But the thing is, Sidney never gave me a hard time about it. We ended up playing together the next year and we got along great. There were no hard feelings at all."

And some kids who play up with older players manage to make a team without ever becoming part of that team—that is, they will play together with their teammates on the ice but become marginalized off it. Gordon said that was never the case with Crosby.

"Even before Sidney was sent back, he seemed to fit in with the guys," Gordon noted. "Whenever he was playing up—whether he was 6 or 12 or whatever—he just seemed to know how to act around the older guys and he knew what to say. He didn't make it seem like he had to try to do that. He just knew and made it seem natural. No one ever objected to having him around—you had to respect his game and you had to respect him just for the way he is."

Troy Crosby, on the other hand, was not always as well respected. Reading between the lines of the coverage of the "playing-up" story, it's easy to sense a certain ambivalence toward Troy. In one sports column that ostensibly supported Sidney, a *Daily News* writer described Troy as "no angel"—a strange backhanded bit of incidental colour. It played to the image of the "involved" parent, one who takes too large a role in his youngster's affairs.

According to those who were on the scene when Sidney Crosby was coming up, there was no shortage of regulars at the rink who were something less than angelic. "Some of the stuff that Troy and Trina had to put up with at the arena was awful," admitted Ed Spidel, father of Sidney's boyhood teammate Tim. "There were lots of awful things that were said to him and to his parents by the parents of other players. It had to make them very uncomfortable—it certainly did with Trina. And Troy had to take the role of looking out for Sidney. It wasn't just Sidney's playing up. (Troy) looked out for him in a lot of areas—whether it was teams coming after Sidney or agents or whatever. And Troy had to be firm and sometimes tough in looking after Sidney's interests."

It was a point that wasn't lost on Sidney's friends and teammates. "It might have been easier for Sid than for his parents," Tim Spidel said. "Sid could go out on the ice and take things into his own hands. If someone gave him a hard time from the stands or the bench or on the ice, he'd just play right through it. He'd take it to them. I know things that went on (around the arena) really bothered him, but these people just didn't understand. He was an amazing player and really motivated all the time—but if you got him mad, he'd just play even better. He'd punish you."

☿

Despite the numbers that Sidney Crosby put up, despite the controversy about his playing up, he remained through age 13 a local phenomenon or, at most, a regional one. His teams won city, provincial and Atlantic championships. But he wasn't yet measured against the best in the country in one of the elite bantam or midget competitions. Until then, the greater Canadian hockey community would view him with some skepticism. Some would maintain that he'd have a lot harder time racking up those numbers if he were in a top league in, say, the Greater Toronto Hockey League or in AAA in Montreal or in against the best of his age in Calgary or Edmonton. And they would shrug off Crosby's reputation in the Maritimes because they knew, like Tim Spidel and Carl Fleming, that Halifax was hardly a hothouse for talent, hardly a production line for elite prospects. The skeptics knew that talent was best fostered and developed in other cities in other regions.

These attitudes started to turn in the 2001–02 season when 14-year-old Sidney, all of five-foot-eight and 165 pounds, moved on to play for the Dartmouth Subways Midget AAA team. The numbers stayed the same: he scored a mind-boggling 193 points for the Subways in 74 games. And he was as always playing up, bantam-aged, the youngest player on the Subways and a mere sprout, more than three years younger than most opponents, when, that year, he took a few shifts with the Truro Bearcats in the Maritime Junior A Hockey League.

Crosby led the Subways to the provincial championship and then to victory in the Atlantic regional tournament, a qualifier for the country's top midget tournament, the Air Canada Cup. It was at the Air Canada Cup that Crosby debuted in front of the national media. The tournament was carried by The Sports Network and received notice in newspapers across the country. It wasn't a home game for the Subways but just about the nearest thing to it, being staged that March in New Brunswick.

Ultimately, the Subways fell a game short of the national title. In the championship game, they started out nervously, made a few errors in their own end of the rink and dropped behind Saskatchewan's Tisdale Trojans 3–0 in the first period. There wasn't much suspense after that, though Crosby did have one spectacular moment. Midway through the second period with Dartmouth down 4–0, Jeff Kielbratowski hit a streaking Crosby at centre ice with a tape-to-tape pass and Crosby finished the chance with a flourish. It was the high point in the game for the Subways, who had to settle for a silver medal after the 6–2 loss.

"They definitely caught us by surprise," Crosby told reporters after the game. "We were a little nervous at the start and we didn't get our feet moving. We might have been a little bit tentative playing in front of a national television audience, but we can't use that as an excuse. They beat us and they're a great team."

The champions weren't reluctant about heaping praise on Crosby. The Tisdale captain, Michael Olson, told Crosby during the post-game ceremonial handshake, "You're a hell of hockey player and I'll probably be watching you some day on TV." Olson later told reporters that the Trojans' game plan had one overriding goal. "Our offence is built off our defence. We knew that Sidney Crosby had to be shut down and we knew we had to play strong defensively."

"He's definitely a very special kid," said Tisdale coach Darrell Mann. "For a 14-year-old, I can't believe his mental toughness and his physical toughness. Every team here keyed on him all week long and for him to put up the numbers that he did, is incredible."

The final line of numbers was just as Mann described them, incredible: Crosby led the tournament in scoring with 11 goals and 13 assists in seven games against players two and three years older than him, good for the tournament's most valuable player award.

Brad Crossley, a high school teacher, knew the game. He had been with the Dartmouth program for nine years, four as a head coach before Sidney came along. He also had known the Crosbys for years. He had played in junior with Troy and gone to high school with Trina. He had

Troy's trust on the hockey side and Trina's on everything else. "It was a dream to have a chance to coach a young man like Sidney," Crossley asserted. "You know that you're lucky to get a chance to work with one player like that in your lifetime as a coach. And it was a lot easier for everyone involved because (of the history).

"Even as one of the younger players on the team, he set the standard for work and intensity. He didn't need to be loud. But other guys could see how he went about things in the dressing room and on the ice. He never did things halfway. His commitment was total. It's a cliché to talk about a star making everyone on the ice a better player—usually it just means that a star creates scoring chances and some guys bank in some rebounds or he opens up the ice for others with all the attention that other teams give him. But with Sidney it really was true. I could sense it in the room. He made his teammates want to be better. He made them believe that they could be better. They saw what he was able to do—what he had done with himself with practice and work and imagination—and they wanted to get there too."

Darren Cossar of Hockey Nova Scotia described the Subways' performance at the Air Canada Cup as "a breakthrough" for hockey in the province. They were the first team from Atlantic Canada to make it as far as the championship game in the event's first 24 years. "There was one time back in the '80s when a Dartmouth team—they weren't the Subways back then—made it to the semi-finals," Cossar recalled.

"Probably a couple of kids from that team played in the Q. But this Dartmouth team that Sidney played on was another thing completely. Not to take anything away from Sidney at all, but there were other talented kids on that team too. Obviously Sidney was the most gifted player on that team but the Subways had some depth of talent—kids like Andrew Gordon who'd go on to play at U.S. colleges. And that Subways team served as an example to teams in Halifax and the rest of the province to show that we could compete with the best in Canada."

Cossar's point about the Subways' silver medal marking a breakthrough is beyond dispute but his take on Sidney Crosby's role is dubious. Never mind that coach Crossley said after the tournament that "we rode on his shoulders for the last seven days and he's pulled us along greatly with a lot of poise." In fact, a few teams that fell by the wayside in the playdowns for the Air Canada Cup featured more than one player who'd be a first-round pick in major junior drafts. The champions that year hailed from Tisdale, a small town in northeastern Saskatchewan, but their line-up featured players from across the province and across the Western Hockey League—11 Tisdale Trojans had been drafted by teams in the "Dub." The Subways, by way of contrast, had but one player, Scott Nause, who had been drafted by a Q team; and, other than Crosby, only Andrew Gordon figured to be a major-junior draft prospect.

After the medal ceremonies, after the television lights were turned off, after the fans left the building, several Dartmouth players spared the arena crew some clean-up work—they grabbed signs and banners decorating the rink. This wasn't just their last midget game. This was as far as they would go in hockey. And they were going to be able to say, like Tisdale's Michael Olson, that they were on the ice with Sidney Crosby. They even had the banners to prove it.

"It's like he gives the team a chance
against anybody."

Effectively Sidney Crosby had come to a crossroads. It must be that way
with prodigies of all sorts. First they overtake the other children, the ones
their age, and the ones older than them. Then they overtake their
teachers, everything their immediate environment can give them. So it
was for Crosby after the Air Canada Cup.

It was clear he would be ready at 15 to compete in the major junior
ranks. But he faced a roadblock for "playing up" like he had encountered
back in Cole Harbour. In many fields, the gifted get doors opened that are
dead-bolted to the run-of-the-mill. Not in junior hockey.

In fact, the Quebec Major Junior Hockey League, the Q, was even
more entrenched in its position on player age than the officials in Cole
Harbour had been: major junior leagues open their doors to 16-year-old
players. In the recent past there have been exceptions made for a few top
15-year-old prospects. They've been allowed to play for teams in cities
where they reside prior to their draft year. Jason Spezza is one example.
At 15 he played for the Brampton Battalion (and his parents had to move
from Mississauga so he could do so). The following year he was eligible
for the Ontario Hockey League draft and was selected by the Mississauga

IceDogs. More recently, in the spring of 2005, the OHL allowed a highly touted prospect, John Tavares, to enter the draft a year early—he was granted status as an exceptional case, because he was the first overall draft pick of his region, a year ahead of his class—like Crosby surely would have been.

Neither the accomplishments of Spezza nor Tavares ranked with Crosby's at the equivalent stages in their hockey careers, yet the QMJHL wasn't about to budge. The Halifax Mooseheads, unlike their minor-league counterparts, were one of the Q's stronger programs and richer teams. And rival teams in the Q weren't about to give them the advantage of a season highlighted by Crosby's services. Some executives expressed concern about whether Crosby was physically big enough and mature enough to stand up to the rigours of major junior hockey; their real concern focused on their teams' chances of competing against another fortified by Crosby's presence. Other executives argued that they didn't want to set an early-entry precedent that players of less ability than Crosby might one day seek to follow. This argument held a degree of credibility. The decision to block Crosby's early entry almost certainly hurt the league's overall business interests—teams effectively voted against an invitation to a gate attraction—meaning that the decision didn't help the prospect, the quality of the league or its bottom line.

Even if he was denied a chance to play with the Mooseheads in the Q, Crosby could have stayed the course and stayed at home—the Dartmouth Subways would have gladly had him back and taken another run at the Air Canada Cup. But that arrangement would have been a lot better for the Subways than for Crosby. He had already been the brightest talent in the midget ranks at age 14. He was more than ready for new challenges. He desperately needed to be pushed. He needed more talent beside him. He needed more talent against him.

But where?

"I'm not sure I'm going to prep school or play junior A," Crosby told reporters at the Air Canada Cup. "Those are the only two things I can do and I'm not really sure yet."

The prep school option came down to one school, Shattuck-St. Mary's, an exclusive private school on a sylvan campus in Faribault,

Minnesota. Shattuck-St. Mary's has but three hundred students, half of them playing in the boys' and girls' hockey program. Other schools closer to home received some consideration, among them Upper Canada College, the Toronto school for the privileged elite. But in truth, UCC's hockey program, though it drew some top student-athletes from across Canada via scholarships and had turned out a few NHLers, paled next to Shattuck-St. Mary's. Shattuck was drawing in not just the best players from the hockey hotbed of Minnesota, it was also attracting many top Canadian prospects, particularly from western Canada. Canadian kids were going to Shattuck-St. Mary's so they could keep open their options for NCAA hockey. (Once a player logs a couple of games with a Canadian major junior team, he becomes ineligible for U.S. college hockey.)

Shattuck-St. Mary's schedule was considered a step up from the competition that players might see in Provincial A in Canada.* This was particularly true for Crosby. Junior A out east, the Maritime Junior A Hockey League, was much weaker than comparable leagues in Ontario or in the west. And though the Crosbys were contacted by dozens of Provincial A programs across the country, any move away from Halifax was likely to meet with some resistance. For several seasons officials in these major junior feeder leagues had been blocking the practice of parachuting in players from other provinces and other countries, ostensibly to promote development of local players. It apparently didn't occur to them that Sidney Crosby or other elite talents parachuting into a league might actually assist development of local players by raising the level of play.

But Shattuck-St. Mary's had no such reservations about bringing in Crosby and others to play with Minnesota's best. Shattuck was too busy running up the score on opponents to hear the complaints about ringers.

Shattuck-St. Mary's has a scholastic reputation comparable to UCC's. Its yearly tuition—$26,500 U.S.—is in the same neighbourhood as UCC's, but Shattuck's reputation within the hockey industry completely

* With 138 teams in 10 leagues across the country (at the end of the 2004-05 season), the Canadian Junior A Hockey League (CJAHL) is the top junior league outside the CHL. Major junior players void their eligibility to play U.S. college hockey, but players in Junior A retain their eligibility. Several teams, like the St. Albert Saints in Alberta or the Pembroke Lumber Kings in Ontario, have produced more NHLers than the total for the Maritime Junior Hockey League. A few Junior B leagues ice teams comparable to the CJAHL.

outstrips the Toronto school. It was well regarded in part because its athletic director had a perfect NHL pedigree: J.P. Parise, a former Minnesota North Star and a member of Team Canada back during the Summit Series in '72. Shattuck also had a growing reputation for developing talent, foremost among them Parise's son, Zach, an impressively skilled if undersized forward.

Sidney's attending Shattuck was not a decision the Crosbys reached in a vacuum. It was, rather, something recommended by players who would be wingers for the phenom off the ice for seasons to come: Pat Brisson and J.P. Barry of the International Management Group (IMG).

It's not clear when the first agent contacted the Crosby household— the parents and son are too diplomatic to name names and cite unsolicited meetings. Suffice it to say, by the time Sidney committed to Shattuck-St. Mary's, IMG's Brisson and Barry had the Crosbys' ears. They weren't yet acting as agents—but just, as they described it to the media, "advisors." It was a veiled way of putting the necessary distance between their outfit and the young player—a distance that would be necessary if Sidney opted to pass up Canadian junior hockey to play the U.S. college game. It's common practice in the industry for agents to have the ears of top collegiate players, though everything is done on a handshake basis and without a paper trail to gum things up. (The NCAA rules here are somewhat contradictory. An athlete becomes ineligible in his or her sport if he or she retains an agent—though the NCAA allows an athlete who is professional in one sport to retain eligibility in another.) Either Brisson, a Quebec league contemporary of Troy Crosby, or Barry, one of the most influential agents in the biz, made a call to Shattuck on Sidney's behalf. Or Shattuck's recruiters initiated talks with the Crosbys who sounded out IMG after the fact. Different accounts of events floated about. The exact blow-by-blow is less important than the players involved and the messages sent.

Message One: The Crosbys, who had overtures from scores of agents, had thrown their lot in with IMG, the original sports agency founded by Mark McCormack and the outfit that built up a thriving hockey practice after Wayne Gretzky came aboard. It was a coup for IMG, which needed an infusion of young talent because of an aging hockey clientele. Down the line, IMG could offer Crosby greater American and international commercial opportunities than the smaller hockey-exclusive agencies.

Message Two: The best hockey talent that Canada had produced in decades was best served by going to the States. It wasn't simply that Sidney Crosby was out of options at home. His choice of Shattuck-St. Mary's was going to prompt more top players to follow and thus effect a flight of talent from the top midget ranks and Provincial A and the like. In the past Notre Dame in Wilcox, Saskatchewan, had been a preferred destination for players not quite ready for junior or others bound for U.S. college. Notre Dame still had famous alumni and lots of lore, but Shattuck-St. Mary's had eclipsed the Saskatchewan school. If there had been a Canadian school or hockey program that represented at least an equivalent opportunity to that offered by Shattuck, then Brisson and Barry, who had roots in Quebec and New Brunswick respectively, would have pushed for it. But they didn't. Nor have other Canadian-based agents who've advised some of the nation's top teenage players to go to Shattuck (and made phone calls to the school on their behalf). All the white papers commissioned by national officials and all the summit meetings into the future of hockey couldn't produce a more damning indictment of the game below the major junior level in Canada.*

"I remember the day when (the Crosbys) made the decision on Shattuck," Ed Spidel explained. "I remember Trina just being so relieved that it was over and done with. She was going to miss Sidney and he was going to miss his parents and (his little sister) Taylor. But things were getting tougher for Troy and Trina at the arenas. There were a lot of demands on them. There was a lot of attention. And some people just said awful things to them and to Sidney. Another season, especially after all the success that the Subways had at the Air Canada Cup, was going to be too much for them."

* In 2005 the players ranked first overall among teenagers eligible for the QMJHL and WHL drafts were both enrolled at Shattuck-St. Mary's. Angelo Esposito from Montreal had told a team in the Q that he was leaning toward attending a U.S. college; the Quebec Remparts selected him in the first round of the Q's 2005 entry draft and he agreed to play for Patrick Roy's team. Jonathan Toews of Winnipeg had made it known he was open to the idea of playing in the WHL. The Tri-City Americans selected him with the first overall pick. But Toews had a change of heart and, as of this writing he is planning, like Zach Parise before him, to attend the University of North Dakota.

Before Crosby made his way to Minnesota to enroll at Shattuck-St. Mary's, Hockey Canada invited him to the Halifax Metro Centre to hang out behind the scenes with the country's top juniors. They were in town for the national under-20 team's evaluation camp, a prelude to the World Junior Championship, which Halifax was going to host at year's end.

The arrangement was the handiwork of Stan Butler, the coach who ran practices at the IMG summer camp in Los Angeles. Butler had coached the world junior team the previous winter and Marc Habscheid had been one of Butler's assistants. So Butler made a call to Habscheid, who was given the head coaching assignment for the 2003 world junior games. Habscheid did more than just offer him a pass to the arena. He installed Crosby as a stickboy and made sure he stayed in the team's dormitory and took part in all planned team activities. The tag-along went to school on the experiences of the players, many of them first-round draft picks.

"I'm just trying to absorb a lot," he told the Halifax *Daily News* at the time. "You can tell they're focused and they want to go somewhere, and they really want to represent their country."

Crosby was hardly undercover in his apparently lowly role with the team. "We heard all about how good he was going to be," Jason Spezza said. "He didn't skate with us, but sometimes when we'd be coming back for our afternoon practice, he would have gone on the ice during our lunch break. You could tell that he had something special happening. He wasn't a great big guy and he had a baby face, I guess. But when we saw him just skating, playing around, well, we all know what it's like. It was easy to tell that he had some real amazing skill. And then when he came off the ice, you could tell he was in amazing condition, not just for a 14- or 15-year-old, he was in shape like a pro."

Spezza said the message that he tried to impart to Crosby wasn't that complicated. "I told him that there are going to be a lot of things said and written about you and you're going to get pulled in a whole bunch of directions. And I told him that no matter what goes on, have fun. Don't forget that it's supposed to be fun."

Spezza remembers today that Crosby wasn't just listening to his message, but saw it play out on the ice and in the Canadian team dressing room. "Any camp like that has some pressure in it—guys trying to make an impression and trying to make the team," Spezza explained. "But we had a lot of guys who knew each other and who got along and had fun when it was time to have fun. And he saw that there wasn't any attitude or anything like that. He was a few years younger but we treated him like he was one of us."

Crosby, too, left a lasting impression with the players at the camp, Spezza said. "He just wasn't like most other kids his age. He got along with everybody, you know, having a laugh. That much you'd expect. But you could tell he was really watching every little thing that was going on."

As it turned out, Spezza wasn't made available to the Canadian junior team that winter—the Ottawa Senators didn't release him back to the program. But he did have a couple of bronze medals and a silver medal from his three trips to the under-20s.

At the arena that August, Crosby handed sticks to many players who made it to the world junior final against Russia in Halifax the following January. They had a good run but in the final they were outmanned by a team that featured one top talent, Alexander Ovechkin, who was already the top junior in the world eligible for the 2004 draft. When the Canadian juniors watched the Russians celebrate their victory, they couldn't have known that the kid handing out sticks of gum on the bench at the summer camp would one day get a chance to avenge their defeat.

J.P. Parise started out by trying to downplay Crosby's arrival. He gave it the no-one-is-bigger-than-the-team approach, straight out of the manual that all U.S. high school and collegiate coaches seem to commit to memory. "With all due respect to Sidney we've had lots of good players in this program over the years," he told me.

Certainly the local papers bought that line, suggesting Sidney Crosby "might be the next Zach Parise." The younger Parise had graduated from the Shattuck-St. Mary's program the previous spring and enrolled at the University of North Dakota. Accordingly, the papers argued that Crosby could effectively fill the void left by Parise.

That didn't pass the laugh test. J.P. Parise never had reporters from their hometowns calling the athletic department for weekly updates on the progress of Ryan Malone (who'd star with the Pittsburg Peguins), Jack Johnson (the top ranked defencemen eligible for the 2005 NHL draft) or J.P. Parise's son Zach. And even if a couple had been written about in their local papers, the buzz around Sidney was at another level. That season, for instance, a film crew came down to shoot footage for a documentary that would wind up on CBC. Zach Parise was a great high school player, an excellent collegian, just not a prospect who deserves to be mentioned in the same breath as Sidney Crosby.

J.P. Parise later admitted that certain qualities set Sidney apart from the other "good players" in Shattuck's program. Parise was immediately struck by the way the heralded new recruit went about his business. It wasn't simply the work ethic hockey cliché, "first one on the ice, last one off." And it wasn't that Crosby found his way to the arena whenever he had spare time. No, what struck Parise was what Crosby did when he was *on* the ice. "He would work on little things, almost like little games, just playing with the puck on his stick," Parise said. "He would practice making it look like he had lost control of the puck—like it bounced up off his stick or dropped back in his skates—but really he never was out of control. He just wanted it to look like that so he could get a defenceman leaning. You see, say, Kobe Bryant, doing the same sort of thing, looking like he's in trouble, in close quarters, and then you realize you're in trouble. I can only imagine that he was visualizing defenders, linemates or whatever. But it wasn't just a little fantasy game. I'd see Sidney practicing some little move or fake one day and then he'd be doing it full speed in a game the next day."

Though Shattuck varsity coach Tom Ward said Crosby "fit in very well with his teammates and in the program," this 15-year-old didn't try to hide the fact that he was at times homesick, missing his friends and family: "It has been lonely. At the start it was really hard, but once I started playing hockey every day and the guys were really good to me, it got easier."

Crosby quickly befriended another sophomore at the school, defenceman Jack Johnson from Indianapolis. Johnson's parents apparently had greater means than the Crosbys—the Johnsons actually moved to Minnesota to promote their son's hockey development. Different positions, different backgrounds, different countries, but still Crosby and Johnson managed to find common ground. "We used to compete with each other in everything," Johnson said. "In that way we were the same. If we were throwing a baseball around then the first one to drop it lost. If we were fooling around on the ice, the same thing. We'd always have these one-on-one challenges."

For a school year Crosby lived in the players' dorm and had his every waking moment scheduled by the coaching staff. Other kids might have balked. Sidney said he loved it. On the ice, his game continued to flourish. Against players as old as 19, Sidney led Shattuck-St. Mary's to a national title, capped by a win over Team Illinois, an all-star squad, in the championship final. Sidney led Shattuck with 160 points in 43 games. That was almost 50 points ahead of Drew Stafford, Shattuck's second leading scorer, who would go on to be Buffalo's first-round pick, 13th overall, in the 2004 NHL draft. Sidney shot to smithereens the notion that he might be "the next Zach Parise." In his sophomore season, Parise had racked up 70 fewer points than Crosby's total.

As one NHL scout explained: "The most remarkable thing about (Crosby's) statistics is that Shattuck did nothing to pad them or really help him run up the total. It's a high school program that goes out of its way to reward upperclassmen, the seniors, a lot of the time at the expense of the underclassman. So these (upperclassmen), like Stafford, were getting more ice time than Crosby in anything but the closest games when you had to play your best against their best. If anybody had any doubts about (Crosby) being special, they were all gone by the time he was playing for Shattuck. We knew these other (Shattuck) kids were players, good players. Crosby was years younger and he was lapping them."

That was the consensus among scouts, but it's worth noting that it was never a point of complaint for Crosby, not during his time at Shattuck, and not in the seasons after. "I had a great time there," he admitted. Not one complaint? Not even sleeping in a dorm? "I liked the whole experience."

And the attention he received at Shattuck-St. Mary's didn't seem to bother his teammates at all. This is more remarkable than it might initially seem, because, on this count, the U.S. hockey culture is very different than it is in Canada. In the U.S. the rivalries between players can be much more intense. For example, the top 1988-born player in the U.S., Phil Kessel from Madison, Wisconsin, opted to go to college in Minnesota because his youth league teammates enrolled at the University of Wisconsin. Though the University of Wisconsin has a strong hockey program, though it would have been easier in many ways for Kessel to stay at home, he and his family had tired of the sniping of other players. Yet there were nothing but kind words that came out of Shattuck about Crosby.

By all accounts Crosby was the model player and the model student. "Not that it would be impossible (for players) to have any issues with him—if they did, then *they* are the problem, not him," said coach Tom Ward. "Sidney made himself part of the program. He just wanted to fall in with everybody and he did. He wasn't Sidney Crosby, the sensation down here. He was pretty anonymous and he liked that. He got tired of all the attention he was receiving at home and in Canada. He was a good teammate, a good classmate, and, I'm sure, a good friend. For us he was a very good student and an outstanding player. But he was also as close to a regular 15-year-old kid as he could be. He could walk down the hallways of the school and just be like anyone else. No worries about people wanting your autograph or saying stuff to get under your skin. He was a special player, make no mistake, but he wasn't a special case."

"He's down to earth for a kid being tagged with the label of the next Gretzky," added Zach Parise. "He's an even better person than he is a player."

⊕

There was but one special consideration that Sidney Crosby received at Shattuck-St. Mary's. School officials cleared the way for him to play for the Nova Scotia team at the Canada Winter Games in New Brunswick.

The Canada Winter Games date back to 1967 and were once a much higher profile event in Canada. Though they don't get the attention they once did, the hockey community still watches them closely. The competition is a good indicator of the progress of top prospects. Scouts from the major juniors eyeball the talent, as do recruiters from U.S. college programs. And what was true of regionalized competition at the under-17 Challenge is even more true at the Canada Winter Games—because the nation's talent is split up along provincial lines. Inevitably, the larger provinces make hay at the expense of the Nova Scotias and PEIs.

Brian Burley, Nova Scotia's manager, downplayed his team's prospects. "We've got some kids that are playing well in the major midget league, and I think they'll do okay. As for placing at the Games, I'm not really sure. It's hard to say until you see them playing totally as a team." (Let the record show that Burley was most likely the first and almost certainly the last coach to write Sidney Crosby's name in a line-up and not lead off with Crosby as the key topic in a discussion of his team's prospects.)

Burley might have been sandbagging because the players tell a different story today. Scott Vanderlinden, a defenceman from Antigonish, thought Nova Scotia had a chance to skate with the best in the country, in large part because of Crosby. Vanderlinden had played against Crosby in tournaments since he was seven years old. He had played for a Pictou County team that lost to Crosby and the Subways the previous year—in overtime of Game 5 in a best-of-five regional playoff series. "We probably had a deeper team than the Subways, even though they went on to the finals of the Air Canada Cup," Vanderlinden said. "No knock on them at all but Sidney was the difference. We lost 3–2 and he was in on all three goals. I was looking forward to finally playing with him rather than against him."

A lot of players in the Nova Scotia line-up were getting their first chance to play with Crosby after years of facing him, including Chad Anderson. "Everywhere we'd go at the Games people would ask us about Sidney," Anderson remarked. "If everyone in Canada didn't know about Sidney yet, then at least everyone in hockey had heard about him."

At 15, Crosby was the youngest player at the Canada Winter Games; he was also captain of the Nova Scotia team. "It sounds strange, but the truth is Sidney was a natural leader, even though he was younger," said Vanderlinden, who wore the "A" to Crosby's "C." "I'd played with guys with a lot less talent who got a bit of publicity and were all full of themselves, getting big heads. But Sidney just made you want to do whatever you could—if you had it in you, you had to leave it on the ice. It was all through his example."

"With Sidney it's like he gives the team a chance against anybody," Anderson said. "He just changes your mindset. And it's something when you're on the bench or on the ice and you see him. Even if he's having a bad game or having trouble with someone shadowing him, at some point he just makes up his mind, picks himself up and just makes things happens. He *refuses* to lose."

Though his squad had only a couple of significant prospects for the major juniors, his were the must-see games for scouts throughout the tournament. Likewise, virtually every media story coming out of the hockey competition focused on Crosby. For the most part, the attention of scouts and reporters didn't faze him. "I know that if I play to my capability, they're going to keep coming."

One question on the minds of scouts and reporters continued to press: would Crosby go to the Quebec league the next season or would he stay on at Shattuck and keep open the option of going to a U.S. college? Like he had throughout the school year at Shattuck, he skated around the question as nimbly as any bit of footwork on the ice. "I'm trying not to worry about it right now," he admitted. "It's something that will take a lot of time to decide, it's a life decision and I'm not going to rush it. I'm just going to have fun playing hockey and at the end I guess I'll have to figure out what I want to do with my life."

Crosby scored the winning goal in Nova Scotia's upset 3–2 overtime victory over heavily favoured Manitoba one night. The next, he shot the lights out against Prince Edward Island, potting four goals, including one end-to-end rush that had scouts in attendance dropping their clipboards.

As good as Crosby was against lesser competition, he had to be even better to keep Nova Scotia in the game against Alberta, the early tournament favourite. More than half the Alberta players were regulars in the Western Hockey League, which a lot of NHL scouts regard as the strongest major junior league.* In contrast, not one of the Nova Scotia

* Among the Alberta players who weren't drawn from the Western Hockey League was Scottie Upshall, who'd later serve as captain of the Canadian team at the world juniors and be selected by the Nashville Predators in the first round of the 2002 NHL draft.

players had any experience in the QMJHL, regarded as the softest of the major junior loops.

Though the Nova Scotians managed to stay close throughout the game against Alberta and though Crosby had several glorious scoring chances, the favoured westerners came away with a 4–1 victory. Crosby picked up an assist on the lone Nova Scotia goal and started to run the Albertans in an effort to light a fire under his teammates.

"Really, I think that loss to Alberta was our best game," Scott Vanderlinden said. "We needed to win to advance in the tournament. And I don't think that outside our room a lot of people gave us a chance. But Sidney was just great in that game. It was a lot closer than the score."

Said one NHL scout: "I can't think of one of the top players—not Gretzky, not Mario, not Orr—who was ever put in a situation like that. Whenever they were in against the best ... they weren't ever with a team that was so far behind everyone else's. If you look at Crosby's Nova Scotia team, it would have been hard for any other player beside him to even make the Ontario team. Other than one or two players, none of them would even get a look."

In fairness, the scout was only in his early 40s, not quite old enough to remember the Oshawa Generals when Bobby Orr first arrived there. Several years ago, when Orr was representing top prospect Jason Spezza and Spezza became the property of a godawful Mississauga IceDogs franchise, I asked Orr about his experience at age 14 when he first reported to the Generals. "It was a terrible situation," Orr confessed. "To say that we were the worst team in the league doesn't even start to describe it. We were a young team and we had no chance almost every night. We were beaten and we were beaten up. There was nothing that any one player could do to change things in that situation. Now, if a top young player were put in that situation, there'd be an outcry in the hockey community. But things were different then."

It wasn't a terrible situation for Sidney Crosby at the Canada Winter Games, but there was no mistaking his team for a medal contender. Crosby didn't carry Nova Scotia as far as he did the Dartmouth Subways. Nova Scotia didn't make it as far as the medal round. The team managed a couple of wins in the opening round and made Ontario sweat for its victory. The Nova Scotians wound up their tournament with a 5–4 loss to Saskatchewan in the game for fifth place, Crosby picking up three assists in the losing cause. As manager Brian Burley noted, though the team was only a couple of goals out of playing for a medal, the sixth-place finish was a significant improvement on Nova Scotia's ninth-place standing at the previous Games. And really, the one difference between those two teams, between a sixth-place finish and a ninth, was Sidney Crosby.

All said, Crosby had no real competition when it came to player-of-the-tournament honours. He racked up a tournament-leading 16 points in five games, even though opponents' game plans once again had him squarely in the crosshairs.

☺

The achievements of the Dartmouth Subways in the Air Canada Cup, the Nova Scotia team at the Canada Winter Games and the Shattuck-St. Mary's Sabres might have escaped the everyday notice of the national sports media, but hockey scouts from major junior teams and the NHL were well aware of Crosby's participation. And so too were hockey fans and players in Nova Scotia. Darren Cossar of Hockey Nova Scotia makes a case that the individual with the greatest influence on the game in the region was Sidney Crosby, even before Crosby was old enough to get a driver's licence, just short years removed from taking shots on his grandmother in the basement.

Cossar points to the recent performance of the erstwhile whipping boys of the under-17 circuit. "In 2005 Team Atlantic won its first medal at the World Under-17 Challenge, a bronze," Cossar explained. "In five years we've seen Team Atlantic go from a team with almost no chance to a contender. Five years ago, it was a team drawn from midget AAA players. This year practically the whole team was made of players who were loaned out by their teams in the Quebec Major Junior Hockey League."

Cossar admits that a number of factors contributed to the uptick, not the least of which was the presence of the Halifax Mooseheads and other Quebec Major Junior Hockey League teams in the region. "Young players are watching these teams and saying, 'I can do that ... I can play there,'"

Cossar said. "It used to be that major junior was some far-off dream, something that wasn't accessible. But now that the kids are growing up with these teams, it becomes a goal to them. It's within their reach. They see that the last three years the top picks in the Quebec league draft were players from Nova Scotia. Funny thing is, the numbers at the grassroots haven't changed, but there's a difference between 18,000 kids playing for the fun of it and 18,000 kids playing with a goal in mind—whether it's making the Q or doing well in a national midget tournament."

"I've been teaching at hockey schools the past couple of summers and I know there's been a huge change," Chad Anderson said. "The kids coming up are as talented as you'd see anywhere. And they're committed. In the old days, no Nova Scotia players would get invited to the (Canadian) under-18 program during the summer. This year, five got invited. Sidney deserves a lot of credit for it. It's like 'Be Like Mike' with Michael Jordan. I don't think these kids think they can be right there with Sidney, but they want to follow him."

If the Dartmouth Subways and Team Nova Scotia represented the possibility for success to the new generation of players in Atlantic Canada, then Sidney Crosby, with his accomplishments at Shattuck, has come to represent the possibility for individual greatness. Yes, young players in the Maritimes might look up to Brad Richards, the Prince Edward Islander who led Rimouski to a Memorial Cup in 2000 and won the Conn Smythe Trophy in leading the Tampa Bay Lightning to the Stanley Cup in 2004. Richards would certainly rank as a role model, a player worthy of youthful aspirations. He figures to be, barring injury, an automatic choice to play for All-Star teams and for Canada in major international tournaments. But Crosby's career curve starts somewhat higher than Richards did and is rising more rapidly. It's Crosby who truly inspires.

"There's a big difference between all those kids playing for fun and all those kids playing to follow Sidney Crosby," Cossar pointed out. "He has shown them what's possible."

"We see tendencies very early."

Canadian hockey officials didn't know Wayne Gretzky's potential successor was in grade school when No. 99 took his last turn on the ice. But he was. And if you were watching him then, shooting pucks in his basement or playing with friends, Crosby would have looked an awful lot like the average Canadian boy, age 11.

Could anyone have predicted Sidney Crosby's genius then, before his breakthroughs with the Dartmouth Subways, the Shattuck-St. Mary's Sabres and Team Nova Scotia? His coaches claimed they recognized it. But could someone who was watching for the first time have foreseen that Crosby was going to emerge as the top prospect in a generation? Two men believe they could have. They believe they can explain and even identify what sportswriters inevitably describe as "the intangibles"—qualities possessed by a great athlete or a championship team that are impossible to define.

These prognosticators aren't the habitues of rinks around Halifax who had watched Crosby as a young man. No, neither of these experts has ever seen him play. In fact, both of these authorities only heard of Crosby when I first interviewed them.

David Hemery understands elite athletes better than most coaches and even the players themselves. In fact, Hemery was an elite athlete himself, a gold medal winner in the 400-metre hurdles at the Mexico City Olympics in 1968, and also, a former world record holder. He worked for many years as a coach and a consultant to athletes and teams. He has also dedicated his adult life to the study of elite performance, in sport, in business, and in other fields. His might seem a curious case. When he won gold in Mexico, you'd think Hemery felt fulfilled, blessed or entitled; instead he was overtaken by other concerns. "Why me?" he asked. "And why not others?" Digging deeper, he asked why it was he and not his brother who had become an Olympic champion. These questions became a focus of his work.

Starting in the early '80s, Hemery interviewed athletes from around the world and across the spectrum of sports: Olympic athletes such as Sebastian Coe, championship jockeys such as Lester Pigott, tennis players such as Chris Evert and race-car drivers such as Jackie Stewart. He had them submit to a battery of 88 questions about their family backgrounds, their youths, their training practices and their philosophies about sport and life. The interviews were intense, some lasting more than four hours. In effect, Hemery was something like a law-enforcement profiler. But instead of looking for markers to future criminal activity, Hemery was looking for markers recurring in the lives of sports legends.

In 1986 Hemery published his findings in *The Pursuit of Sporting Excellence*. (An updated version with more research, *Sporting Excellence: What Makes A Champion?* appeared several years later.) Some 20 years after his original work, Hemery acknowledges that sport has changed dramatically.

"Because of professionalism, the abundance of money going into sport, the pressures on athletes to perform are much greater today than they were in previous generations," Dr. Hemery submitted. "We've seen the advent of sports schools and sports academies for young athletes, largely because of the promise of professional millions. We've seen the advent of sports agencies, which will find young athletes and invest time and resources in them (because) the more money these athletes make down the line, the better the agency fares. And we've seen athletes willing to compromise themselves and the traditional values of sport, particularly in the case of the use of steroids and other performance-enhancing substances. The motivation to use steroids is largely the product of financial incentives—the better you do, the more money you can make in professional sport, the more income you can generate from commercial opportunities.

"Then there are the advances in sports science. Now athletes are working with nutritionists, kinesiologists and all manner of sports scientists—not just at the elite or international level, but at the (grassroots) level."

All said, Dr. Hemery maintains that the character of athletes has remained constant. Circumstances have changed dramatically, yet Hemery holds that the "humanity" of athletes in his original study closely matched the humanity of today's athletes.

"In my original study, I didn't just gather information from active or recently retired athletes," he explained. "I interviewed athletes spanning several generations. The common threads ran across generations and I'm convinced that would be true today. Changes in society have been significant over the past 10 or 20 years, but how much more than in the preceding decades? Not significantly enough to change the findings, I believe. The very basic elements—those motivations, competitive will and other elements of character—would be a very close match."

Many of Hemery's findings seem obvious. For instance, the athletes in his survey tended to come from two-parent families that were loving and supportive. They also tended to have played several sports in their youths and achieved a degree of success in each, but specialized in their mid- or late-teens.

Some of the findings are puzzling. Birth order, for instance, yielded strange results. First-born children tend to have an out-sized representation in a number of fields, with many becoming successful businessmen and CEOs, for example. Yet among athletes, the disproportionate plurality existed among second-born children—the one possible explanation being that the younger sibling has in the eldest an always accessible mentor an a competitor to play up against without having to leave the home.*

Other findings were instructive. For instance, Hemery found that 90 percent of respondents described themselves as highly competitive and in constant pursuit of a challenge—that is, they always looked to *achieve* in the games they played. "It was not only a one-on-one race to the nearest tree ... but (also) an inner drive, a quest for self-improvement and self-challenge."

It might not sound so exceptional, except when the athletes themselves started to describe how they were driven and, in one case, both literally and figuratively, how that athlete drove himself. Said Britain's Steve Cram, a former world-champion middle-distance runner: "I'm awful (about being competitive). I time myself driving to training every day." Arnold Palmer who also described going out on the course as a tyke with a single sawn-off club and getting around nine holes on his own in 60 strokes—and then 50 and 40, each of those occasions being memories he could recall vividly a lifetime later.

It was easy to see this competitive wiring in Sidney Crosby. It played out not just on the ice but elsewhere: it might sound strange for a champion athlete to compete against himself driving to a workout, but no more strange than wagering with teammates on who could finish a meal first.

Likewise, athletes in Hemery's survey often competed as hard in workouts or pickup games as they did in international events. Another Briton, middle-distance runner Sebastian Coe, said he sometimes ran past the breaking point in training sessions that others thought of as fun runs. Coe spoke of "just having to do it." Hemery noted a common disconnect among Coe and the others. "The level of competitiveness bore no relationship with the lack of importance of the occasion," he wrote.

Hemery could well have been writing about Crosby playing the hot-potato volleyball game in the parking lot before the game against

* On this count Crosby doesn't seem like a good fit, unless you factor in Troy's relative youth when Sidney was born. With Troy in his 20s stopping shots in the basement, he could have passed for an older brother. Wayne Gretzky, a first-born. Bobby Orr, a second-born. And Mario Lemieux, a third-born.

Switzerland at the under-18 tournament. Or about Crosby throwing a baseball around with Jack Johnson at Shattuck. Indeed, these vignettes did not just begin to answer "why him?"—why Crosby succeeds and transcends—but also "why not him?"—why those others fell short.

One of the athletes originally profiled by Hemery was Wayne Gretzky. He was in fact the only hockey player in the study. Today, Hemery remembers Gretzky as an extraordinary case, markedly different from any of the other star athletes.

"What stands out about Wayne Gretzky was the role that his parents played," Hemery recalled. "They clearly raised him with certain values and wisdom. They were involved to an extraordinary degree in his career—much more than most of the athletes I surveyed—yet they put great value on establishing a balance in his life. So often we see parents push too hard. And in cases like this the young athlete pushes back and loses interest. That was clearly not the case with Wayne Gretzky. His father had an expert level of background in the sport. (Walter was a junior B coach when Wayne was tearing up age-group leagues in Brantford.) And the decision to take his son out of (Brantford) and have him play against better competition left him open for criticism. In other circumstances it could have been reckless. Ultimately, though, the decision proved to be a wise one."

The Gretzky case wasn't quite unique. For instance, Seb Coe's father was also deeply involved in his son's career and training, yet the elder Coe had no background in track and field. Instead, he committed himself to researching the sport and taking a scientific approach to setting up a training schedule.

I described for Hemery Troy Crosby's involvement with Sidney, and said that it seemed to parallel Walter Gretzky's role with his famous son, a role that carried right into the last days of a Hall of Fame career. Even the hard decision that Walter and Phyllis Gretzky made about sending Wayne to Toronto mirrored the decision to send Sidney Crosby to Shattuck-St. Mary's. I also told Hemery that in my years in the sport I found that many, if not most, players in Canada can point to their parents' constant support. Many had been coached by their fathers. Many had skated with them. They had underwritten the costs not just of equipment and league fees, but of hockey schools. They routinely drove hundreds of miles to see their sons play. Might there be a cultural component to the game—or even to the game in this country—that puts a premium on parents' participation? Might the dispatch of a young boy to a hockey outpost far away from home likewise be just part of the culture of the game—less an individual decision than a rite of passage?

"There could well be (a component) specific to the culture of the game of hockey or specific to the game of hockey in Canada," Hemery said. "That there is a common thread running through the lives of several or many elite athletes in hockey—but not in other sports to an equivalent degree—would suggest that. It might be a matter for study."

I then asked Hemery about the evolution of his own studies—if, looking back on his work, he had undervalued or overlooked any qualities of character in the athletes he surveyed.

"In my original research and the writing of *Sporting Excellence*, I didn't place high enough value on awareness and self-responsibility," Hemery admitted. "By awareness, I'm speaking of an awareness of self and of things around the athlete. By self-responsibility, I'm speaking of the understanding that ultimately the athlete can only depend on himself or herself … (and) that the athlete must accept responsibility for victory and defeat."

It sounded so anachronistic. Hemery seemed to be talking about a sporting world of the long past—not about his own era in the late '60s, but more like the one pictured in *Chariots of Fire*. Where were values in sport in the first decades of the 21st century?—where you could find athletes behaving disgracefully every time you opened the sports pages, where athletes were so utterly disconnected from reality, who lived in cushy bubbles, who enjoyed the entitlements and special privileges and exemptions that went with today's Professional Sporting Life. You want athletes who understand the day-to-day lives of fans? In basketball you had Latrell Sprewell, who once assaulted and choked his own coach at a practice, claiming that making $10 million a season wasn't enough because he had to provide for his family. You want champion athletes who understand self-responsibility? In baseball you had Barry Bonds claiming to be a victim of racism between trips to a grand jury investigation of a steroid lab. In hockey you had Vancouver's Todd Bertuzzi crying crocodile tears after his apparently career-ending assault on Colorado forward Steve Moore.

No, the stuff that Hemery described seemed to be lifted straight out of the Boy Scout's manual. Values that might have once been embraced were now passé. And yet for the champions interviewed by Hemery, those who reached the summit of their sports, those who enjoyed long, distinguished careers, values did matter.

A sense of common decency does cut across decades and sports. When I think of those whom I've talked to through the years, this holds true even more. For Gretzky certainly. Mario Lemieux too. Ray Bourque. Steve Yzerman. They all fit. And then there were the Canadiens. Jean Béliveau was the standard, but then there seemed to be a team-imposed sense of dignity expected of the Canadiens of yore. There were things that had to be done and things that were just not done. If you were outside the Canadiens code, you were moved on to other teams. You can see it in the way Serge Savard or Bob Gainey carry themselves even to this day. Or Ken Dryden. Or even Saku Koivu.

The life values that Trina Crosby tried to instill in Sidney were a simpler version of those described by Hemery. *We taught him to be a good person and treat others like he wanted to be treated. It wasn't complicated. We asked him to treat people with kindness and respect his elders. He's sensitive to other people. He's thoughtful.* This might explain why Sidney expressed an early desire to play for Montreal. Not a matter of geography. Nothing to do with his father getting drafted by the team. It could have been, quite simply, a values-based desire. To go some place where there had been a code, where it still seemed to apply.

In the first 30 seconds of any conversation with a scout about Sidney Crosby, he'll mention something to do with Crosby being "clutch." As Tim Burke said, "When he needs to, he can get it done." "When he's needed most," another scout in Breclav added, "he plays his best." There are one hundred variations on the theme.

The best way to sort out players is to put them in pressure situations: some perform worse than usual under pressure, others play as if oblivious to it, and the tiniest group plays better when the stakes are highest. If Crosby were just a *skilled* player—if he could just skate fast, shoot hard, perform drills impressively—he would still be considered an elite prospect. What separates him from other top prospects is the fact that he is a clutch performer. That's what excited scouts on his run through the Air Canada Cup, Shattuck-St. Mary's and the Canada Winter Games. And when he debuted so impressively at the under-18s in Breclav in 2003, pulling Canada through tough games against Finland and Switzerland, it just confirmed the fact that Crosby was, indeed, a clutch performer.

Ask some professional athletes about clutch performers and they'll tell you there is no such animal—players play and respond to situations as best they can. Ask others and they'll claim they possess something that makes them stand above their peers. Baseball Hall of Famer Reggie Jackson, for one, used to argue it was "character" that made precious few players—himself foremost—clutch performers.

Like Jackson, Roland Carlstedt believes there are in fact clutch performers. Moreover, Carlstedt believes he has successfully isolated the cognitive elements that make up the psychology of clutch performers— something significantly more advanced than Reggie Jackson's "character" theory. And to cap it off, Carlstedt is convinced he's on his way to understanding how to predict who will be a clutch performer and who will struggle in pressure situations.

Dr. Roland Carlstedt, a licensed clinical psychologist and the chairman of the American Board of Sport Psychology, is the author of *Critical Moments During Competition: A Mind-Body Model of Sport Performance When It Counts the Most.* As Dr. Carlstedt describes it, in sport a "cascade of images" passes through an athlete's consciousness during performance. It is not just a stream of consciousness so much as a waterfall. During performance, the athlete will remember similar situations when he has performed well, or perhaps a coach's words in the dressing room before the game. Some of the cascade he can control. Sometimes he can stay "on message." But at other times, random thoughts just pop up. Maybe it's a shopping list or something about his parking space. Sometimes such distracting thoughts are overtaken by other distracting thoughts he'd like to suppress but can't. Memories of similar situations when he's failed. Tough losses. Or maybe that his team will lose.

In spring 2005, Dr. Carlstedt was recruited to fill a guest role in sport's unintentionally comedic but most popular soap opera, *The Days and Lives of The New York Yankees*. At that point, Alex Rodriguez, the infielder who was reaching the midway mark of a 10-year quarter-billion-dollar contract, confided to the press that he had been seeing a therapist. Not a physiotherapist, but a psychotherapist. *The New York Times* contacted Dr. Carlstedt and asked if it were possible that A-Rod might be psychologically disposed to struggle in clutch situations. Dr. Carlstedt qualified his assessment by saying he couldn't "scientifically analyze him from a distance but judging from a distance ... " He then did a quick analysis from A-Rod's thumbnail bio: "He's troubled about being abandoned by his father. He's had situations when he has not performed well when it counted most. He might very well be the type who will ruminate on a negative thought at the crucial moment, who may be saying, 'I hope I don't fail. I'm getting paid $25 million and this is when I have to succeed.'" If it had been the *New York Post*, the headline might have read: DOC TO BOSS: A-ROD'S A CHOKING DOG. Nevertheless, if Carlstedt's judgment wasn't borne out by Rodriguez's regular-season stats, then it went a long way to explain his worst moments and subpar performance against Boston in the 2004 American League Championship Series.

There's a working model for Dr. Carlstedt's findings, an explanation of the clutch performance phenomenon based on three athlete traits: subliminal attention, subliminal reactivity and subliminal coping. "Athletes who are high in neuroticism/subliminal reactivity and concurrently high in hypnotic susceptibility and low in repressive/subliminal coping under stress do not exhibit the protective dynamic exhibited in the ideal profile," he told the *Times*. In other words, those who don't measure up in the clutch are the ones who can't get the negative thoughts off their minds at key moments.

Further investigation led me directly to Dr. Carlstedt who offered the layman's version. "There are three factors in play with the psychological aspect of clutch performance," he told me, "a specific constellation of psychological traits that can predict success in pressure situations. The three are a) an athlete's ability to focus, b) his ability to handle stress and c) his ability to keep intrusive thoughts at bay. These factors can be monitored and measured. For instance, heart rate is an effective measure of the ability to handle stress in a variety of situations, not just in sports. A high achiever in academics for instance, will likely prove to have no anxiety leading up to a test or an exam."

With the right balance of these three factors, clutch performers tend to be able to control the cascade. And what they can't control pours out positively nonetheless. They can focus. They can concentrate. They can think good thoughts. There's a balance of the three traits that shows up in those who perform best under pressure.

I asked Dr. Carlstedt if it were possible to judge the psychological foundations for clutch performance in a player only in his teens, someone like Sidney Crosby. Dr. Carlstedt said it was in fact "not too early" to go this route with Crosby. He suggested the cognitive underpinnings of the adult are long in place by the time an athlete reaches his late teens. "We see tendencies very early," he told me. "They continue to develop while the athlete matures and solidify when an athlete is in his early 20s. But for the exceptional athlete, the one who will best perform in pressure situations, those tendencies will be apparent in his teens—in fact, they should stand out."

I didn't try to get Dr. Carlstedt up to speed on the Sidney Crosby story to that point. All said, Crosby seemed, unlike Alex Rodriguez say, an unconflicted soul. A happy home life. Friend to all. He also appeared to be able to reach a state of absolute focus. And Crosby's ability to focus—to get lost in practising alone, visualizing opponents—is one of his hallmarks.

Funny though, much of what Crosby has been lauded for doesn't seem to have an impact on clutch performance—at least for Dr. Carlstedt. Take conditioning, for example. Coaches and NHL scouts admire Crosby's dedication to gym work and the attention he pays to fitness. Yet the idea that conditioning is key to clutch perfomance—that fatigue makes cowards of us all—doesn't really stand the measure of Dr. Carlstedt's research. "The best-conditioned athlete will struggle in pressure situations if he is deficient in certain (cognitive) traits," Carlstedt told me. "And no degree of improving his physical conditioning on its own will have any significant impact on his clutch performance." Which is to say, it's one thing if your heart is racing because of exertion, it's an entirely different and less promising thing if it's racing due to fear of failure.

Not surprisingly, an athlete's all-out efforts to help improve clutch performance often don't help at all and can be (in the worst cases) counter-productive.

I presented a scenario to Dr. Carlstedt: if an athlete hopes to score a goal in a championship game and stays after practice each day, firing hundreds of pucks on goal to perfect his timing and mechanics and touch, could it compound negative rumination? That is, with all the practice, could the athlete be placing more pressure on himself? Dr. Carlstedt allowed that it was in fact possible and, maybe in some athletes, not only likely, but inevitable.

I remember watching an American Hockey League game with a scout years back. The puck came to a forward in the undefended slot. A perfect scoring chance. It was the type of chance Mike Bossy would have one-timed for a goal in a blink of an eye. This time, though, the forward all but fanned on the puck. It fluttered end-over-end. Take-out shots in curling have more steam on them than this one did. The scout turned to me and said: "For 160 feet, this guy is an NHLer. It's the last 40 feet that keeps him in the AHL. For 20 minutes a game he looks like an NHLer, but for a couple of hundredths of a second—when he gets the puck on his stick for a scoring chance, when he needs to produce—he doesn't. Good almost all the time, unable to rise to the occasion. And that's the scouting report on practically all these guys (forwards). Given a chance they can't score. Not because they aren't good players. Not because they're not fit or hungry. Just because they don't have it."

That was the conventional wisdom in hockey. And like a lot of the game's conventional hockey wisdom it lacked nuance—subtle as a slash on the wrist, but hard to dispute. They don't have it so they can't play in the NHL. It didn't even matter what *it* was or that no one took the time to define *it*. All that mattered was they didn't have the requisite *it*. That minor league forward who fanned on the puck didn't score, but an NHLer would have. That's what separates the two. And whatever you put it down to is immaterial in the world of NHL scouts.

Sidney Crosby obviously possesses *it*.

Sadly, for those who don't possess *it*, there's not much hope of ever acquiring *it*. Career minor leaguers don't find a scoring touch. They don't break out at age 30. It would be easier for them to change their fingerprints than their games. The athlete who struggles in the clutch is almost certainly destined to always struggle in the clutch. Dr. Carlstedt argued that, like Alex Rodriguez, an athlete can address some of the factors affecting clutch performance by working with a psychologist—but the doctor also suggested that there's only so much that science can do. "I doubt very much that an athlete (with a negative profile) can ever get close to that ideal balance of traits."

Dr. Carlstedt describes his work in the field of clutch performance as "a breakthrough." And he's exploring "real-world" applications for his finds—predicting the success and failure of individuals in the most intense, pressure-filled jobs imaginable. He's been looking at brain surgeons, air-traffic controllers and fighter pilots, among others. Carlstedt says his papers have been peer-reviewed and the only knocks he's received have come from closed minds in the press and in the sports establishment. He's convinced, however, that even the hold-outs will come around. "If you're going to draft a topnotch quarterback, for instance, and invest millions of dollars and years in his development, you shouldn't leave anything to chance."

I told him I suspected Sidney Crosby would probably have an open mind about being tested, probably even a curiosity about it. NHL teams might be a tougher sell, though.

⊛

Could Hemery and Dr. Carlstedt have predicted Sidney Crosby's genius for the game? Hemery would likely have picked up certain markers in his competitiveness. Dr. Carlstedt might have been able to track his cognitive traits. But maybe the most important point was Hemery's about responsibility and accountability. Maybe it's not crucial that an institution recognizes genius early on—or at least not as crucial as a youth recognizing his gift and treasuring it. Being responsible with it. Acting accountably. Making the most of genius. Not wasting *it*.

— S E V E N —

"Sidney can handle almost anything
that comes along."

"The next time you see me skating, it'll be with my kids," Wayne Gretzky said in 1999 when talking about his retirement plans. It was his way of saying he wasn't going to be coaxed back into uniform, that his will to play had been exhausted. Maybe he intended it literally. If so, it didn't hold true.

Seasons passed and Gretzky didn't put on skates. And then he took a turn in the spotlight when, in November 2003, the NHL took the game outside in Edmonton for the Heritage Classic. The Oilers and the Canadiens faced off on a frigid Saturday night. As a pre-game attraction, oldtimers from the two teams played a game of shinny. Certainly no greater number of Hall of Famers and Stanley Cup rings have ever been involved in a pickup game. Gretzky was there, the headline name, evoking the glory days of the Oilers franchise.

The next day, the press raved about the occasion and about Gretzky getting back on the ice for the first time since his retirement.

But the press had it wrong. The first time Gretzky skated after 1999 was an even more momentous occasion, though it was out of the hockey season and witnessed only by a few. In July 2002, Gretzky showed up at an arena in Los Angeles where IMG had brought in a bunch of its top young prospects. For several seasons the agency had made it a practice to stage a development camp for its elite clients who were in their teens and early 20s. This was added value IMG could offer when it came to signing talented midget- and junior-aged players. Thus, first-round draft choices skated beside players who had NHL experience. Young prospects from rival teams and from rival nations were, for a week or two, just part of Team IMG.

Gretzky showed up at the rink in part because he had been IMG's headlining client for years and, though he could not be affiliated with the agency due to his role in Phoenix's management, he was still on good terms with the agents of some of the hold-overs.

And on this July day, Gretzky went from casual spectator to something else. He had heard rumbles in hockey circles about Sidney Crosby. On this day Gretzky was seeing him for the first time. It was like Einstein spying a gifted kid running through complicated equations on a blackboard in a lecture hall. He wanted to get his skates. He wanted to skate with Sidney Crosby.

At 14 Crosby was by more than a couple of years the youngest player at the IMG camp, the youngest ever invited to it. "He saw everything on the ice," Gretzky would later tell me. "He saw the game the same way I did when I was 14. He just had these incredible skills and a real love of the game—an incredible desire to do whatever it takes to be better. He's the best talent to come along since Mario and what makes him different (from the stars who came along before) is the attention to conditioning and work in the gym."

Stan Butler ran IMG's summer camp for several seasons and was conducting the drills the day Gretzky came to the arena. Butler worked with phenoms when he was a coach and general manager of the OHL's Brampton Battalion and a (two-time) head coach of the Canadian under-20 team. He worked daily with Jason Spezza in Brampton when the centre was 14 and 15 and at the world junior tournament a couple of seasons later. He worked in the national program with Vincent Lecavalier and Brad Richards at the under-18s. He worked with Rostislav

Klesla, the best junior defenceman in the world. He quickly recognized that Crosby was a player at another level.

"It is the vision thing that's like Gretzky," Butler said. "Maybe more than just seeing where players are at any time on the ice, but a sense of where they are going, what they're going to do and where the puck is going. It's awareness-vision, instincts and feel all rolled together. You think, 'Oh yeah, he guessed right that time.' But then you realize that he's not guessing because he's right practically all the time."

It could have been nothing more than a great memory for Crosby and a special moment for a few select IMG players and officials. But something came out of that camp that would follow Crosby wherever he went.

A year later, at the conclusion of another season of ever duller, ever less creative NHL hockey, Wayne Gretzky was asked by a reporter if anyone could ever beat his league scoring records. Gretzky answered: "Sidney Crosby. He's dynamite." Crosby was the only one Gretzky named. On the basis of what he saw out in Los Angeles, he was not only enticed to put his skates back on. He was moved to name his successor.

A few months later I asked Gretzky about the idea of naming a kid—then still only 15—as the one candidate to break his seemingly untouchable records. Was there any danger in attaching a kid's name to such a prediction? "From everything that I've seen, Sidney can handle almost anything that comes along," Gretzky told me.

☙

Gretzky anointed Crosby at a critical juncture in the teenager's career. The month before, the Rimouski Oceanic drafted Crosby with the first pick overall in the 2003 QMJHL draft. It seemed a risky selection for the Oceanic. Teams in the Q had been burned by first-round picks who were looking at U.S. colleges as an option. Some kids never came to terms with the teams that drafted them. Not first overall picks but picks high up in the first round. The Oceanic won but 11 games the previous season and could ill afford to burn up the top selection in the draft.

It had to look problematic. While at Shattuck-St. Mary's Crosby had a chance to see a hockey scene where the college game, and not the NHL or major junior, reigned supreme. In Minnesota young players grow up wanting to be Gophers, wanting to wear the big M on the University of Minnesota sweaters. But it wasn't just that Crosby was exposed to the U.S. college environment. No, he was actively recruited and even made visits to three schools in the U.S., including the University of Minnesota. For some players, U.S. college might be out of consideration simply due to their poor grades, but Crosby was an above average student. At Shattuck-St. Mary's Crosby had been preparing to graduate a year early, to get to college a year ahead of his class.

Rimouski, though, had been through the tough sell before.

The Oceanic was a still freshly pressed expansion franchise back in 1996 when it landed the first pick in the Q's midget draft. There wasn't much debate about the best available talent. Vincent Lecavalier was a gifted forward from Montreal's West Island. If it just came down to merit, then Rimouski's choice was easy. But Lecavalier and his parents hadn't been thinking about junior hockey—or at least not junior hockey alone. The Lecavaliers had aspirations not limited to the arena. Vincent's older brother Phillipe attended Clarkson University in New York on a scholarship. Though not a pro prospect, Phillipe skated off with his degree at the end of his four-year collegiate career. When Vincent was tearing up peewee leagues in Montreal, he dreamed, and his parents planned, that he too would attend college in the U.S. on a puck scholarship.

"Yvon and Christianne (Vincent's parents) are blue-collar people who only want what is best for the kids," said agent Bob Sauvé, who had known the family long before their younger son was a prospect. "They wanted Phillipe and Vincent to have a chance to be educated. Their minds were not focused just on hockey." Like the Crosbys, the Lecavaliers made the decision to send a son to a distant school while he was still in his mid-teens. But the Lecavaliers had an agenda that wasn't a factor in the Crosbys' plan. For their younger son to go the U.S. college route, Lecavalier's parents recognized that he would have to develop not only his hockey skills, but his skills in a second language too. So they arranged his enrollment at Notre Dame College in Wilcox, Saskatchewan, home of the fabled Notre Dame Hounds hockey program.

When Lecavalier checked into his six-man Notre Dame dorm, he was issued a bottom bunk. Each night he looked up at the mattress of a kid from Murray Harbour, PEI: Brad Richards. "When we first got there, we would just lay awake in our bunks wondering what we got ourselves into," Richards told me. "We were so far away from home, so isolated. There were a lot of (first-year) guys crying every night, wanting to go home. The only place we were free was on the ice. And even there we were the only guys in Grade 9 on the team. Most of the guys made the team only after being there for a year. Eventually they accepted us, but at the start they resented us being there."

The Lecavaliers had a plan but they ran into a problem that made U.S. college less attractive. Like Crosby, Vincent Lecavalier quickly outgrew prep school hockey, even Notre Dame's solid program (he had 52 goals and 52 assists in 22 games). While Lecavalier realized he needed a move for the sake of his game, his parents hoped he would stay on at Notre Dame. "I had to convince my parents that (going to major junior) was the best thing," Lecavalier told me.

Lecavalier at 15 understood already what NHL executives, scouts and players knew. Yes, some will endorse U.S. college hockey for developing skill. But the consensus is that, when the time has come, legitimate NHL prospects—at least those in North America—are best served by an apprenticeship in major junior.

In recent years major junior hockey has come under fire. Media pundits have criticized the franchises for focusing on generating profits at the sake of player skill development and player education. And more than a few experts at the hockey summits have advanced the idea that major junior hockey in Canada should adopt the European model—fewer games, more practice, a lot less time on the bus. Truth be told, if you hang around a junior team long enough it does seem to be a bit of a grind, and, for many 19-year-olds who have not been selected at the NHL draft, a dead end. Under the standard junior contract, all that franchises can offer a player is an educational guarantee, tuition, residence and books for post-secondary studies, a guarantee that stays in place after the end of the player's junior career. The franchise is only off the hook if the player signs a professional contract. The guarantee, however, often turns out to be an empty promise because many young men don't look after their books in high school. Either the demands of playing the game don't give them time enough to maintain a decent average, or they blow off classes because they're convinced that one day they'll be making NHL millions.

An NHL career was no fantasy for Lecavalier, though. At 16 he was inspiring the same sort of comparisons as Crosby was years later. "The best player out of the Quebec Major Junior League since Mario Lemieux," pronounced Roger Dejoie, the Oceanic coach during Lecavalier's time there.

It might not have seemed like a rosy picture to some—a young man, a phenom, who would have had his pick of U.S. colleges but instead embarked on his junior career in a town of 40,000 on the wind-swept south shore of the St. Lawrence, 280 kilometres east of Quebec City. Yet when I went out to Rimouski at the start of the 1997–1998 season, Lecavalier hadn't just bought into the program—he could have been president of the local chapter of the Chamber of Commerce.

"I was able to attend a private school close to the Rimouski Colisée, so school was okay," Lecavalier told me in 1997. "I didn't care how many people there were in Rimouski—there were more than at Wilcox. Here everybody knows who you are when you go out in the streets. That's pressure, but it's good pressure. Maybe if I was playing in Montreal or in Hull it would be different."

The greatest benefit of playing in Rimouski, Lecavalier said, was the chance "to focus on hockey and school." In fact, Lecavalier's agent, Bob Sauvé, made the case that Rimouski's isolation was an asset, not a liability.

"If another team had drafted Vincent, he would have stayed at Notre Dame and gone the U.S. college way," said Sauvé, whose son Philippe was an Oceanic goaltender. "The team being so far away was not a negative. It was a positive. There weren't going to be the distractions that he'd have in the bigger cities. And there's tremendous support from the Oceanic organization.

"It used to be that players wouldn't go to Rimouski. Now (1997) because of Vincent, because of a contending team and a good organization, they're begging to go there."

It was clear after a few days with Lecavalier in Rimouski that the only thing small-time was the setting. The franchise proprietors, the Tanguay family, also happened to own Quebec's largest chain of furniture stores. Victory in Rimouski was good for the family's standing in the province.

As such, the Tanguays had invested in a great hockey environment. The Colisée in Rimouski was a boxy, utilitarian edifice in the middle of town but it more than served its purpose. Capacity crowds of 5,063 were automatic. Of that number at least 700 were in standing room. The only thing blocking hundreds more from pouring in was the fire code. And when local cable started televising every home game, the crowds still packed the place.

Lecavalier got big-city perks too. It went beyond free green fees at the many golf courses in the area and a wave-in at any restaurant or club in town. Before the '97–'98 season opener, for example, a local paper showed Lecavalier accepting the keys to a courtesy car, a '98 Cavalier "toute équipée."

Lecavalier knew he had to play junior hockey and, as it happened, he landed in a great situation. He and the kid in the upper bunk at Notre Dame, Brad Richards, both went to Rimouski and both prospered by doing so. After two seasons and some eye-popping statistics, Lecavalier was selected first overall by Tampa and went straight to the pros. Richards, who arrived in Lecavalier's second year in Rimouski, led the Oceanic to a Memorial Cup championship in 2000. Maybe they would have been excellent pros no matter where they played, but by all accounts they enjoyed and benefited from their time in Rimouski.

The town and the team were still unknown quantities back in 1996 when Lecavalier first arrived. They weren't by 2003 when the Oceanic drafted Crosby.

The Oceanic had a lot on the line with the selection of Crosby, but so too did the QMJHL. The Q needed some good news. It had teams in remote regions, out of the province and out of the country, but not a single franchise in Montreal, Quebec's largest urban centre.[*] Regarded as the weakest of the three loops comprising the Canadian Hockey League,

[*] In 2004–2005 when Crosby last played in the Q, the league consisted of 16 teams divided into three divisions. The West included Rouyn-Noranda, Shawinigan, Gatineau, Drummondville, Victoriaville and Val-d'Or. The East included Rimouski, Chicoutimi, Quebec City, Lewiston (Maine) and Baie-Comeau. The Atlantic Division included Halifax, Moncton, Cape Breton, P.E.I. and Acadie-Bathurst.

the Q had usually sent fewer players than the Ontario or Western leagues to the Canadian under-20 team. Some NHL organizations had made it a much lower priority for scouting than the OHL and WHL. Yes, it had turned out Lecavalier and Richards, but it was also the league that produced famous flop Alexandre Daigle. Sure, because of goaltending guru Benoit Allaire and other imitators, the Q churned out solid puckstoppers like Jose Theodore, Roberto Luongo and J.S. Giguere. Still, the Q was third and apparently fading like the memories of Lecavalier and Richards in Rimouski.

Crosby looked like a potential risk for the Oceanic. After all, the team's executives didn't know if the Crosbys would balk at having their son play in a town that was 99 percent francophone. They didn't know if the Crosbys might follow the lead of Eric Lindros and family; Lindros, the heralded prospect of the early '90s, was taken by the Soo in the OHL draft and by the Quebec Nordiques in the NHL draft and refused to play for either team. The Soo was too far from his Toronto home and Quebec was too, well, French, or at least, too far out of the mainstream to maximize his marketing potential. Or so the stories went.

Nevertheless, Rimouski made its pitch, not knowing whether the Crosbys would play hardball. At this point the details get a little fuzzy. Canadian Hockey League rules prohibit teams from offering financial inducements to players. Teams are instead limited to paying a weekly stipend that might run between $60 and $100 a week, not a lot different than back in Gretzky's day. But all this is just how it plays in the rule-book—not real life. Rumours have it that general managers pay upwards of $100,000 Canadian to top prospects. Big bucks (off the books) are also involved with every European who makes his way to the CHL. Back when Ilya Kovalchuk was a junior he was demanding $200,000 to come over to play in the Q—effectively pricing himself out of the market. If this seems out of line, keep in mind that CHL franchises are for the most part profitable businesses, and in many cases, licences to print money. If coaches or general managers can routinely command six-figure salaries, then the players should be entitled to their piece.

For the record, no one on either side of the Rimouski-Crosby negotiations will talk specifics. Sure, they volunteered that the team was going to provide an English-language tutor to help Sidney finish his high school diploma by correspondence. And they let out the fact that Sidney wanted tickets for every game, home and away, set aside for underprivileged kids. There was no harm in leaking anything that cast league, franchise and player in good light. "You have to believe that Rimouski wasn't going to risk alienating Crosby and his parents by not being fair and straight with them," said one scout who works in the Q. "You also have to believe that the Crosbys weren't about to get shorted and completely understood Sidney's value to the franchise. They had the agents (IMG) right there. If they got $150,000 a season and a couple of other deal-sweetener bonuses for the playoffs, then the team got fair value and so did the Crosbys. That's what the market is today."

Fact is, if the team had signed Crosby for $60 to $100 a week and nothing more as CHL rules stipulate, then the Oceanic and the Tanguays would be more deserving of criticism than if they had cooked a side deal for six figures. Because, as it was, Crosby made an enormous difference. The team stood to make a windfall with increased attendance, playoff dates and merchandise sales. Back in 2003 Rimouski drafted the top player available in the Q draft. By the time he headed off to the national under-18 team's summer camp in Calgary at the start of August, the Rimouski franchise had something else entirely, a still 15-year-old kid who had been hand-picked by Wayne Gretzky as his succesor. This had the phones at the ticket-sales office ringing off the hook. The next one cometh. *Le prochain étoile.*

For the Crosbys, money wasn't Rimouski's ultimate attraction. What was true of Lecavalier was true of Sidney Crosby. Both ran out of challenges at the highest level of hockey below major junior. What Troy Crosby had said back in Cole Harbour held. "We want what's best for his development. Everyone should be challenged to play at his best, otherwise it's just a waste of time." It was true when Sidney was 12. It was even more true when he was turning 16. Another year at Shattuck-St. Mary's would have been a waste of Sidney's precious development time. Rimouski, on the other hand, was going to challenge him. And in the interim there would be an intermediate step up: the summer under-18 invitational tournament in the Czech Republic.

EIGHT

"We know you do not feel good tonight but you will all be champions someday."

Breclav, Czech Republic
August 13, 2003

The morning after the victory over Switzerland, the members of the Canadian under-18 team were starting to file into the dining room at their hotel. Their eyes were heavily lidded. Their yawns barely stifled. These were the effects of their exertions and the symptoms of jet lag. Despite the shot in the head he had taken in the second period, despite all the ice time he logged and despite that long stretch he spent knocking a volleyball around in the noonday sun, Sidney was up early. He was sitting at a table warily looking over a plate of eggs floating in grease and a hot dog posing as sausage, evidently the Czech breakfast of champions. I asked if it would be alright to join him and he didn't beg off. I then asked if he had a favourite pre-game meal. About this, and seemingly everything else, Sidney was commonsensical in a way that almost any other teenager wouldn't be.

"I don't want to get into any superstition that I can't control," he told me. "I like my routines. I'm superstitious about a bunch of things. I dress right before left. After I finish working on my stick before a game I never let it out of my sight. I don't just put it in the rack. But a pre-game meal, that's something I can't control."

Few adults give that much thought to mundane details of day-to-day life, yet Sidney Crosby's life was one that he had already examined at length by his 16th birthday. From the breakfast table to the arena and all places in between, the young man seemed keenly aware and self-aware. Nothing was done on impulse or whim.

If his superstitions were so calculated, I presumed the major decisions in his life were even more intensely considered.

I asked him about the biggest decision of his hockey career so far, the decision to sign on with Rimouski instead of holding out for a hockey scholarship from a U.S. college.

"I visited campuses," Crosby explained. "I was really looking at U.S. college as an option. The quality of the game in college is really high. And I think I'd have liked being on campus. But (going to college) would have meant another year at Shattuck and trying to finish two years of high school in one. I'm a decent student—a good one—but that would have been a really tough year. I liked Shattuck. I loved the dorms and everything to do with the school. And I want to go out there the first chance I get to visit some of my friends. But I didn't really want to go through (doing two school years in one). And if it was going to take two (more) years at Shattuck, then junior looks even better."

After a couple of days of surreptitiously scoping Sidney around the hotel and the rink, one thing came clear: as much as the spotlight found him on the ice, he seemed determined to get lost in the crowd and disappear into the background away from the rink. He pulled this off by seeking the median. Hanging around the hotel, some players wore t-shirts featuring death-metal bands and sleeves cut off to showcase shoulder-to-elbow tattoos. Others went for "gansta rap" stylings or with bleached blond hair spiked up in surf-punk mode. Not Crosby, a fan of new country, the rare 16-year-old who listens to Toby Keith and Shania Twain. Here at the breakfast table Sidney looked like he walked right out of a milk commercial, clean cut, freshly scrubbed. His thick brown hair had been blown dry. He looked boyish without seeming boy-bandish, handsome without seeming vain or overly concerned with fashion. He wore a Team Canada golf shirt, Roots shorts and flip-flops. His clothes appeared to be ironed. He was neither the loudest nor so shy that he stood alone. Others were offering up scouting reports on the waitresses, some making their plays. Sidney just laughed along.

Another thing had become clear in those days of watching Sidney and the under-18 team: as much as he tried to blend in, it was clear he was a special case. This point was driven home by a scene that unfolded later that morning in the dining room.

Near the end of the team breakfast one of the trainers threw out a brainteaser for the players to kick around. It was a part of the morning routine. This morning's riddle went as follows: it's a food; you throw away the outside and cook the inside; you eat the outside and throw away the inside.

There was much humming and hawing and bad guesses from all corners. And then Crosby went to say something. Or at least ...

"Hold on, hold on," coach Bob Lowes said. "Sidney, do you have it?"

It was a small point. It sure had the makings of a great metaphor—let the boy-wonder come up with the answer. But more important than that was the coach's obvious effort to ensure that Crosby, the youngest player, was *involved*. That the older players didn't squeeze him out. That he was brought into a group of players who had already played together and against one another in under-17 play and in the CHL. Lowes didn't stop the guessing for anyone else, just for Crosby.

At this point, though, I sensed, if anything, Crosby would have felt more at ease if Lowes hadn't gone out of his way to include him. "No," Crosby told him, a little sheepishly. You might think that anyone so accustomed to being in the spotlight wouldn't be self-conscious in such a setting—but only if you've forgotten what it's like to be 16 and surrounded by people you've only just met. Or if you didn't know that the worst thing one could possibly be was a special case. "I've never considered myself bigger than any person I ever played with," Wayne Gretzky said, defining in one sentence the difference between his attitude and Eric Lindros's, and at the same time providing a prescription for behaviour becoming athletic genius. Crosby didn't want to be *bigger*. He didn't even want to be *different*.

After a couple of minutes, the guessing died down. The first up with the correct answer was the team's No. 1 goaltender, Julien Ellis-Plante. Ellis-Plante was the team's designated iconoclast, as you might expect given his position. Despite the hyphenated half-anglo name, Ellis-Plante's English was ragged but it was no impediment to solving problems of logic. It seemed he walked around tuned in to his own private frequency, but when it came to the morning brainteasers—to thinking outside the box—he had been lapping his teammates.

Quiet fell over the room. Ellis-Plante didn't look up from his plate. He knew the answer, just not the English word for it.

"*Maize*," he mumbled.

Shuck the husk, cook the inside. Eat the kernels, throw away the cob. The correct answer: corn.

Breakfast was winding up. I asked Crosby if he thought he had it tougher than most of his teammates on this under-18 team—having gone to the U.S. for a year, having to head out of his province and comfort zone to play junior. He didn't buy it. "I don't think about what's fair," he said, after choking down his eggs and washing the taste out of his mouth with the Czech equivalent of Tang. "I just make the most of whatever situation it is."

It's tempting to presume that genius isn't coached. Or even that genius resists coaching, that it unfolds naturally, organically, independent of outside influence. It might be true in many cases. It didn't look to be true of Sidney Crosby.

At the morning skate prior to the Canadians' critical contest against the Czech Republic, the final game of the opening round, coach Lowes blew the whistle to gather the team for a chalk talk—to outline a play or a drill. Crosby busted it to get to the front of the pack. When Lowes drew up something with his felt pen on the erasable board, Crosby was down on one knee right in front of him, staring up. His eyes traced the lines as they were drawn. Crosby's teammates stood by and looked at the diagrams, though they'd occasionally glance away, or bend at the waist to catch their breath. They listened to the details, while Crosby was lost in them. It wasn't something he put on for effect or to curry the coach's favour. Fact was, nobody noticed. Not his teammates—because of his position at the front, they could only see his back. Not the assistant coaches—they were down the ice gathering pucks. And not the coach—he was to busy scanning the ranks to make sure that his point was hitting home.

Crosby displayed that level of attention Rick Bowness had described. *Soaks up the game like a sponge. Wants to learn about things that can make him better.*

Afterward I asked Lowes about Crosby's approach to practice. "It goes past what we do on the ice," Lowes told me. "He's the one who wants to see any video that we have. He's the one who wants to see the scouting reports or asks questions."

I mentioned to the coach Crosby's philosophy of making "the most of whatever situation it is." Lowes said it seemed to carry over straight from his game.

"When you watch what he does on the ice or even break it down on tape, it seems like he makes the right play. If he passes, you don't say afterward that he should have shot. Or the other way around. He gets the best chance possible out of every puck possession. Maybe it's not a great scoring chance. But he doesn't take a shift off. He doesn't take even part of a shift off."

It's a theme that plays out in one form or another all through Crosby's life. If it's less than ideal, then he'll make do and he'll more than get by. It might be a game situation as unpromising as a two-on-three rush on a penalty kill. It might be a life situation like having to shoot pucks in the basement because the weather is too lousy and no neighbourhood rinks are available. And so it was this day at practice. The team was going to the rink, so why not make the most of it? Why not try to get something out of it? Going through the motions, mailing it in and feigning interest are the stuff that doesn't seem to be in his make-up. His positive attitude was more than refreshing. It was humbling.

Later that day Crosby was trying to make the most of a brutal situation, one presented by a talented Czech team energized by 6,000 raucous fans and a referee who wouldn't see anything Canada's way. Hockey Canada gives its players a first brush with international play at the summer under-18s and it's a tough initiation.* A tournament in Scandinavia would be more benign. The World Cup in the Czech Republic featured tough crowds, motivated home teams and, worst of all, the shabbiest refereeing outside of professional wrestling. Crosby was getting a full dose of all three. The Czechs were working Sidney discreetly. As soon as the ref's back was turned they swarmed him like pickpockets on a three-piece suit. If he was within reach, they elbowed and sticked him. Even when the ref was staring right at them they chipped away with impunity. They didn't try to drop the bomb on him like the haymaker to his head in the Switzerland game. Instead, the Czechs just set up a gantlet of hooks and holds and never let Crosby gather a full head of steam. After all, there were only so many penalties the ref could call on the home team. Welcome to international hockey, Sidney Crosby.

The host Czechs had a 1–0 lead through two periods. The Canadians were still very much in the hunt. Crosby was creating chances. One time he was sure he had scored, and even started to raise his stick in the air. But Czech goaltender Marek Schwarz had his number that time—a sprawling glove save. Between the homer ref and a goaltender having the game of his young life, Crosby was plainly getting aggravated. Several times he pleaded his case to the ref. Other times he looked skyward, as if for help. Still, with 20 minutes to play, the Canadian teens still looked like

* Hockey Canada has boasted about the performance of its under-18 team in the summer tournament, noting that the 2003 team was looking for the program's eighth consecutive victory in summer play. In fairness, the tournament has been a hodgepodge over the years. One year it was a four-team tournament in Japan, featuring an over-matched host team playing the Russians, the U.S. and Canada. In Lecavalier's year it was a three-team affair with the host Czechs, Slovakia and Canada. Only in the past few seasons has the field filled out with teams from most of the strongest nations. In August 2003, the summer World Cup tournament had a better complement of players eligible for the NHL draft than most previous years. However, many players who have played on the Canadian under-18 team in the summer have been unavailable for the World under-18s in the spring because of commitments to their major junior teams; the same is true of a few American and European players who play in the CHL.

they could pull it out. The stage was set for Crosby to do something special, like when he scored in the shootout in Canada's win over Finland, or when he authored three goals in three shifts against Switzerland.

Over the years a few of the brightest talents in Canadian hockey made their breakthroughs in the summer under-18 tournament. In fact, the scouts in Breclav were starting to compare Crosby's play at the tournament to that of Rick Nash's two years earlier. Nash, the first overall pick of the Columbus Blue Jackets in 2002, scored a hat trick and two assists in a 9–4 win over Russia in the game that clinched the championship. And Vincent Lecavalier's performance back in 1997 was almost magical: though allowing only nine shots on goal and dominating play, Canada trailed the host Czech team 2–0 with less than four minutes remaining. Lecavalier sparked a furious rally capped by the championship-winning goal with less than 30 seconds remaining in regulation, a one-man effort that scouts likened to Crosby's breathtaking slalom run through Switzerland's defence.

I spoke to a couple of NHL scouts in attendance and they were down on the Canadian team's chances. "They're not going to get calls," said one. "And really once you get by Crosby and (Brampton Battalion winger) Wojtek Wolski, their forwards aren't really generating much."

Their message was plain: in other years the Canadians had brought teams with much more depth, with players just a year away from playing in the NHL. In 2001, for instance, Rick Nash played with two other players who would jump straight from junior into the NHL at age 18: Eric Staal, who went from Peterborough to the Carolina Hurricanes, and Pierre-Marc Bouchard, who jumped from Chicoutimi to the Minnesota Wild. Crosby lacked that quality of support on this under-18 team.*

I suspected that Troy Crosby was thinking as much. For most of the game Troy had been standing alone in the back rows of the stands. He looked in a bad mood. Trina had been sitting with a few other parents of

---

* All but four of the Canadian under-18 players eligible for the 2004 NHL draft were selected in the first four rounds. Defenceman Cam Barker went third overall to Chicago and then, surprisingly, back-up goaltender Devan Dubnyk went 14th overall to Edmonton. The core of the blueline went late in the first round and early in the second: Mark Fistric (Dallas, 28th), Andy Rogers (Tampa Bay, 30th) and Michael Funk (Buffalo, 43rd). The highest-drafted forwards were Kyle Chipchura (Montreal, 18th) and Wojtek Wolski (Colorado, 21st).

Canadian players and was cheering and talking. Troy looked too annoyed to socialize. No matter, during the second intermission I walked over to him and introduced myself. Troy stood up, revealing dimensions that suggested he might have been a hard-hitting defenceman or an enforcer and not a goaltender back in the day; his hands were like meat hooks, though he didn't offer one to shake. He glowered when I mentioned that I wanted to interview him. I told him I had spoken to one of Sidney's "advisors" from IMG, J.P. Barry.

That didn't break the ice. "J.P. never mentioned you," Troy said, just before walking off.

It left me thinking it had to have been easier to be Walter Gretzky in the '70s than it was to be Troy Crosby circa 2003. Walter flooded the backyard rink, coached some Junior B hockey and was seen as a genial figure; any criticism of his sending Wayne to Toronto to play minor hockey in his early teens was quickly forgotten. Troy, on the other hand, heads off a rogues' gallery: parents trying to match Sidney with their daughters; agents trying to squeeze out IMG; and the media, with much more to come. I figured he must have practised that glower he trained on me. As the Crosby family gatekeeper, he shut down a lot of people who tried to smooth-talk him.

I put Troy's shortness down to his son's struggles on the ice.

In the third period Sidney ended up with a couple of glorious scoring chances but was stoned by the Czech netminder again. The hosts scored another goal late in regulation and added an empty-netter in the dying seconds for a 3–0 win. The score could easily have been reversed with a timely bounce or two. It was a hard loss to swallow, especially with the refereeing, but it didn't do real harm to Canada's chances in the tournament. With their opening two wins, Canada advanced to the elimination round, regardless. If they had beaten the Czechs, then they would've met Russia, in Breclav, two nights later. Instead, the Canadians would play the U.S. in the semi-final in the Slovakian spa town of Piestany. There was a bus ride to Piestany and a border crossing, but the way the Canadians looked at it, it seemed a more favourable matchup.

After the game, the Czechs fans poured out of the arena to celebrate in the parking lot, chanting "Ceske, Ceske." At some point they moved from beer to hard liquor. Their heroes from the winning side came out of the dressing room to lead the celebrations. The Czech players knew which dressing room the Canadians were in, so they parked themselves outside an open window and serenaded them with taunts. The Canadians would have to make their way through a couple of hundred of them to get to the team bus, a disaster waiting to happen. Soon the parking lot looked like a beer garden and out into the middle of it walked Sidney Crosby searching for his parents. He eventually found them. But he had to wade through a sea of inebriated Czechs.

After 15 minutes the Canadian coaches went to the side door of the arena. They realized that Sidney had gone out into the parking lot and that the team bus was locked. The rest of the team remained inside. As soon as the coaches ducked their heads outside, the taunts from the Czech fans grew louder and angrier. Fearing a drunk might take a swing at Sidney, the coaches called him back into the dressing room. A loss in an opening-round game they could explain or rationalize to their bosses back at Hockey Canada. Allowing the future star of the national program to be swarmed by liquored-up hockey hooligans—that's definitely not the report you want to file from your watch.

Troy Crosby grimaced like he had a toothache. Trina looked shaken. So too did Sidney by the time he made it back inside the arena. The Canadian contingent, holed up like hostages, waited it out for an hour until the party broke up.

Breclav, Czech Republic
August 14, 2003

The Canadians had the day off. It was much needed. They had played three tournament games in three days (and an exhibition contest the day before that). Factor in the travel from the training camp in Calgary, and it's easy to understand why the players were shuffling wearily around the hotel the morning after the loss to the Czechs. At breakfast, Lowes gave the news to his players: no practice, strictly R & R. The only scheduled activity was going to be a ride on the team bus into Brno, the Czech

Republic's second largest burg. Just to be in a city setting was going to be a bit of a reprieve from the quietude of their countryside hotel.

☙

On the ride in to Brno, I asked two of Crosby's teammates, Wojtek Wolski and Evan McGrath, about their already heralded centre. I asked the indelicate question about players, prospective top draft picks, having to watch from the bench while the coach sends out Crosby for shift after shift. It was, I suggested, far easier for his friends on the Dartmouth Subways to accept than for players who are stars on their junior teams and, in many cases, future pros.

Wolski said that egos weren't being bruised, that the players put the good of the team ahead of personal agendas. "I never heard anybody complain. And nobody really can complain. From the first day of training camp everyone has seen how hard he works . . . in practice and in games. And nobody can complain about how he's playing. He deserves everything he has."

McGrath, who played for the Kitchener Rangers in the OHL, concurred. "Everybody here understands what Sidney's got," he said. "And each (player on the team) knows what his role is and we're happy with that. Each of us is trying to figure out if we're going to play (at the next level, the NHL). But that's for later on. I'm sure there are more unhappy guys on most major junior teams than there are here. (On a major team) players have only got so much time to show what they can do and might feel like they're not getting a fair chance."

McGrath's point was a good one. He had watched that exact story unfold with his older brother Brett. Brett had gone to the Ottawa 67's a few seasons before and had shown a lot of skill when he first arrived; for whatever reason, though, his career stalled. Others soon passed him in Ottawa's plans. Maybe a trade to another team would have advanced his career and given him a chance to showcase himself for NHL scouts—but the 67's held on to him just as insurance until his junior eligibility ran out. He then went on to university, with not much to show for his time in junior except a bagful of what-might-have-beens and should-have-been-betters.

In Brno, the team was taken on a walking tour led by a local historian who looked and sounded like George Costanza's mother. She took the team to a castle on a hill overlooking the city. Nobody was tuning in to her spiel. The players would have preferred to be skating. Sidney walked between Troy and Trina. Troy was still going over the previous night's game. "They're holding your stick on rebounds," he told Sidney, who nodded but otherwise didn't reply.

The bus took the group from the castle to the plaza downtown. The players had two hours of liberty. Sidney's reaction was that of any red-blooded 16-year-old. He waved goodbye to his parents and fell into a pack with players seeking out a cornerstone of global youth culture, McDonald's. They spent their time scoping out local girls, like judges in a beauty contest. From the chatter it was easy to sort out which players read *Maxim*. Sidney just smiled and chowed down adolescent comfort food. He's usually particular about his food and this would not have been his first choice, but even Rotten Ronnie's, as the players called it, was an improvement on the gruel out at the hotel.

By the time the players made it back to the bus, none had bought postcards or souvenirs. A few players, goaltender Ellis-Plante among them, bought monster toy Uzis that fired plastic bullets. The coaches' eyes were rolling. There was no way that they were going to allow the players to carry the guns in their belongings on the flight home. Just let airport security guards get a load of that stash on their X-rays. But, if nothing else, it served as a reminder that these were boys they were coaching.

Back at the hotel Sidney Crosby had an hour to talk after he finished a phone interview with CBC Radio's news desk in Halifax. He went back to the room that he shared with Wolski and two other players. They were flopped on couches, watching television. Sidney apologized for the once-worn clothes strewn across the floor. He dialed Halifax and made it through the interview without a stutter or stumble: "We outplayed the

Czechs ... I was surprised by Wayne's comments ... it's really early for any talk like that." Just as he hung up, someone in the hall yelped. His roommates bolted. The gunplay with the toy Uzis had started. Man down.

Against the backdrop of boys being boys, I asked Sidney how he acquired the kind of skills that haven't come along in Canada for so many years.

Most athletes, adult professionals or precocious teens, would have shrugged and offered don't-knows. But just as he makes the best of every opportunity, so too did Crosby try his best to make the best of the question. He said bloodlines were a factor. It wasn't just his father who had been a player. In fact, he made it sound like his gift was matrilineal. "My uncle Robbie Forbes played in the Q and in Europe," he said. "He was a legend back home. He played senior hockey there and in Newfoundland. He played a lot of different sports." He mentioned other cousins, Forbes MacPherson, who was a career minor leaguer, and Robby Sutherland, who was captain of the Halifax Mooseheads in the QMJHL before playing university hockey with his twin brother, Brian.

Sidney admitted his game wasn't simply a by-product of hockey genes. "I played as much as possible," he said. "Whether it was organized games in a league or shinny at our local rink. I grew up in Cole Harbour. We were in a row of townhouses and there was a bunch of us who always played together. I'd knock on doors after school and on weekends, trying to get guys to come out to play. And we had a really good bunch of players. We called it 'our dynasty.' We won a lot of championships.

"It was the same way for us in baseball. We had a great team, a great bunch of guys who played together. I played catcher (because) I liked to be involved in the game all the time. I liked having the game go the way I called it. And we had a real shot at playing in the Little League World Series when I was a kid. We were that good. It didn't happen though. I had to give up (baseball) and concentrate on hockey and I was pretty sad about that—I really loved the game. I still wish I could play."

I asked him what was toughest about being Sidney Crosby—was he a target of resentment from coaches, players and parents. He allowed that there might have been "a few bumps" but said he had "a lot more friends than enemies" in sport. He said he had built up a list of more than two hundred contacts on his MSN Messenger, friends from back home, former teammates, guys whom he met at hockey camps.

I asked him when he knew that he wasn't like everyone else. "When I was seven I knew I had a talent," he said without a smidgen of brag. "That year I was playing up, against players a couple of years older than me. I scored 300 points or something, 150 goals."

It was a polite answer and a believable one. The only believable one. It strained credulity when Wayne Gretzky said he didn't think he was any better or more important than anybody else. Likewise, Bobby Orr used to feign modesty, aw-shucks-ing his way through interviews. Crosby, however, wasn't about to ignore the obvious. It wasn't a matter of ego. He scored three hundred points and nobody else did—he was different. He was being pursued by agents and nobody else was—he was different. His play caused a lot of tension in Halifax and nobody else's did—he was different. At age 14 and out of challenges close to home, he had to go far away to advance his career and nobody else had to—he was different.

A knock. The unlocked door opened. A teammate holding a razor and clad only in a towel stood before us. "Oh Sid, you're doing an interview," he said. "Never mind. I just wanted to show you my moustache." The kid had no hair on his face.

Sidney shut the door, sighed and picked up exactly where he left off. "My parents were real young when they had me. They lived at my grandparents' house when I was little. I used to take shots on my grandmother in the basement when I was two or three. She wasn't easy to beat. My parents had to struggle sometimes, I guess ..."

Here he skipped by some stuff that I already knew: that Troy's job as an administrative assistant in a law office put food on the table but not a heck of a lot more sometimes; that it had been harder for Sidney than his teammates in many ways.

"After games on weekends sometimes, my parents and I would go out and deliver flyers. That was to get enough money to pay my league fees. We made it something like a family outing. No matter what, my parents made sure that I had good equipment, never secondhand."

I asked him if he had ever envied those players whose families didn't have to deliver flyers, if he had ever felt cheated when he saw a teammate throw his equipment bag in the back of a Beamer.

"Honestly, I never did."

Sidney seemed to be earnest. He also seemed to stand well apart from most of the players on this team. Too many of them strode about the hotel as they had through much of their young lives, with self-involved sneers and a sense of entitlement reinforced by clippings from the sports pages. These were Canadian hockey princes. That's the state of the junior game these days. Go to the major junior arenas and you can spot the Prince of Swift Current, the Prince of Guelph and the Prince of Sherbrooke. Many on this team were the manor born, albeit in the principality of hockey. They were the fruit of a hockey culture that often prices out even the middle class with $400 skates, $100 sticks, and sundry other expenses that run up into thousands of dollars a season.

If Sidney never resented delivering flyers after games, he possesses something as rare as his skills and twice as valuable.

"Of course it gets easier from here," he said.

True in one sense: his parents would never again have to scratch up money for equipment. In no time manufacturers would be paying Sidney to wear their wares. Nonetheless, I suggested that it wasn't going to be easier now that Gretzky had designated him as his heir apparent.

Crosby insisted that fame wasn't going to change him. "My parents always told me: remember where you came from, work hard and good things will happen. I just try to be the same as I was as a six-year-old kid going to the rink."

An honourable sentiment but an unrealistic one. If he was going to make peace with fame and wind his way through future trials, it would soon be time to put boyhood behind him. He would never have to deliver flyers again, but otherwise life was certainly going to get harder in many ways.

The morning before the semi-final, the coaches gathered at a table in the hotel dining room. The assistant coaches, Dave Cameron from the St. Michael's Majors and Pascal Vincent from the Cape Breton Screaming Eagles, were working up a bet. Cameron, a real chatterbox, said Sidney was going to be the Quebec league's leading scorer by Christmas. Vincent, as soft-spoken as Cameron was brash, said he was willing to bet against it. Vincent cited a couple of factors—Rimouski would have back the same players who won just a handful of games the previous season, and the Q, like the other major junior circuits, was regarded as a league for 19-year-olds. Even though the Q was supposed to be more free-wheeling, Vincent wasn't able to let go of the notion that a 16-year-old phenom could eclipse players, top players from Montreal, Quebec City, Europe, wherever. Even though Vincent had watched Crosby author a couple of minor miracles here, the coach felt obliged to stand up for his league. Maybe Vincent thought Cameron was taking a dig at the Q. And maybe Cameron was—saying Crosby would lead the Q in scoring, leaving unsaid the belief that such a thing just couldn't happen in the Ontario league or out west.

Then head coach Bob Lowes, whose shaven head and hard features gave him the countenance of a prison guard, pressed Vincent, whose Cape Breton team was going to face Crosby during the Q league season. "Are you going to goon him?" asked Lowes.

Vincent maintained that his team wasn't going to take that route. Cameron got the needle out, implying that if Cape Breton wasn't going to goon Crosby, then they'd be the only team in the league that would take the high road. At first I thought Vincent's position to be a matter of respect for the game and for the phenom himself—once you knew Crosby and coached him, how could you send out a lug to take him out? But later I concluded that Vincent might have been a step ahead of Cameron. Vincent wasn't going to adopt old-school brutality as a strategy just by default. What had worked best against Crosby at this tournament wasn't Switzerland's attempt to cause him bodily harm, but rather the Czechs' blanketing him—a carpet-bombing rather than one attempted nuclear strike.

Piestany, Slovakia
August 15, 2003

The Canadian bus pulled into town in the late afternoon. For these teenagers it was just another stop on their European tour, just the site of their next game. The semi-final against the U.S. was situated in Piestany. The name didn't mean anything to them. It was just another line on their itinerary.

But this Slovakian spa town was the site of one of the most infamous moments in Canadian hockey history. Back in January 1987, not so long after Sidney Crosby was conceived and while the rest of the players on this Canadian under-18 team wore diapers, the national junior team led by Brendan Shanahan and Theo Fleury had a chance to win a world title. The Canadians needed a one-sided win over a Soviet team that had underachieved throughout the tournament. But in the final game of the round-robin tournament, with Canada leading and perhaps threatening to deliver the rout required for the gold, the U.S.S.R. team instigated an epic bench-clearing brawl. It wasn't just players trading punches. It was as close as international hockey has ever come to trench warfare. Defenceman Greg Hawgood was knocked out and suffered a broken nose from a head butt. One Soviet held down Stephane Roy while another kicked him in the head. The referee ordered the arena staff to turn out the arena's lights. And the Czechoslovakian army filed onto the ice in the dark to escort the teams off. A kangaroo court of international hockey officials convened and threw both teams out of the tournament.*

In the aftermath the media jumped all over the Canadian Hockey

---

* Not surprisingly, officials from the other teams in the competition voted unanimously to kick Canada and the Soviets out of the tournament and wipe their games from the official record. Finland, which was in the best position to win the tournament going into the last game, came away with the gold, though the victory was somewhat tainted.

Association's program. Commentators and newspaper columnists criticized the players for allowing themselves to be goaded into the fight; the coaches for letting the players jump over the boards; and Canadian hockey in general for turning out players who dropped their gloves whenever opponents gave them sideways looks. Though the Soviets and Canada would play a few times afterward—including a Canadian win over the Soviet juniors in Moscow the next winter—Piestany was the last shot fired in hockey's Cold War. A few years later the Soviet Union collapsed and a lot of the mystique surrounding this rivalry disappeared—how much mystique could survive among players who now shared the same agents, who played on the same Canadian major junior teams?

The semi-final at this summer's under-18 tournament in Piestany, however, was going to be the latest installment in the new international hockey rivalry that replaced Canada vs the Soviet Union. Maybe it plays out differently for the fans and the media, but at ice level nothing these days compares to the heat generated by U.S.A. vs Canada. It's the Soviet-Canadian dynamic turned inside out. In the old days, the Soviet and Canadian teams knew nothing of each other and the dialogue was nothing more than a few four-letter epithets that had greater international reach than Esperanto. It was a rivalry ground in ignorance and suspicion. In U.S.A.-Canada matchups, it's a matter of familiarity breeding contempt. The players faced each other in tournaments since they were tykes and the trash-talking is comparable to that in the National Basketball Association. Not that the trash-talking ends with the horn—no, the players take bragging rights back to their teams and rub it in, the Americans giving it to any Canadians on their college teams or the Canadians to any U.S. players on their major junior squads.

The Canadian under-18s weren't up to speed on the historical significance of Piestany, though a couple seemed to recall video of the brawl. Perhaps it was a good thing, because otherwise, they might have thought a curse was attached to the town. A generation and a couple of political transformations later, Piestany's bad karma lingered. There were portents of trouble at every turn. Sidney's wingers were on the limp: Evan McGrath with an ankle bruised by a slapshot in the Czech game, Wolski with stretched ligaments in his right knee. (Wolski had been on crutches in Brno the day before, a cause of real griping on the walking tour.) The bus ride to Piestany was a two-hour, day-of-the-game grind. It was 30°C outside and not a lot cooler inside. The ice-making equipment was strictly Communist Bloc hardware, so a couple of spots in the corners gave it the consistency of a slushee.

Worst of all, the bottled water on the Canadian bench was carbonated. Blame rested not with tournament organizers—no nefarious conspiracy here—but with team staff that fetched it from a local market before the game. The players weren't about to drink the gassy stuff because it would have had them burping. But if they didn't drink it, they were going to dehydrate, probably well before game's end given the sauna-like conditions. (For reasons known only to them, Canadian officials didn't dispatch anybody to hunt down water after the warm-up when they realized the screw-up—despite the fact that a gas station a five-minute walk from the arena had shelves lined with bottled water.)

All of this was unknown to the American parents who occupied a block of seats at centre ice. A dozen or so waved large flags while others simply wore them. Theirs were the only voices heard in the arena. The few Canadian parents to make the trip were drowned out. Otherwise the arena was vacant, the people of Piestany not having a rooting interest in the semi-final. And it seemed there was as much action outside the arena as inside—a photographer working the game had his car stolen though three soldiers were stationed in the parking lot.

The game had a through-the-looking-glass quality to it, even stranger than the circumstances surrounding it. In the first minute the Canadians took two penalties, two marginal calls. It couldn't have been a bleaker beginning. And then the American families took up the chorus of "U-S-A, U-S-A"—just the thing to bring already hot Canadian blood to a boil.

It was the perfect scenario for a Canadian meltdown (or desiccation, as the case was). And yet over the next two minutes the Canadian teens managed to find resolve and composure that many veteran professionals lack. They managed to kill a five-on-three power play, thanks to Rizk, who ran around the ice recklessly throwing himself in front of shots from the point, and goaltender Ellis-Plante, who was landing in a puddle every time he flopped to the fast-melting ice.

The Americans soon sagged. With his hobbling linemates McGrath and Wolski gutting out every shift, Crosby went to work. In a two-minute stretch at the end of the first period, Crosby set up two power play goals, a point blast by defenceman Cam Barker and a rap-in off a rebound in a goalmouth scramble by Alex Bourret. Canada was up 2–0.

But the game turned 180 degrees after the intermission. Twenty seconds after the drop of the puck, the Americans got a goal on a seemingly harmless shot from a kid familiar to many on the Canadian team, Tyler Haskins, a forward from Ohio who had played the previous season with the Guelph Storm of the Ontario league. The Canadians reeled. For the next 19 minutes the U.S. stormed the net, firing 15 shots at Ellis-Plante, putting two more past him. Even the "U-S-A, U-S-A" cheers from the American families weren't rousing the Canadian teens. No, the bench was a collection of heads hanging, shoulders slumping and faces grimacing.

The arena was fast heating up—one temperature reading had it at 24°C. And down at ice level Canadian team manager Scott Salmond was laying into officials and the ice-maker who couldn't guarantee that the surface was going to last till the end of regulation. That the ice was pud-dling and that the puck was sticking were the least of Salmond's concerns. At some point conditions might have become unsafe for play. To have a player injury result from bad ice wouldn't be a blow to the Czech organ-izers so much as a blow to the Canadian or U.S. programs.

Going into the third period, 21 of the Canadians didn't know what hit them. But Crosby did. The Americans were pounding him and hoping he'd shy away. They were slashing him on the gloves and delivering fore-arms and whiplash-inducing elbows. They were counting on wearing him down and maybe even breaking him. A couple of times when the Americans headed off Canadian rushes and started in the other direction, Luke Lucyk, the biggest U.S. defenceman, already NHL-sized at 6-foot-1 and 210 pounds, held Crosby down, pinning his back to the ice with a stick across his chest. Crosby was giving up 30 pounds in the wrestling match.

I met an NHL scout at the snack bar—the concessions crew thank-fully hadn't raised the price of bottled water—and I asked him about the beating Crosby was taking. He wasn't sympathetic, noting that whatever the Americans were dealing out was "the price Crosby will have to pay." When I told him of Pascal Vincent's claim that he wasn't going to goon Sidney in the Quebec league, the scout laughed it off. "Everyone's going to try it, but will it be effective?" the scout wondered for a second. "No, you goon him and you'll give his team a power play or maybe a four-on-four, which is all good for Crosby. What the Americans are trying is what gives you the best chance. Shadow him. Lean on him. Chip away."

The Americans stuck with their strategy through the third period. What proved to be the most effective way to stymie Crosby was tried and true, as old as the game itself: nightmare-inducing goaltending. On a couple of his best chances, what looked like sure goals, Crosby was stoned by American netminder Cory Schneider. Other times Lucyk body-slammed him. And yet Crosby kept on firing and Lowes kept sending him out—10 minutes into the frame Crosby seemed to be out on every other shift. And in spite of the workload, the heat and the poor man's Perrier on the bench, and with the Americans up 3–2, Crosby got a second—or third—wind. With less than three minutes left in regulation, Crosby set up Mike Blunden, a forward with the Erie Otters, for the tying goal. With the tournament on the line, Crosby lived up to Tim Burke's assessment. *When he needs to, he can get it done.* With the game heading into overtime, everyone in the rink was thinking he was likely, almost certain, to do it one more time.

For five minutes the overtime period passed uneventfully, just a bunch of cautious one-man-in dump-and-chases. It seemed likely that the game was heading to a shoot-out, but then the American blueliners were caught napping and Crosby slipped behind Lucyk for a clean breakaway, from the centre redline in. The Canadian bench and coaches stood and yelled as one. But otherwise the arena was so empty and quiet that I could hear Crosby's skate blades cutting the soft ice. With three strides he was in flight, cutting from the right side into the middle of the ice. I happened to be standing behind the glass at that end of the rink, beside the goal judge's seat, the closest thing, I suppose, to the sensation of having Crosby come in on you in a game situation. Crosby tried to deke Schneider on his stick side, a shift right and left, again, a move I could hear as much as see, the stick hitting the puck and ice together. But the goaltender made a sprawling save. Crosby was so far ahead of Lucyk that he had time to take the rebound behind the net and try a wrap-around. This time the goalie dove from one post to the other to make the save.

The Americans then took control of the puck and headed straight up ice. Crosby gave chase, but he was too late. Lucyk cranked a seemingly harmless shot from the blueline, unscreened. Ellis-Plante swiped at it and missed. The Americans won with their first shot in overtime, a goal credited to Michael Taylor on a phantom deflection. The Canadians had to stand while "The Star Spangled Banner" rang in their ears. It drowned out their sobbing.

After the game many of the Canadian teens complained they were drained by the lack of water. Sidney didn't grouse, but he told Wolski he didn't have a drink all game.

Parched and downcast, the Canadians packed up and rode the bus into downtown Piestany for a post-game meal. There they got word that the Russians had upset the Czechs and would play the Americans in the gold-medal game. Canada would again play the Czechs, this time for the bronze back in Breclav.

The best restaurant in downtown Piestany turned out to be a safe haven for an oppressed minority, who so far, remain overlooked by Amnesty International: Slovakian jazz musicians. To the strains of "My Favorite Things" and past a gallery of portraits of Miles Davis and Duke Ellington, the Canadians were ushered to the only unoccupied tables in the smoky room. "We would like to welcome the Canadian team," the band leader, a saxophone player, announced. "We know you do not feel good tonight but you will all be champions someday."

The band then broke into John Coltrane's "Nocturne," a fitting tribute to the team's melancholy. Nobody talked. Everybody had a thousand-yard stare on. Sidney's chin rested in his chest. He didn't even raise his head when the chicken dinner arrived. The players had lost their appetite—for dinner and for this tournament. This was the last place they wanted to be. They wanted to be on the plane home. They wanted this tournament behind them.

At the end of the long, silent ride back to the hotel, Scott Salmond, the team's manager, stood up at the front of the bus. "I'm not going to bull-shit you," he told the players. "Tomorrow's game will be the last chance a bunch of you have to wear a Team Canada sweater. It's up to you whether you want to play or not."

Salmond was an unlikely candidate to have reamed out the players. Perhaps the coach should have said a few words. But at this point, even Bob Lowes looked beaten by the evening's events. So Salmond delivered the state-of-the-team message himself. It was an attempt to shame and anger the princes, and at the same time, appeal to their patriotism. It was no Gipper speech. Fact was, in contradicting the Slovakian sax player about all these young men being "champions someday," Salmond only stated the truth. Some years half the players from the under-18 program eventually wind up making the Canadian under-20 junior team. And some years only a handful make that next step up. After a couple of losses and two tighter-than-comfortable wins, players on this team should not have had any illusions about this tournament being just another stepping stone on their inexorable march to the NHL. It was one thing for Crosby, another thing for many, if not most, on the bus.

Breclav, Czech Republic
August 16, 2003

Team Canada arrived at the arena the morning of the bronze-medal game. The players didn't skate. They made the trip to shower because the water was off at the team hotel. Sidney was the first out of the dressing room. He sat cross-legged on the ashphalt beside the team bus, his head hanging again.

He explained that he recieved bad news the night before. "Rimouski called," he said. "They want me to report (for training camp) right after the tournament. I was supposed to go home after the tournament for a couple of days to rest. I'll have played six games in seven days. I'll have flown from Halifax to Calgary for training camp to Vienna and back to Toronto and out to Quebec City or whatever. Get off the plane, go straight to practice. I've run out of clean clothes."

He paused.

"That sucks," he said.

He'd get no sympathy from the scouts. Whenever a coveted teenager opts to play junior instead of going the U.S.-college route, rumours circulate that money is behind the decision. Connect the dots, the scouts will tell you.

Just then I thought about what Gretzky said. *We were making 21 bucks a week and I was just as happy as I am today.* Just as it was tougher to be Troy Crosby than Walter Gretzky, it was going to be tougher for Crosby in Rimouski than it was for No. 99 in the Soo. Even before Sidney Crosby entered junior, he had commercial opportunities and fame beyond what Gretzky knew in the OHA, in the WHA, even as a sensational NHL rookie. And yet at what cost? Once Crosby got to Rimouski, his every move would be scrutinized. By the townspeople, by the media, by the scouts. Had his last private moment already passed?

And what was awaiting him? In the Quebec League he would fall under the vigilant gaze of NHL scouts. In the NHL, everyone would want a piece of him. Sports-television networks, cameramen and soundmen were going to be tracing his every step. His life was going to give way to "Sidney: NHL Reality Show." The natural, unguarded moment was soon to be a thing of the past. Here, now, before being called in from the playground, he had one last chance to be a boy.

Still, the Czechs' gloating the other night really burned Crosby's ass. "The way they acted after the game made me sick," he said.

Now on the bus he turned and looked up. "We're not riding to the game tonight with that thing there," he said.

"That thing" was a Czech flag. "There" was high up over the driver's head on the windshield inside the team bus. The flag was hung there, above a Team Canada banner, by the bus driver, a local named Karl. Karl had been an unhappy camper since Canadian officials let it be known that a four-pint lunch was not considered an appropriate tune-up for a day's chauffeuring.

Soon Evan McGrath was standing at the door to the bus and anxiously trying to get the attention of Karl, who was sitting in the driver's seat with his nose in a newspaper.

"Karl, Karl, problem, problem," McGrath yelped. He pointed to the rear of the bus. "Flat tire," and then made a hissing sound.

Karl got out of his seat and off the bus. While he was doing a quick inspection, Sidney clambered up at the front like a kid on monkey bars, standing with one foot on Karl's seat and the other on the steering wheel. He reached up to the flag. McGrath got word to stall and bought time by taking Karl around for a full multi-tire inspection. Finally the flag was down. Sidney clambered back with the banner tucked away. The look of innocence served him well when Karl sat back in his seat and noticed his treasured Czech colours gone. It was refreshing to see that Crosby, so careful to do and say the right things, was capable of a little boyhood mischief.

☺

The Canadian team opened the bronze-medal game hitting every Czech in sight. It might have been an attempt to intimidate the host team or, more likely, it might have been a petulant response to Salmond's challenge from the night before. It was, however, self-defeating. The ref led a procession of Canadians to the penalty box—four minors in the first nine minutes—and the players never got the message. It was 1–0 Czech Republic after the first period; 4–2 after a second period that featured six Czech power plays to a single Canadian turn; and the worst was yet to come. The final score was 8–2—and this time the Czechs and their fans didn't wait for the post-game party to taunt the Canadians. Again they celebrated like it was a gold-medal game, New Year's and Mardi Gras all at once. To Crosby's credit he didn't quit. The same might not have been said of his teammates. Crosby did lose his composure midway through the last dispiriting frame, taking an unsportsmanlike conduct penalty. Jeers rained down on him when he slammed the penalty box door.

A half-hour later, Sidney was red-eyed and downcast standing beside his parents in the parking lot beside the bus. Troy was blasting Scott Salmond about Rimouski demanding that Sidney go directly to training camp. He said there was supposed to be "an understanding" with the CHL. Salmond said it was out of his hands. It was the message he was getting from upstairs. Troy looked completely pissed. So did all the Canadian players when they got word that the U.S. had just defeated Russia in the gold-medal game in Piestany. "Should have been us," Evan McGrath lamented.

Coach Lowes called for his players to board the bus. Sidney was the last one on. After he gave Trina a hug, he came up to me without solicitation. "This was an embarrassment," he concluded. "I'll always remember this. Next time you can write that we get the gold."

I told him I'd like that. I also told him to lose his luggage and force the Oceanic to spring for some new clothes. He shrugged. He wouldn't do anything like that. It just wasn't in him to even think about that. He boarded the bus and gave the banner back to Karl the bus driver. It wouldn't have been much of a souvenir anyway. It wouldn't have been right for it to take a place beside a banner from the Canada Winter Games in his personal hall of fame. And nothing from this tournament was going to be featured that prominently in his display of sweaters, pucks and trophies. He waved out the window to his parents.

It had been fun while it lasted. It had been a learning experience and after so many great moments it ended here in frustration. But now, effective immediately, Sidney Crosby was property of l'Océanic de Rimouski. From here on it was going to be different. He had been a peewee, a bantam, a midget, a high schooler, even an international player. Now he was a Canadian junior. Under contract. The game he had loved as a boy now owned him as a man.

NINE

"The thing that's not in the notes is the fear
in the defenceman's eyes ..."

Crosby went to Rimouski sooner than he wanted but that didn't have a negative effect on his play. In fact, he exploded out of the blocks in junior.

"The first exhibition game we played in Rimouski that fall, the arena wasn't sold out," Oceanic PR official Yannick Dumais recalled. "Everyone around here had heard about Sidney but wondered how he'd adjust to the Q. He had four goals and four assists and we won. I was thinking that those would probably be the last empty seats of the season."

In mid-September Crosby won the Q's player of the week award in his first week in the league. And he took the award again seven days later. Across the fortnight he racked up 10 goals and 8 assists. Then he was named the Q's player of the month and was given the same honours by the Canadian Hockey League. He ran out to an early lead not just in Quebec league scoring but in the overall CHL scoring ranks as well. His teammates immediately realized what type of player the club had landed. Mark Tobin, a scrappy winger from Newfoundland, started calling Crosby "Gretz," because of the Great One's assessment of Crosby and because of the vanity number that Crosby took in Rimouski, No. 87, which goes to his birthday, August 7, 1987, in other words, 8/7/87. Crosby shut down the "Gretz" talk quickly.

The Canadian sports media started to pick up on the unfolding Crosby story, but NHL scouts filed the most compelling accounts of his first games. I chased down scouts who had made it out to Rimouski or caught Crosby on the road in the first two months of the 2003–04 season.

Christian Bordeleau, a veteran scout who works Quebec for the NHL's Central Scouting Bureau, couldn't wait to see what all the buzz was about. He made it a point to make it out to Crosby's first regular-season junior game, a game at the Aréna Dave Keon in Rouyn-Noranda.

"Right from the first shift he was dominating play," Bordeleau said. "He's the first man in on the forecheck and he's so fast he's the first guy back when play goes the other way. After a few minutes, it's clear his skill is unbelievable. He does a lot of things that Gretzky did. He passes like a pro, everything on the tape—so much that the kids on his team, guys who are maybe not that skilled, aren't ready for it. They're not expecting it. He's playing way ahead of them, thinking way ahead of them. He never takes a shift off. Early on I'm thinking that maybe size is going to be a drawback. He's five-foot-ten, 185. But then I see he's not really getting pushed off the puck. He has incredible power, so with this low centre of gravity he's hard to hit and when he hits you, you know it.*

"After the second period, I thought I had seen everything I needed to see. They (the Oceanic) were losing 3–0 but he'd done everything but score. I could never have guessed what was going to happen."

Bordeleau was no neophyte. He was not a man to be easily impressed or surprised by something he saw on the ice. He played in hundreds of games in the NHL and the WHA. He played with Jean Béliveau as a Montreal Canadien and with Bobby Hull as a Winnipeg Jet. He played against scores of Hall of Famers. But what he saw in the third period that night was something lifted out of a storybook.

Philippe Lauzé opened the scoring for the Oceanic on a power play goal less than five minutes into the third period. At that point, Crosby took over. He proceeded to score a natural hat trick over the next 10

---

* Bordeleau came to understand the source of Crosby's power later that season. "When I measured the kid (for NHL Central Scouting) I saw how the kid is built. His legs are like a weightlifter's. He looks small but he had incredible development for a 16-year-old."

Sidney Crosby waiting on the draw in his familiar Rimouski Océanic
whites. No. 87 represents his year of birth, 1987.

Busting up the wing during a prep game in Kitchener for the 2003-2004
world juniors. Crosby's explosive speed makes him a constant threat,
even deep in his own end.

A March 2004 playoff game against Shawinigan. Crosby takes a blast from the top of the circle, as Dany Roussin (15) waits on the rebound and Marc-Antoine Pouliot (78, at left circle), spins off for the corner.

Final game of the Memorial Cup, 2005, against the London Knights. Here Crosby jams on the brakes in mid-flight, forcing the play to develop around him. Such intuitive playmaking has hockey pundits comparing him to Wayne Gretzky.

Veteran hockey scouts often note Crosby's childlike love of the game.
Above his joy is palpable, as he and Dany Roussin explode out of the
neutral zone leaving behind a much-bewildered Quebec City
Remparts opponent.

Sidney Crosby learned to shoot in the basement of his grandmother's house. A Whirlpool dryer was the net; his grandmother was the goaltender. The result is something fearsome: perfect balance and a turn of the blade for incredible velocity and pinpoint accuracy.

Sidney signs autographs for young players from Toronto's East Enders Ticats. Always gracious with his time, Sidney gives kids, often not much younger than himself, extra consideration.

If you can't stop him ... Above, Crosby gets introduced to Canadian junior hockey by Dominic D'Amour of the Gatineau Olympiques, during the 2003-2004 QMJHL season. Below, Brandon Prust of the London Knights does everything but sit on Crosby during the 2005 Memorial Cup in London.

At age 17 Crosby was already the most sought after hockey interview on the continent. Here Crosby shows just how comfortable he had become in front of the camera, doing an on-ice interview with a national sportsnetwork at the 2005 Memorial Cup.

At the centre of it all. Sidney Crosby prepares to break out with defenceman Francois Bolduc, deep in the heart of the storied Quebec City Colisée.

minutes, all the scoring that Rimouski would need for a 4–3 victory. "It was really amazing stuff," Bordeleau exclaimed. "It was like it took him two periods to figure out the league. Rouyn knew he was coming and couldn't stop him. The tougher the situation, the more important a goal is, the better he plays. Each goal was one more spectacular play or deke or shot. For a player in his first game in the league, stepping up a level, it was just incredible stuff."

Like Bordeleau, Mike Racicot thought he had seen it all. In fact, you could make a case that he had seen more than anybody else in the Q. Regarded as the dean of Quebec scouts by his peers, Racicot had scouted the region for the Buffalo Sabres for 33 years. He had filed reports on Guy Lafleur who led the Quebec Remparts to a Memorial Cup title, and Mario Lemieux and Pat Lafontaine when they set Q scoring records. And before he latched on with the Sabres, he had seen other stars, such as Gilbert Perreault, come up through the league. He remembered the Q from a time when the Montreal Canadiens literally owned it—every player in the league was the property of les Habitants because the NHL granted the franchise a territorial hegemony on junior hockey in the province. Yet Racicot was blown away by what he saw when he first worked one of Crosby's games.

"I saw him early in the season," Racicot explained. "All the skills that you can measure in a player, he's at the very top of any rating: speed, skating, passing, finishing chances. But what makes him stand out more than players who come along in other years is his vision. It's hard to compare someone to Wayne Gretzky, maybe it's not fair, but he sees situations so quickly, reads play. He sees things on the ice, plays developing, before anyone else in the arena. He made a couple of passes that had me jumping out of my seat. Scoring is down all over hockey—in the NHL, in junior—but if he had come along when Lafleur or Lemieux or Bossy were playing, he'd score 200 points instead of 130. It's the chance to see something like Sidney Crosby that keeps you in scouting."

Daniel Doré is the Boston Bruins' chief scout for the Quebec league. Back in the '80s, Doré was a giant on the left wing of Drummondville and Chicoutimi and was drafted fifth overall by the Quebec Nordiques in 1988. He didn't stick in the league, playing only 16 games as an 18-year-old and one game the following season. Nonetheless, Doré later found his niche as a junior scout.*

Asked to compare Crosby and Vincent Lecavalier at the same stage, Doré was cautious, calling Lecavalier "an exceptional junior." But he made it clear that, as a junior, Crosby ranked in an even more exclusive category. To make the point, he pulled out his scouting report from an early-season game. One notation: "Perfect pass." Next notation: "Perfect play." In the skills categories that appear on the Bruins' standard scouting form, Crosby was given the highest possible rankings—across the board.

"Really, my notes can't tell the story," Doré said. "This is one of those cases when words don't do justice."

Doré put his notes and reports back in his case and shrugged. He used his own playing experience to colour in between the lines. "The thing that's not in the notes is the fear in the defenceman's eyes when Crosby is coming down the ice, one on one. I can see that fear and I know what it feels like. It's not just that Crosby has such great speed and puck-handling skills. He has an amazingly quick mind for the game. He reads a situation instantly. He knows a defenceman's weaknesses—sees how (the defenceman) is trying to compensate, and makes a decision while going full speed. Crosby will come down the ice five times on a defenceman and beat him five different ways. He's so confident. It takes a lot of nerve just to try the things he does. Maybe what makes him different from Gretzky or some of the other super-skilled players is how he goes into traffic down low. He is absolutely unafraid of contact with bigger players."

You didn't have to be a hockey man to appreciate Sidney Crosby. In fact, some who didn't have scouts' passes appreciated Crosby in an altogether different way than the guys drawing NHL paycheques. Take season ticket holder of Seat 7 Row D Section 9, located right behind the Rimouski penalty box. Suzanne Tremblay wasn't quite the average fan of the Oceanic. Between 1993 and 2004, she represented largely sovereign-

* Back in the 2003–04 season, Doré was able to dine out on his recommendation of Patrice Bergeron to the Bruins. A second-round draft choice, Bergeron went to the Bruins' training camp lightly considered by management. He not only started the season with the club, but finished it in a regular role, scoring 16 goals, and even played for Canada's gold-medal winning team at the 2004 world championships.

tist Rimouski as a Bloc Québécois member of parliament in Ottawa. Tremblay made it to Rimouski's Colisée as often as she could back when Lecavalier and Richards played there and Crosby's arrival made it an even higher priority for her. She described the Oceanic as "outside politics" and pointed to the fact that she supported the team even though Éric Forest, a vice-president of the team, once ran against her as a Liberal candidate in the riding. "For 60 minutes we're hockey fans, not sovereigntists or federalists," she noted.

Suzanne Tremblay described Crosby as "a remarkable young man, a great player and also a wonderful person." She said that many players, francophones from Montreal and Quebec, and anglophones from the Maritimes, embraced life in the community, but few so quickly as Sidney Crosby. "When he went out in the community, he was talking to everybody, whether it was in stores, the supermarket, at restaurants. He was trying to speak French. I think, no matter the situation, he wants to do the right thing. When he passes kids in a playground, he stops and gets in the game with kids. They have rubber legs afterward—they say they can't believe it's Sidney Crosby. But he makes time for everybody and he's always respectful. I hope for an independent Quebec, but that doesn't mean that I don't like or respect anglophones—and for sovereigntists, I believe this is the attitude. I respect Sidney Crosby and not just for hockey."

☺

In November of Crosby's first year with Rimouski, Hockey Canada invited him to its evaluation camp for the team that would represent Canada at the world juniors in Finland. It was only the sixth time a 16-year-old had been brought in to the under-20 program.*

Sixteen-year-olds had a very mixed record with the Canadian world junior team. Gretzky led the world junior tournament in scoring as a 16-year-old in 1978. In 1990 Eric Lindros was already billed as the game's

---

* The youngest players to dress for Canada at the world under-20s: Bouwmeester, 16 years 3 months; Crosby, 16 years 5 months; Spezza, 16 years 6 months; Lindros, 16 years 10 months; Gretzky, 16 years 11 months.

next great player and lived up to the hype, taking a regular shift and fitting in seamlessly with a gold-medal winning Canadian team. In 2000, Jason Spezza and Jay Bouwmeester earned bronze medals with the Canadian team that went to Sweden, but they played very small roles there. The two returned the next season to play more prominently with a Canadian team that again took the bronze, on this occasion in Moscow. On their third trip, Spezza and Bouwmeester and the rest of the Canadians came up just short in a spirited final against the Russians in Pardubice, in the Czech Republic.

But there is also a cautionary tale involving a 16-year-old invited to try out for the world junior team. Back in 1995, Dan Cleary, a winger from Newfoundland who was causing a small sensation with the Belleville Bulls, was invited to the under-20 team camp. Cleary, who was touted as the likely first overall pick in the 1997 draft, had been the subject of several profiles in the national media. But Cleary was a late cut—at least some scouts thought he should have made the team—and it seemed to shake his confidence. Cleary was cut from the Canadian junior squad the next two seasons, 1997 and 1998, and his stock with NHL scouts plunged when he reported to the summer under-20 camp 15 pounds overweight. Cleary ended up being drafted 13th overall by the Chicago Blackhawks and has continued to slide down the slippery slope for several seasons. He is now little more than a fringe NHLer.

Crosby, though, seemed to be heading into the under-20 camp with a full head of steam. He was proving Pascal Vincent wrong, not only leading the Q in scoring, but running away with the race. Would he break out at the world junior level like Gretzky? Would he take a strong supporting role like Lindros? Would he be mostly a spectator like Spezza and Bouwmeester? Or would it all go wrong like it did for Cleary?

Just at that point a black cloud blew in.

One night in front of a sellout crowd in Rimouski, with the Oceanic leading the Quebec Remparts 4–0, Crosby set up behind the net. He already had scored his 25th goal of the season in the first period and had assisted on two goals by Dany Roussin. In other words, Rimouski was cruising, putting on a show for the hometown fans. When the Quebec defenceman didn't chase him, Crosby did something that he had only tried in practice. Something he had fooled around with. He pressed down on the puck with the face of his stick blade on the forehand side, then lifted the puck up, letting it sit in the curve of the blade—a standard lacrosse move. Still in lacrosse mode, he worked a chest-high wrap-around past a stunned Quebec goaltender. It was sword work worthy of Zorro, but it would have been soon forgotten—that is, if it hadn't been for a videotape of the game and if it hadn't been Sidney Crosby wielding the stick.

Commentator Don Cherry hammered Crosby on *Hockey Night in Canada* the following week. Cherry has made his millions with a shtik that plays to hockey lowbrows and one element of his shtik is an abiding belief in "the code," rules of behaviour for players that are unwritten but understood, unchanged since his playing days in the '50s and '60s, unquestionable by all and sundry. "I like the kid," Cherry said while tape of the goal rolled. "But this is a hot dog move ... the Quebec Remparts are going to remember that the next time they play. He's gonna get hurt. They're gonna grab the mustard and put it all over him."

Your average teen might be terminally embarrassed when, say, a teacher blasts him in class. Imagine being the whipping boy for the game's most influential voice on your country's most watched television show. Talk about your *Carrie* moment.

Fortunately for Crosby, the rest of the media didn't see it Cherry's way and instead upbraided Cherry for his over-the-top attack. Jack Todd provided the most colourful counterpoint in the Montreal *Gazette*. "Don Cherry must have reached the age where his idea of a thrill is heading out for bingo night without his Depends," Todd wrote, "because when he decided last weekend to use his national bully pulpit to pick on a talented 16-year-old kid, Cherry was definitely having a senior's moment."

And down home the people who had watched Crosby grow up threatened a boycott of *HNIC*. One letter to *The Daily News* labelled Cherry "a bully and a loudmouth" and suggested there were "thousands of Nova Scotians out there wishing they could take a crack at Cherry, whose pimp-like dress clashes with his would-be bravado."

Even in the face of such lampooning (or perhaps because of it), Cherry didn't let up. On *HNIC* the next week, he said the public reacted to his comments "like I said something about the Pope." Cherry explained that he criticized Crosby "to warn the kid (about) what can happen." He then took a shot at the Quebec league. According to Cherry, the league is soft and French players are "floaters." "You might be able to get away with it there," Cherry said, but Crosby would pay the price in the NHL or any other pro or junior league. Cherry backed up his case by airing an interview with Detroit's Brendan Shanahan, who said he'd be "looking to take the head off" a player who pulled a stunt like Crosby did in Quebec.

Cherry then went after Troy and Trina Crosby. "His parents evidently don't know anything about that stuff," Cherry said. "Someone should have told him not to do it."

I called Troy a few weeks later and he brushed off Cherry's tirades. "There's no use talking about something that ignorant," he said, not angrily so much as dismissively.

Sidney was unapologetic, but still seemed shaken when I asked him about it. "I know the unwritten rules," Sidney said. "My father taught me all about respect in the game. I didn't try to embarrass anybody. A reporter in Quebec even went to the Remparts goalie and asked him if the goal (embarrassed him). He said it didn't—that I was just trying to put the puck in the net."

Sidney admitted it wasn't quite a play made on the spur of the moment—that he had seen a college player score on the same move on TV and afterward practised it.

By the time Sidney reported to the world junior camp, the controversy about his lacrosse-style goal had died down. The issue had turned instead to whether Crosby could make the team, or even make an impact.

There was little question about the former. Hockey Canada didn't want another situation like Dan Cleary's. If Crosby was going to be invited, then team staff had to keep open one of the 13 forward roster slots for him.

The latter was a more difficult call. Conventional wisdom made Crosby's playing a lead role a long shot. As Oilers' amateur scout Kevin Prendergast told the *Edmonton Journal*: "It's a pretty good tournament with a lot of 19- and 20-year-olds. Against the low-end teams, he'll probably do well, but against the high-end teams ... I think this will be a learning process for him."

It was a prescient reading of the situation, though perhaps not for the reasons Prendergast expected.

Mario Desrochers of the QMJHL's Lewiston Maniacs was the coach of the Canadian team and he said all the right things, everything that made it seem like the door was wide open for Crosby. "I'm not looking at whether he's 16, 18 or 19, or whether he's English, French or Italian," said Desrochers. "I just want the best 22 guys."

And the Canadian team's chief scout, Blair Mackasey, endorsed Desrochers' approach. Crosby was, Mackasey said, "a 16-year-old playing against the best 18- and 19-year-olds in the world, which is a challenge for anybody. But he certainly proved at the world under-18s last summer and at the Canada Games last year that he deserves the opportunity."

Crosby certainly got the opportunity, and, as Prendergast predicted, his best moments came against Team Canada's weaker opponents. In fact, Crosby became the youngest player ever to score for Canada in the tournament's history when he potted the final goal in a 7–2 opening round victory over Switzerland. "It wasn't even anything I knew until after the game," Crosby said. "I never really think about age, but when they brought that up, it was definitely pretty special."

The puck was sent to the Hockey Hall of Fame.

Crosby added another goal in a 10–0 victory over an even more outmatched opponent, Ukraine. But again, like Prendergast predicted, Crosby struggled against the better teams. He didn't make the scoresheet in Canada's 3–0 victory over Finland. He picked up three assists in two wins over the Czech Republic, but most of his work was limited to power-play shifts. Though Canada rolled undefeated and effectively unchallenged into the final against the U.S., Crosby played less and less with every game. He didn't score another goal. In fact, the biggest news Crosby made at the tournament was when he fell victim to a prank—his teammates bound him with hockey tape in a mattress and left him in the elevator in the team's hotel.

For 40 minutes in the final, it looked like a gold medal was going to be his consolation, but then the Americans rallied from a 3–1 deficit to score a 4–3 victory. It was painful enough for Crosby to watch Canadian goaltender Marc-Andre Fleury, the first overall pick of the Pittsburgh Penguins in the 2003 draft, make a horrific gaffe on the winning goal. Crosby's pain was compounded by the fact that he was reduced to being a spot player in the final—he had little more influence than when his teammates left him as the meat in the mattress sandwich.

Hockey insiders disagreed somewhat about Desrochers' handling of his youngest player. "There's no way he shouldn't have played all through the tournament," said one major junior coach who watched the tournament. "He was just more skilled than a lot of the other guys and he would have really been able to do some things on the (oversize European) ice surface. But there was no second-guessing (Desrochers) with the team winning the way (it) was, right into the final."

An NHL scout at the tournament outlined another view, which backed Desrochers' decision: "It was a tough spot for (Desrochers) because the best-known player he had was the youngest. He had to go with the players that he thought he could win with and look after both ends of the rink. Crosby's great with the puck and good in the other end of the rink—better than almost any 16-year-old you'll see defensively. But not better (defensively) than an 18- or 19-year-old with two or three seasons of junior experience and playoff hockey."

Players on the Canadian team weren't about to question Desrochers in the wake of the silver-medal finish. Mike Richards, a forward with the OHL's Kitchener Rangers and a first-round draft pick of the Philadelphia Flyers, suggested that the team and the tournament had to be kept in perspective. "Before the tournament we were the underdogs and we went to Finland with a really young team, probably the youngest team that Canada ever sent," Richards said. "A lot of people talked about (the 2004) tournament being a stepping stone for the next year. It was supposed to be a learning experience for players like me who were still going to be eligible for (the 2005 tournament in) North Dakota. And that was true for Sidney. I don't think it was fair to expect Sidney to play a big role with the team—it's a lot to expect of a 17-year-old, forget about a 16-year-old."

When I asked Crosby about the experience he was surprisingly upbeat. "It was a disappointment to lose in the final the way we did," he told me a few weeks after his return. "But otherwise I liked the whole experience. It was great."

"Even the prank?" I asked him.

"Even that. It was great to be in a situation like that. With a team (like Rimouski) you get to know guys over months—a whole season, maybe even two or three seasons. With a team like the world junior team, a bunch of players have to come together in just a few days."

Was it a little easier to accept the silver medal knowing that you and a lot of your teammates would be back the next year?

"It's right at the top of my goals for next year," he concluded.

— T E N —

"The way you handle yourself and the way you play
is the way you get respect."

Rimouski
April 2, 2004

The first junior playoff game of Crosby's career was not the personal
showcase that his first exhibition game and first regular-season contest
had been. For 59 minutes les Cataractes de Shawinigan had kept Crosby
off the scoresheet. He couldn't see just one thin ray of daylight. Every time
he turned around he was grill to grill with Nicolas Desilets, a disagreeable
19-year-old defenceman. Every time Crosby thought he had time or space
to make a play, Desilets had an arm or stick hooked around him. Every
time the ref's back was turned, Crosby was getting an elbow in the ribs
or a slash on the wrists or a facewash. Crosby's talent shined through
occasionally—a slippery move here, a knowing head fake there, a how'd-
he-see-that pass through traffic. He also showed a combative streak, a
willingness to literally carve out his own space, looking like a peach-fuzz
Peter Forsberg. But Crosby was able to generate only a couple of scoring
chances and on those occasions he was stoned by, yes, Julien Ellis-Plante,
the flaky goaltender from the under-18 team. When the puck came back

to Crosby in the slot, Ellis-Plante had answers for him, just like he had answers for the brainteasers over breakfast in the Czech Republic.

Just a couple of nights before, Crosby had beat a path to the podium at the QMJHL's award show: top rookie, top rookie scorer, top scorer overall, most valuable player and, the Paul Dumont Trophy. "There isn't a word in English for the Dumont," Rimouski official Yannick Dumais tried to explain. "It's the award for the player who brings the most sunshine to the league." But if Crosby's playoff debut were your first glimpse of the phenom in action, you might have wondered what all the fuss was about. You might have suspected that his stats—59 games, 54 goals, 81 assists for 135 points—were somehow trumped up. You might have doubted that he was in fact the most prolific 16-year-old in league history. Or that Mario Lemieux's numbers as 16-year-old with Laval paled by comparison.* The 5,000 fans crammed into le Colisée de Rimouski knew all these things but were now seeing the one thing they never imagined: a near-total eclipse of their sunshine boy.

Thanks to the play of forwards Marc-Antoine Pouliot, a first-round draft pick of the Edmonton Oilers, and Dany Roussin, Rimouski was clinging to a 2–1 lead in the third period. With about five minutes left in regulation, les Cataractes started to take the initiative, controlling the puck and peppering Oceanic netminder Cédrick Desjardins with shots. The pressure continued into the last minute when Shawinigan pulled Ellis-Plante in favour of an extra attacker. It looked ominous for l'Océanic when Shawinigan forced a face-off in Rimouski's end. The situation looked even darker for Rimouski when Crosby lost the draw and the puck came back to the 200-pound Desilets at the point. Then, Crosby stepped in front of the slapshot. Five thousand went silent, scouts in the crowd winced, and the hearts of Rimouski's coaching and management staff rose in their throats.

I recalled the words of two NHL scouts. Tim Burke talked about Crosby being "fearless," but this move verged on recklessness. Daniel Doré talked about Crosby making the "perfect play" in difficult

---

* Mario Lemieux, who turned 16 on October 5, 1981, recorded 30 goals and 66 assists in 64 games for the Laval Voisins, 16th in the league overall. Claude Verret of Trois-Rivières led the league in scoring with 162 points in the 1981–82 season.

situations, but this maneuver would only have been perfect if a third-liner had made it, or if it was pulled during the seventh game of a championship series. His will to compete—that desperation to play just one more time, to continually raise the stakes even when on the losing end—I thought that all this had overtaken him. Unable to put his mark on the game one way, he would do it another way using anything but judgment and caution.

The puck caught flush on Crosby's shinpad. It hit in a good spot. A couple of inches one way or another and it might have shattered an ankle or broken bones in his foot. If it had caught him differently maybe his knee would have taken the force of Desilets' blast. But everyone saw the franchise, the game's future, flash in front of his eyes. Then, suddenly, play in real time started again: Crosby, not missing a beat, skated toward the loose puck, beating Desilets to it. Crosby then coolly fired it the length of the ice and into the undefended net for the clinching goal.

He threw up his arms, seeming more relieved than overjoyed. He had not won the game with spectacular skill. He had merely clinched it with a gutsy defensive play, something that showed just how rounded a player he had already become.

But Sidney Crosby wasn't just looking ahead at a few more playoff games of tight checking by the likes of Desilets. He was facing the playoffs *and* another whole season in the Q, another long winter of checkers being on him like the crest on his sweater. And some reasonable onlookers might have guessed that this somewhat unremarkable game showed that Crosby still had lessons to learn.

Rimouski
April 3, 2004

I had arranged to meet with Crosby after a midday practice. It was a school day but there were no conflicts for Crosby or the other anglophone players. Their session with their tutor was scheduled around practice.

NHL practices are closed to the public. So too are many, if not most, junior practices. In Rimouski, the Colisée is public property and l'Océanic don't bother to secure the doors or head off any rubberneckers. On an average day a couple of dozen spectators sit in the stands, like they did when Vincent Lecavalier and Brad Richards were with the team, like they did the season before when the club won only 11 games. Playoff fever, however, created a spike in attendance this day. I counted 50 citizens of Rimouski watching practice and you could tell that their eyes were following Crosby around the ice, watching the kid who was winning trophies and making Rimouski a destination for NHL scouts.

I spoke to one fellow, Pierre Blier, who made attendance at practice his daily routine. When time for his first coffee break rolled around, Blier drove down from work to the local Tim Hortons and then met up with the regular attendees in the stands. "For us, the Oceanic is more than just games on a Friday and Saturday night," Blier said. "It's an everyday thing. Part of our community." One of the onlookers told me his son was playing at a neighbourhood outdoor rink one day earlier that winter and, sure enough, out skated Sidney Crosby, and a couple of his teammates, for a game of shinny with the school kids. Not a public-relations event staged by the club, just an impromptu skate. Others in his cluster of regulars nodded in agreement. It had the ring of truth. Assistant coach Guy Boucher told me the team had on one occasion ordered Sidney to take a day off from practising, effectively locking away his skates. He responded by calling home and asking his parents to send out a second pair so he could get to a neighbourhood rink to work out on his own and play shinny.

It wasn't just that Crosby and his teammates were wrapped up in the game. No, at another level they were engaged to the community. "Everybody has a story about Sidney and the team," Blier began. "Everybody sees the players out in the town. Just think about it—it's not an autograph. It's something more—Sidney and these players out playing (shinny) on the little outdoor rinks with little kids and their fathers— things that these kids will be able to tell their children about one day. The one funny story I have was Sidney coming into the Tim Hortons doughnut shop and there were a bunch of kids, little kids, sitting at a table. So Sidney bought a box of doughnuts and gave it to them. After he left they were trying to figure out whether they should eat them or keep them as souvenirs.

"It was very big for us here when Vincent Lecavalier came because it was the first time that it gave us a chance to win. When Brad Richards came, we had a team that could win a national championship. But now we know what it's like to have a winning team. Now we have a program, a winning program. A tradition. Sidney Crosby was something different. The community (embraced) Vincent and Brad as players very quickly, but people like Sidney in a different way. I don't know if it's because he's a different player."

Crosby was good to his reputation and good to the cliché, first one on the ice for practice. There were no cheers from the spectators in le Colisée, half of whom were sitting in seats, half standing beside the goal judge's perch at the north end of the arena. They all watched him, fixed on him, but kept up their conversations. I eavesdropped as best I could and when in doubt I asked for help with translation. They talked about last night's game, about Crosby's frustrating night, about the prospects of l'Océanic advancing beyond Shawinigan and going deep in the playoffs. They dwelt on the micro-Sidney, not on the macro-Crosby. They didn't seem at all concerned about what Crosby might mean to the NHL some day, which corporate outfits might chase him down to hawk their wares, where he might fit in the sport's pantheon. To them he was not yet a brand. He was still a 16-year-old hockey player. This was the stuff that made Wayne Gretzky as happy in the Soo as he ever was as a millionaire hockey icon.

Fans don't generally get to see the biggest names in hockey practice, to see them fool around with a puck in a spare few minutes before a skate begins. Suffice it to say, some players can do everything but make the puck talk. What yo-yo champions can do with string and disk, the best players can do with puck and stick. Crosby is one of those players. Skating at medium speed he stickhandled like Curly Neal dribbled a basketball. That infamous lacrosse wrap-around shot was nothing in this show of skills. But those in the arena were hockey fans, many of them coaches of other teams or parents of players in youth leagues—that is, they appreciated talent. And even though this pre-practice warm-up was akin to LeBron James showing up in someone's driveway to try out some new elements for a dunk contest, the onlookers didn't express any particular surprise nor do anything so gauche as applaud. They had seen it all before. Most recently, yesterday and the day before yesterday.

A few minutes later, Rimouski coach Donald Dufresne took the ice and so did Crosby's teammates. And then practice looked much like it did at any other junior rink with any other junior team. Yes, Crosby stood out in the same way he did in a game: the deft touches; the ability to adjust stride and speed in a fraction of a second to take a pass; and the clinical finish on scoring chances. If there was one thing you didn't see in a game situation but saw in practice, it was a little extra flourish on dekes. And Crosby again was the first one to hustle to centre ice when Dufresne called the players. Again he was there in front of the erasable board, staring at the X's and O's for the next drill or play. It certainly hadn't been a show Crosby put on for the Canadian coaches at the under-18s practice. That was just how he went about business.

When practice ended, the people in the arena filtered out, back to their homes or back to work. I met Crosby in the players' lounge, a room that featured wall-sized photo enlargements from the turn of the 20th century, portraits of bygone Rimouski teams dating back to a time not long ago when businesses backed teams. During games, the lounge was a makeshift tavern. There were no kegs for the players in the early afternoon, just a ping-pong table that was wheeled out for post-practice tournaments. And so, with heavy metal the soundtrack and with the sound of a ping-pong ball bouncing back and forth, I caught up with Crosby. When I asked him about the game the night before, he smiled and shrugged. "It was just nice to get a win and to get the rust off," he said. (Rimouski had a bye into the second round of the playoffs because they won their conference during the regular season.) "I was pretty excited— I don't know if I'd say anxious about it. And (defenceman) Desilets is a tough guy to be out there against every shift."

Then I asked about Rimouski. Like he was lifting his material from Daniel Doré's scouting reports, Crosby described his situation on the south shore of the St. Lawrence as "perfect." He said that playing in

Halifax, Quebec City or any of the larger stops in the Q couldn't improve on what Rimouski was offering. He admitted that sometimes he felt "stuck in his house," that "house" being a basement apartment he shared with team tough guy Eric Neilson. And he said that most nights at home, after covering his homework for the team tutor, he and Neilson watched DVDs—and there weren't too many action films he hadn't seen at least once. It sounded bleak, but Crosby said he had no problems with the quality of life: "The focus here is the team. This team has had a lot of good players come through ... and has done well developing them."

In precocious, league-defining talent, Crosby was right up there with LeBron James who had been selected first overall by the Cleveland Cavaliers the previous spring. Their lifestyles, however, were starkly different. You could make a case that basketball prepares its future stars for greatness by giving them an early taste of the perks to come, while hockey seems to go out of its way to keep its best humble. LeBron took ownership of his Hummer as a high-school phenom; Crosby depended on Neilson's one-wheel-in-the-scrapyard Mazda of uncertain vintage for rides around town. LeBron starred in nationally televised high school games; Crosby's home games were shown on a community television station. LeBron played across the U.S. in major arenas; Crosby played in the Quebec major junior league, a.k.a. the Q, which features a team in the remote mining region of Val d'Or, but not one in Montreal.

In making the best of his stay in Rimouski, Crosby became an anglophone hero in a town as French as pea soup, as Québécois as poutine. Parents who voted for Quebec's separation from Canada bought their sons and daughters Rimouski sweaters with CROSBY printed boldly on the back; and they scrambled to get his autograph. It turned Roch Carrier's children's story, *The Hockey Sweater*, inside out. In Carrier's story a Québécois boy is horrified when he orders a Rocket Richard Montreal Canadiens sweater from an Eaton's catalogue and receives instead a Toronto Maple Leafs sweater, the very symbol of the *maudit anglais*. But now it was not the sweater of Quebec's own cultural icon that was the object of desire, but one with the name of an anglo on the back. If hard feelings lingered over Eric Lindros snubbing the Quebec

GARE JOYCE

128

Nordiques years back, Crosby put them to rest with modest attempts to say *bonjour* and *merci*.

"English-speaking guys have excelled in the league," Crosby told me. "Pat LaFontaine is one. My dad played against him. He said (the American-born) LaFontaine was really liked. My father told me, it doesn't matter what language you speak. The way you handle yourself and the way you play is the way you get respect. I want to learn more French. I'd like to get to where I can do interviews next season. I feel like I understand a lot already. It's going to be a matter of time."

With the heavy metal still pounding, I hit him with Q's and he responded with A's. Some of Crosby's observations were predictable. Like all other players jumping from midget ranks or prep school to major junior, the speed of play and the size of the players forced him "to make quicker decisions" on the ice. Clearly, given his regular-season numbers and given that he was going to become the first 16-year-old ever named Canadian Hockey League player of the year, he made the adjustments quickly, and everyone else was left struggling to adjust to him.

I had to broach one subject that made Crosby uncomfortable, but he already had enough media savvy to see it coming. Before the playoffs started, Crosby was embroiled in a controversy not quite on the scale to match the Cherry imbroglio, but enough to be a blow to his growing reputation. In March of his first junior season, the story out of Rimouski was that Crosby might not dress for already sold-out games in Quebec and Lewiston, Maine. As the story had it, Oceanic management was fed up with referees putting away their whistles while the boy wonder was mugged and roughed up. The rumour was a public-relations disaster.

"It's a laugh that Rimouski would accuse anyone of gooning players," one junior coach complained. "They've got a big team with more slugs than almost anybody in junior hockey."

Sidney said he had nothing to do with any planned protest. He acknowledged that some in hockey circles and the media presumed his father had pushed for it. But he said that just wasn't the case. "It was like the *Hockey Night in Canada* thing," Sidney recalled. "I didn't see it coming. I just don't want anything special from anybody. I don't want special treatment one way or the other."

(When I asked Troy Crosby later about it, he was even more emphatic. "It didn't come from Sidney or me," the father said. "Sidney can handle himself. That's the way it's always been.")

Crosby, however, admitted there was something to the idea that teams had made him a target of gooning. His reputation had preceded him. "The pre-season was the worst," the young phenom said. "Being a rookie, teams wanted to intimidate me. I wasn't going to let it happen and my teammates were standing up for me. And after the world juniors it was pretty bad too—a lot more stuff going on, 5 or 10 fights sometimes. One game had five fights in the first 15 seconds."

It seemed, however, that the fights and the finished checks didn't bother him so much as the hooks, holds and interference that bogged the game down. It was an issue that caused Mario Lemieux to retire from the game back in 1997. It was the stuff that allowed the ordinary to compete on equal terms with genius, that allowed house painters to compete with artists. "Watching classic games (from the '70s and the '80s), it's unbelievable how much fun was in the game," he said, his eyes lighting up. "It's down and back, end to end. Basically, they were letting players play. There weren't a lot of systems. The odd team might trap but the only reason a team did that was (because) it was less skilled. Now Detroit with so much talent plays the trap. You wonder what would happen if one team stepped up and said 'Let's play hockey.' But you'd really need 20 teams to do it."

While Crosby dutifully answered questions about the season's rough spots, just talking about this ideal game of hockey—the possibilities for improvements—seemed to lift him. I threw a little cold water on him at that point, countering that even convincing 20 NHL teams to abandon the trap wouldn't do it—if one other NHL squad were succeeding with it, others would follow. "I think there are some things they can do to open the game up," he said. "I hope they try."

As we spoke, hockey's rumour mill was floating speculation about Crosby passing up the next season in Rimouski to play in Europe. As it went, part of the motivation stemmed from fears that a thug in the Q might try to get his 15 minutes of infamy by putting Crosby on ice. And supposedly, part of the motivation was based on money—there'd simply be more of it in the European pro leagues. Perhaps one day another phenom will challenge the NHL's draft rules in court and seek draft eligibility at age 17. But for Crosby, it all would have been an exercise in futility—fighting for the right to play in a league that looked ready to be shut down by a lockout. There wasn't going to be a challenge from Crosby, no seeking of a new set of rules just for him. "There's still a lot for Sidney to learn in junior. And it's still the best place for him to develop," Troy told me.

The Crosbys and Sidney's brain trust were well aware of the hostility that was directed toward the Lindros family—when Eric balked at playing in the Soo as a junior, though the Soo was good enough for Wayne Gretzky; or when Eric snubbed Quebec City after the Nordiques selected him first overall. Still, the rumours about Sidney jumping to a European pro league lingered. And the Crosbys endured.

"We have a good team this year," Sidney said. "We get almost everybody back next year. It would be great to make a run at a league title and the Memorial Cup (the Canadian national junior championship)."

At that point Neilson, Crosby's ride, arrived in the lounge. Neilson looked like your standard-issue Canadian junior third-line tough guy, a 19-year-old who forgot to shave this week, last week, and the week before, who walked around with perpetual bedhead and whose wardrobe featured a fine selection of black t-shirts with metal-band logos. His job on the ice, protector of Crosby's interests, was pretty much his responsibility as roommate. I asked him if it was difficult for Crosby to adjust to Rimouski. Neilson wasn't about to embarrass his roommate, the franchise that was placed in his trust. "All first-year players are probably a little homesick sometimes but he already spent a year away from home," Neilson said. "He calls home every night and his father makes it out to a lot of our games. We're always doing something. He's an average guy."

Neilson and Crosby then disappeared. And a couple of minutes later, the music in the lounge was drowned out—the sound of Neilson's car starting.

I met up with the coach, Donald Dufresne, in his office after talking to Crosby. Dufresne, a hometown boy, a thick-set, amiable Rimouskois, had a healthy stretch on NHL bluelines in Montreal and Edmonton, among others, and scoffed at the idea that any special responsibility went with coaching a prospect of Crosby's calibre. "I don't think that anybody talks much about who coached Bobby Orr or Gretzky or Mario," he pointed out.*

I then asked Dufresne about the story of the planned but aborted sit-out. He didn't deny that the team considered it, but he claimed it was a misunderstanding. "We worried about Sidney running out of gas," the coach stated. "He had been playing since August. He had travelled a lot. We ask him to play a lot. It would be tough on any player but especially a 16-year-old who hasn't played at this level before or played as much. We were already in the playoffs. Really, it was for his own protection. We were just worried about him getting injured—not getting gooned. Nothing that came from Sidney. Nothing that came from anyone else (his father and his agent)."

Everyone in the junior ranks and the hockey media regarded Dufresne as a good coach and a good guy. Crosby hadn't landed in an unstable situation like Gretzky had, and he certainly hadn't locked horns with Dufresne. It wasn't Dufresne who had coached l'Océanic to their Memorial Cup championship with Brad Richards—no, in 2000, general manager Doris Labonté was behind the bench. Nonetheless, Dufresne had Crosby's confidence and seemingly, that of Labonté and ownership.

"Sidney has been a pleasure to coach and what he's helped us do here—to go from the bottom of the league to the playoffs in a season— has been great for the franchise," Dufresne remarked. "And our main guys should all have a year or two (of junior eligibility) left. We get practically everybody back next year."

According to NHL scouts working the Q, Rimouski under Dufresne's

---

* Wren Blair coached Orr at Oshawa; Gretzky was coached by Muzz McPherson and Paul Theriault at the Soo; and Lemieux was coached by Jean Bégin at Laval.

stewardship had become a decent team—but not a true championship contender. That was going to take time, Crosby's continued emergence, and a goaltender. The team's goalie in the 2004 playoffs, Cédrick Desjardins, didn't inspire a lot of confidence and l'Océanic was in deep negotiations with Cory Schneider, the American goaltender who had stoned Crosby at the under-18s in Piestany the year before. Rimouski had drafted Schneider in the 10th round in 2003. If it had been a challenge to convince other anglophone kids to come to Rimouski, it would be doubly tough to recruit a kid from a place where college hockey rules, where the Beanpot and not the Memorial Cup, is the ultimate prize.*

Dufresne wanted to make sure he wasn't portrayed as a coach looking past the playoffs that were just now under way. "I think we can win next year, but the reason is, I think we can win this year," Dufresne said. "I don't want our players looking at this like it's a two-year program … like we should peak next year. I want them to play like there's no tomorrow. That's my job."

◉

Eric Neilson kept a watch over Crosby. Donald Dufresne wrote Crosby's name into the line-up and sent him over the boards. And Christian Bouchard was responsible for the care and feeding of hockey's boy wonder.

Bouchard, 29, and his partner, Christine St. Onge, both Rimouski grade-school teachers, were Crosby's and Neilson's billets. The players lived downstairs from the couple and Bouchard did most of the cooking and almost all of the translating for the household. Bouchard described Crosby as "a careful young man … serious about his hockey, his diet and his schoolwork (but) fun to be around."

Bouchard met Crosby back when l'Océanic selected him in the Q's 2003 draft. The Crosbys were testing the waters, seeing what life would be like for Sidney if he played in Rimouski. And seeing where he'd be

---

* The Beanpot is an annual Boston-based battle royal, a half-century-old hockey tournament bringing together teams from Boston College, Boston University, Harvard and Northeastern.

living during the season was a crucial factor in the decision to commit to the franchise.

The role of billets in junior hockey is an uncelebrated one. If left to his own devices, the average teenager's diet, health and welfare would go all to hell in a hurry. It's true of most teens and players alike. Some 20-year-old players are allowed to live on their own. But for the younger players, billets give their lives structure. Billets balance between being landlords and surrogate parents. And Bouchard made it sound like performing this balancing act with Crosby was easy.

"I'd say he's like the average teenager in a lot of ways," Bouchard said. "He likes to have fun, to watch hockey and movies on television, to go on the computer and the internet. He likes to joke around with Eric or Christine—she doesn't speak English and he's just learning French. Those are the average things. But he's not like an average teenager when it comes to food. On every box, he's checking the ingredients, the calories, fat. Sixteen-year-olds don't do that, but Sidney does."

Bouchard said Crosby and Neilson were "no trouble" and he and his partner were enjoying their first year serving as billets for l'Océanic. "We would do it again, whether it's Sidney and Eric that we get back or someone else," Bouchard concluded.

Before Game 2 against Shawinigan, I went to dinner with IMG's Pat Brisson, who went to lengths to point out that he was "an advisor," not an agent. Perhaps his relationship with Crosby was at that time understood, and would be formalized at some later point. Clearly, with Crosby attending IMG's summer camps, with the agency "advising" on arrangements at both Shattuck-St. Mary's and Rimouski, and with Brisson making several trips from his home base in Los Angeles to Rimouski, a lot would have been riding on only an understanding and a handshake. He was in fact working as Crosby's representative and, truth be told, IMG had a lot to offer Crosby—it was hard to imagine that another agent could ride in and squeeze out Brisson and J.P. Barry. IMG's most famous hockey client had been Gretzky, but over the years the agency had built up a star-studded list that featured, among others, Mats Sundin, Daniel Alfredsson, Sergei Fedorov, Alexander Mogilny, and Jaromir Jagr. IMG's hockey division thought internationally and acted internationally. As one of their agents in the field explained it to me, IMG wanted to have the biggest name or two in each of the major hockey-playing nations. IMG also wanted names who could cross over—who could be marketed without regard to borders and beyond hockey's niche. Gretzky had been the face of hockey to those with only a peripheral interest in the game, and Brisson believed there was good reason to think that Crosby could fill that same role.

"He's an incredibly well-grounded young man," Brisson said over a bowl of mussels and frites at a restaurant overlooking the thawing St. Lawrence. "The way he's managed to keep his composure in the face of all the attention that he's generated and all that he has to go through on the ice, it amazes me. And people just like him. You come away from meeting him knowing that he's something special."

It might have seemed premature. After all, the night before, Crosby had been shut down but for the empty-net goal. And maybe some could have accused Brisson of seeing what he wanted to see, letting the fact that Crosby was his client influence him.

But Brisson had learned about the Q from the inside. He played four seasons in the league starting out with Verdun and then moving on to Drummondville and Hull. Along the way he befriended Mario Lemieux. Brisson maintained that Crosby faced far tougher challenges than Lemieux or Gretzky. "When we played in the Q it was a lot more wide open than it is these days—a lot more fun to watch and a lot more fun to play in," Brisson told me. "Now there's so much holding and interference. It just makes what Sidney is able to do that much more incredible."

☾

NHL Central Scouting's Christian Bordeleau talked about Crosby taking 40 minutes to figure out the Q in his first regular-season game. It took him just a little longer to figure out the post-season brand of the game—a full 60 minutes. A few minutes into the second period of Game 2 against Shawinigan,

Rimouski led 4–0. Crosby scored twice, one at even strength and the other on a power play. He also created chances for teammates on every shift.

But then Rimouski took two minor penalties just seconds apart. A long five-on-three power play gave Shawinigan a little hope. Coach Dufresne sent Crosby out to take the draw in the Rimouski end. "A 16-year-old shouldn't even be on the ice in that situation," Dufresne said later. "But Sidney was on a roll—he thrives on more ice time when he has momentum going for him. And Sidney brings skills and speed that I've never seen in a 16-year-old."

Les Cataractes had never seen anything like it either. Crosby played the passing lanes and stayed a stick's length or two off the puck, just as you'd expect a player would in a five-on-three situation. But when Nicolas Desilets got too cute with a cross-ice pass, Crosby pounced on the puck and left all pursuers behind with an explosive burst, just a few strides. You could hear the ice chips fly just before the crowd started to roar. Crosby was half the length of the ice in a flash and bore down on the Shawinigan goal. Julien Ellis-Plante might have been able to answer the brainteasers, but he had no solution for Crosby's mesmerizing deke to the backhand side. It was just about the most spectacular way to close out a hat trick.

Crosby raised his stick, looking triumphant but a little stunned. "I never had scored three-on-five before," Crosby said later. "Once, in peewee or something, I think I scored just as the first penalty had ended. Strangest thing is, after this goal, I threw up my arms and stood behind the (Shawinigan) net. I was looking for a teammate to celebrate with. The nearest one was at the other end of the ice. A hundred feet away. I had to skate all the way back to the bench alone."

Troy Crosby looked on from his seat at centre ice. He didn't clap or smile. He wore the look of someone who had seen it all before and fully expected to see it again. Not so the other 5,000 in the arena. They had watched Lecavalier and Richards but never witnessed anything like this. There was a sense, a collective sense, that even with the thinnest ray of daylight, Crosby was going to shine, he was going to make something happen. And the people of Rimouski would bask in the glow for as long as it shone on the northern St. Lawrence.

L'Océanic went on to sweep les Cataractes. Each game was a little easier than the previous one. Crosby led all scorers with six goals and six assists. In the next round, however, Rimouski ran into a stone wall in Moncton goaltender Corey Crawford. In five games, Crosby managed only a goal and three assists. Crawford gave up just six goals in a five-game series, all the more remarkable considering that l'Océanic averaged more than 40 shots a game. Though Rimouski went into the playoffs seeded ahead of Moncton, most hockey scouts had favoured the New Brunswick team.

When it all shook down, Moncton lost to Gatineau in the Q final. Gatineau made the Memorial Cup but Crosby was given only a ticket to the championships. At the CHL's award show at the Cup, Crosby was given awards as Canadian major junior top rookie and its player of the year, the first 16-year-old ever to come away with the latter prize. Crosby's numbers—59 games, 54 goals, 81 assists—were irrefutable proof that he was a deserving winner. Yet numbers didn't quite capture his game. Moments like that goal playing two men short against Shawinigan defied numbers and words.

ELEVEN

"Having it too easy takes away some of the motivation to strive."

Sidney Crosby went into his second season with l'Océanic on the wrong end of umpteen slashes, cross-checks and miscellaneous assaults in the Quebec league. In other words, he was halfway through the basic apprenticeship for a Canadian-born hockey star. Few elite Canadian kids had gone the U.S. college route: Ken Dryden had gone to Cornell and Paul Kariya to Maine and assorted others to the various U.S. colleges offering decent hockey programs (NCAA Division I hockey, for instance, includes 58 teams). The truly great, however, had come up through Canadian junior hockey. Just look at the first class of hockey stars going back to the days of yore. Maurice Richard (Verdun). Jean Béliveau (Quebec). Bobby Hull (St. Catharines). Bobby Orr (Oshawa). Wayne Gretzky (Sault Ste. Marie). Mario Lemieux (Laval). All had come up through junior hockey. And now Sidney Crosby. But did junior hockey make them? Or did they simply pay their dues and become great on their own?

It's no more conclusively answered than the chicken-and-the egg conundrum. Still, it was not altogether clear whether junior hockey had been as good for Sidney Crosby as Sidney Crosby had been for junior hockey.

Going into his second season with Rimouski, Crosby had already been profiled in the pages of *Sports Illustrated* and *ESPN The Magazine*. When his name came up in discussion on sports-talk radio or nightly TV sportscasts in Canada, there was no need to give the background—if you had even a casual interest in the game, you knew Sidney Crosby and were up to speed on his story. You could have argued that Gretzky or Lemieux or Orr had been better junior players. You might have even been able to argue that Gilbert Perreault or Guy Lafleur deserved a place in the junior pantheon no less prominent than Crosby's.* But there was no arguing against the fact that Sidney Crosby was by age 17 the most famous junior hockey player in the history of the game.

It had a lot to do with his game, of course, but even more with the proliferation of media. Crosby came of age as a player at a time when three Canadian specialty-sports television networks served the market. In Orr's and Perreault's and Lafleur's time, there were only a couple of TV networks of any sort in Canada. Orr and Gretzky were barely out of their teens when, as young NHLers, they had each been named *Sports Illustrated*'s Sportsman of the Year. And yet there's no argument that, even leading up to Orr's and Gretzky's appearances on the cover of *Sports Illustrated*, all the words dedicated to their exploits in all the media only matched the number devoted to 17-year-old Sidney Crosby—a kid just beginning his second year in junior. Even as young NHL all-stars, Orr and Gretzky remained *hockey players*; as a junior, Crosby had been fast-tracked toward something else entirely. He was a phenomenon, a commodity, a brand.

Other junior players must prove they belong in the CHL. Crosby, on the other hand, was so far beyond this that he was being sought out to legitimize an altogether different—albeit quixotic—league. Near the end of the summer of 2004, with the hockey world bracing for the NHL's imminent lockout of its players, two heretofore obscure businessmen, Allan Howell and Nick Vaccaro, announced—with straight faces, power-point demonstrations, but not much else going for them—plans to launch

---

* In his season with the Soo Greyhounds, Gretzky played 64 games totalling 70 goals and 112 assists. Other debut seasons: Lemieux with Laval Voisins: 64 games, 30 goals, 66 assists; Gilbert Perreault with the Montreal Junior Canadiens: 47 games, 15 goals, 34 assists; Guy Lafleur with the Quebec Junior Aces: 43 games, 30 goals, 19 assists. For the 2003–04 Season with Rimouski, Crosby played 59 games and accumulated 54 goals and 81 assists.

an alternative professional hockey league. Presuming that lightning might strike a name twice but bankruptcy only once, these enterprising gentlemen even labelled their league the World Hockey Association (WHA), after the maverick sideshow from the go-go '70s. The old WHA gave the game a few sublime moments (the comeback of Gordie Howe alongside his sons Mark and Marty with the Houston Aeros; and Bobby Hull working magic with his Winnipeg Jets' linemates, Swedish stars Anders Hedberg and Ulf Nilsson). It also offered many ridiculous ones (including teams such as the Miami Screaming Eagles that existed not on the league's trademark white skates, just on paper). The fledgling WHA of 2004, however, did not hold out this kind of promise for either excellence or amusement. Though Toronto goaltender Ed Belfour signed on to be a part owner of a Dallas franchise, the WHA of 2004 was not a league so much as a theory. Nonetheless, one of its first moves was to tender Sidney Crosby an offer of $7.5 million for a three-year commitment, with $2 million to be paid up front. The balance, the organizers promised, would be paid even if the WHA never got off the ground. He was effectively invited to clean out the till and show up for work only if needed.

Crosby did not sign up with the WHA so the organizers' promise was not put to the test. The WHA didn't launch in the fall, nor did it open for business in midwinter as was later promised. It turned out the organizers couldn't come up with a quorum of would-be owners willing to dish out $50,000 for a franchise fee.

Crosby likely didn't miss out on the $7.5 million—or even bus fare— by declining to sign up with the WHA. He also didn't lose his good name because he couldn't have been accused of being out to get as much as he could as quickly as he could. "He has made up his mind right now about where he wants to play," his father Troy said. "He wants to stick by his plan to play another year in Rimouski. He's 17 and he is not playing for the money right now. He feels playing junior is the best way to continue to develop."

Such altruism notwithstanding, by the fall of 2004 it was clear that, whenever the NHL took the padlocks off the arena doors and resumed league play, Crosby's financial prospects were going to pale next to other young stars who had signed with teams before the lockout. In the media coverage of lockout issues, Crosby was already cited as the individual who likely stood to be hurt more than any other by the coming collective agreement.

The National Hockey League was prepared to play hardball with the NHL Players' Association and was targeting rookie contracts as a key place to scale back. The NHL governors thought they had done just that coming out of the 1994 lockout, but a few sharp agents found gaping loopholes in that collective agreement—an entry-level player's salary was capped, but not his bonus money. Thus writing in easy-to-attain performance bonuses basically nullified the rookie salary cap. Joe Thornton had seen $3 million just for dressing as a rookie, and Ilya Kovalchuk had earned in the neighbourhood of $4 million as an 18-year-old in Atlanta. Pundits in the media estimated that Crosby's first contract stood to yield $7 million to $10 million less across its term than if he had come along even a couple of years earlier.

Whatever the case, it was not altogether clear whether the celebrity treatment and the talk about the millions of dollars awaiting him were good things—for Sidney Crosby and for the game.

At this point in his career, you could have made a case that fame was a greater threat to his genius than any opponent on the ice. You could have made the case that the business end of hockey might intrude on his game, might take the joy out of it. And you could have made a case on a related point, that Crosby's celebrity and genius obscured the flaws in the major junior game.

Back at the end of 2001 I received an e-mail from a European hockey journalist. He had received a translation of a story that had appeared in a Finnish sports newspaper, *Veikkaaja*. The author of the article, a reporter named Petteri Linnavalli, was not ambiguous about his opinion of Canadian hockey. He considered the European models for player development far superior to those in place in Canada. In fact, he suggested that Canadian major junior hockey was cruel and inhumane, that it was the closest thing to human-rights violations as you'd find in sport. He claimed that major junior hockey practises "exploitation of child labour." He described Canadian hockey fans as "bloodthirsty." And he criticized the leagues and franchise owners for putting profits ahead of skills development and players' well-being.

The story would have been a passing amusement but for the fact that Linnavalli had quoted an NHL executive. That executive was Linnavalli's Finnish countryman, Jarmo Kekalainen. At the time Kekalainen was the Ottawa Senators' player personnel director and also, somewhat curiously, the only NHL executive of his rank who resided in Europe.

Several of the quotes attributed to Kekalainen in the piece seemed to endorse Linnavalli's criticisms. "I would not put my own son in that league (Western Hockey League) unless I knew that he was so tough that he could handle a few beatings," Kekalainen stated in the translation I received. "The Western Hockey League is a rather barbaric school of life."

Kekalainen made the case that U.S. college hockey was a better system for developing talent. "The university players are at a total different level of conditioning—especially their legs and feet," he argued. "CHL players can skate a long time, but they lack in explosive power a lot."

And Kekalainen expressed concern about the celebrity aspect of junior hockey, the star system. "The player's future depends on how the player can handle his popularity, the media and the environment, and how he can channel it into his own development," he told Linnavalli.

The first thing I did after reading this e-mail was contact a Finnish friend who had worked in hockey circles for more than a decade. He told me he had read the original story and I asked him to check the translation I received. He confirmed that the translation was on the mark.

I then tracked down Kekalainen, who was on a scouting assignment in Switzerland. We had been acquaintances of three years up to that point and had talked regularly. When I mentioned the story to him, everything went frosty in an instant. Some of the more caustic criticisms in the piece reflected Linnavalli's opinions, not his, he said. He told me that he threw out the line about the WHL "with a smile on my face."

Kekalainen said Linnavalli went "overboard" but he also suggested that the CHL shouldn't be above criticism. "Clearly there is a chance for Canada to do a better job with its junior leagues and skill development," he told me. "The article says that the juniors play too many games in Canada, and I think that is true. If it were more of a sport and less of a business, it would be better for the players and the game, but that's not going to happen any time soon. Junior hockey isn't a cheap thing to run. Look, there are more teenage hockey players in Canada than there are teenagers in Sweden and Finland combined. Canada produces more players than any other nation, but it could produce far more players of higher quality than it does right now. I don't think that Canadian junior hockey is child exploitation or anything like that. I do agree with the article that Canadian junior hockey could be better. I say it should be."

The next day my story appeared in the papers and the Senators went into spin mode. In a statement released by the team, Kekalainen said: "I am very disappointed that these comments were wrongly attributed to me in the article by Mr. Linnavalli, even though they were not my words or thoughts on the state of Canadian junior hockey." It was a remarkable piece of backpeddling—you'd have to go to the Ice Capades to find somebody skating backward as fast and furiously as Kekalainen on the English-language publication of his views on the Canadian game. (It also represented a change of heart in less than 24 hours, because I had read each quote in question back to Kekalainen, word for word, and he vouched for them.) The Senators took a few swings at me and the translator, but no matter. The story was out there. An incensed John Davidson chatted it up on *Hockey Night in Canada* and junior hockey officials laid into Kekalainen.

Jarmo Kekalainen had been touted as a candidate for Ottawa's general manager's position that was to be vacated by Marshall Johnston in the spring of 2002. The idea of a European as an NHL GM might have seemed like a progressive move in some quarters, but there was no chance now that the Senators could install any hockey man of any nationality who had slammed grassroots hockey in Canada like Kekalainen had.

Just a few days later I was in a room full of NHL scouts at the 2002 world junior tournament in the Czech Republic. Most of the scouts—and, with the exception of the Senators' crew, the Canadians almost to a man—expressed no love for Kekalainen and congratulated me on the story. One scout, though, lit into me. This fellow, a Canadian who now works for an NHL team in the Sunbelt, had also been an assistant coach for a couple of teams. He loudly suggested that Kekalainen never said what I had put in my report—that my piece was strictly a work of fiction.

"Jarmo would never say those things," the scout said with unwavering confidence.

I tried to clarify the matter. (This came to the considerable amusement of an assembled bunch in the scouting ranks who were watching the incident unfold.) I asked the scout if he had in fact read my original story. He admitted he had not. I asked if he knew I had contacted Kekalainen and read back his quotes—and even had deleted statements he had denied making to Linnavalli. The scout admitted he wasn't aware of those salient details. And I asked the scout if he knew exactly what Kekalainen had said, namely that Canadian hockey could be improved, that it should be more of a game and less of a business. He admitted he had not.

Finally I asked him if he believed that these were opinions Kekalainen genuinely endorsed.

"Oh, we all believe those things," he said. "I just can't believe that he'd say them."

"Are you trying to make my case for me?" I said in utter exasperation.

However strained, the upshot of the argument was crystal clear: there are some things scouts understand to be true but also understand to be unspeakable. And maybe that's the reason Kekalainen's comments sparked such outrage—a case of truth-telling straight out of the emperor's new clothes. I won't sign on to everything Kekalainen claimed, but a couple of his statements I won't dispute. One, Canada has a chance to do a better job with its junior leagues and player development if hockey was treated more like a sport and less like a business. Two, the "star system" in Canadian junior hockey does nothing to advance player development and can be counter-productive in many instances.

As hard as it was for me to defend my story against Kekalainen's defenders, it must have been even harder for Kekalainen to fathom the fallout from his critique of the game. After all, what Kekalainen suggested wasn't so different from what Ken Dryden said of Canadian hockey in his classic tome, *The Game*. When Dryden lamented what he perceived to be the passing of skill development in Canada, he ended up with a bestseller; when Jarmo Kekalainen offered his opinions, he killed his chances of becoming general manager of the Ottawa Senators. You could suggest that one was a Hall of Famer and the other a journeyman with a short NHL career. But really, it boiled down to birthright. As a Canadian and a former Canadien, Dryden could speak his mind; as a foreign employee of a Canadian team, Kekalainen had to mind his manners—and didn't.*

Jarmo Kekalainen didn't know Tim Spidel, but Sidney Crosby's former teammate in Cole Harbour would endorse the scout's take on Canadian junior hockey. Spidel lived through it in his brief taste of major junior hockey, a tryout with his hometown Halifax Mooseheads that soured him on the game.

"When I went to the Mooseheads camp I felt really good about my chances," Spidel said. "I had spent the entire summer working out. I thought that I was ready as I could ever be."

Spidel was prepared to play but not prepared for the game the Mooseheads wanted to play. "I scored in the first couple of scrimmages," he noted. "I made one cut, but as things went on, the coaching staff was going with players that they had drafted and brought in. They had veteran skill guys on their first two lines that were coming back and I wasn't getting shifts with these guys (whom) they had already signed."

Spidel was competing for a third- or fourth-line role against bigger players, not skilled players but tough, physical forwards more likely to punch an opponent's lights out rather than turn on the goal judge's red light. The Mooseheads had a bunch of square holes and were only

* Kekalainen joined the St. Louis Blues as amateur scouting director in the summer of 2002.

looking for square pegs to fill them. That's not to say the Mooseheads were wholly to blame for this approach. If other teams go that route, woe is the team that doesn't. No, the Mooseheads were taking the conventional approach. And with a few square holes to fill, it was Tim Spidel's misfortune to be the round peg. He had something to offer. He had great speed, the explosive quick start and high gear that would place him in the top one percent of kids coming into junior. He had some skill. And though he didn't lack toughness, he lacked size; he didn't play an intimidator's game.

"It was funny," Spidel explained. "The coaches kept on giving me encouragement—telling me how well I was playing. But I knew that something was going on. I don't know if there was anything I could have done to make the team. It was a numbers game. They had commitments. There were deals with agents to bring some players in. I know enough about hockey and I've played with and against some great players, including Sidney."

Said his father, Ed Spidel: "Tim saw something happening in the last couple of years before he went to junior—that the game at higher levels was becoming less about skill and more about the physical stuff. And he realized that teams were going to keep a couple of big enforcers around—that you didn't fill your bench with skilled players who might develop into first- or second-line players."

When the Mooseheads cut Tim Spidel, his heart went out of the game. Moreover, he saw the game differently than before. "Sidney is Sidney, just an amazingly skilled player, and every team will have a place for really great talents," he said. "But major junior teams and coaches are looking for just one sort of player to fill out their rosters, big, physical guys—a lot of them aren't great skaters, a lot can't do much with the puck. So what's Sidney in against a lot of time in the Q? Guys who can't skate with him. Guys who can't go skill-to-skill with him. So they bang and hold and do whatever they can. It's not the way that it should be and I don't think that junior has to be that way. There are skilled players, guys who can skate and play the game, who get left behind."

These days, Tim Spidel doesn't put the blades on much. He enrolled in university and is a sprinter on his school's track team. I asked if he was surprised by what his old linemate had to put up with in the Q. "To tell you the truth, what these guys do is all that they can do against him."

☯

Tim Spidel knew enough about hockey and had seen junior hockey, briefly at least, from the inside out. Still, his was an accurate reading of Sidney Crosby's fix: the best players can't stop Sidney but would try to do it honourably; others would set honour aside and resort to the most brutal tactics, if necessary. Given Spidel's experiences, it was fitting that the worst moment of Crosby's junior career came against the Mooseheads. It was enough to send a chill not just through the Rimouski team and its management, but all through the hockey world. And it was enough to give credence to the criticisms of Jarmo Kekalainen and others who would reform the junior game.

Crosby was off to an amazing start to the 2004–05 season. He had racked up four goals and 18 assists in Rimouski's first seven games. During a game in Rimouski, Crosby was skating across the blueline without the puck when Mooseheads forward Fred Cabana delivered a knee-on-knee hit that left the phenom writhing on the ice. Even before he was helped off, Crosby was yelling at his one-time Canadian under-18s teammate.

"Cabana knew what he was doing," said one scout who works in the Q. "In that situation, given Crosby's role and Cabana's role, it's no accident."

Troy Crosby suggested no less, a tough position when the Halifax media was racing to Cabana's defence.

Cabana, a Philadelphia draft pick who didn't have a goal to that point in the season, was designated as Crosby's shadow for the game. Predictably, the hit provoked a blood-for-blood, eye-for-eye melee. L'Océanic didn't wait for the next game against the Mooseheads. Crosby's teammates didn't wait for the next period. They were, like one junior coach noted, not above goonery themselves.

Cabana was given a five-minute major and a game misconduct, but not before Rimouski defenceman Patrick Coulombe chased him down and drilled him. A couple of minutes later, with Crosby in the dressing room receiving medical attention, Oceanic enforcer Alexandre Vachon jumped Halifax's Czech import Petr Vrana, a non-fighter and the Mooseheads' best offensive threat. Vachon didn't even wait for the puck to drop to start pummelling Vrana. By the end of the first period, 187 minutes in penalties had been dished out. A lot of fair-minded individuals might have judged it, like Kekalainen had the Western Hockey League, "a rather barbaric school of life."*

Crosby came back later in the game—he had two points in Rimouski's 4–2 loss—but the condition of his left knee worsened over the next week, causing him to miss a few games. Crosby, Rimouski teammates and officials, and the rest of the hockey world heaved a sigh of relief when, after the swelling went down, an examination found no structural damage, just severe bruising. QMJHL executives reviewed the tape, interviewed Cabana and even had him submit a written statement about the incident. They made an emphatic statement with their decision: an eight-game suspension. They described Cabana's hit as "dangerous" and suggested that Crosby not having the puck evinced the Halifax forward's premeditation.

Mooseheads' general manager Marcel Patenaude complained bitterly about the suspension. "Did they try to give an example to the other players (with) Freddy Cabana?" Patenaude questioned. "I think it is fundamental in the league right now that we have to look at it to make sure that decisions or incidents are evaluated in a fair way."

Clearly, the league feared that other teams would follow Cabana's and Halifax's lead, with injuries to Crosby and attempts at payback the likely repercussions. There was a legitimate concern that the league, watched more than ever because of Crosby's presence, could be dragged into disrepute. Pascal Vincent said that he wouldn't goon Crosby. He was as good as his word—but that wasn't the real threat, anyway, punching his lights out. No, the greater threat was taking him out at the knees, low-bridging him. Or some escalating stick work that might go terribly wrong.

* In fairness to the Western Hockey League, one NHL scout claimed that Cabana's hit on Crosby was more likely to happen in the Q than out west. "In the Q, Crosby's teammates didn't like what Cabana did. But in the Dub Cabana's teammates wouldn't have liked it either. That's their code. They respect other players—on other teams and on their own teams—who stand up for themselves and who don't do anything that drags the game down or puts teammates at risk (for retribution)."

Was Crosby better for this particular junior hockey experience? It's hard to see how. Did he learn from it? It's easier to believe that he simply survived it. Knee-on-knee hits are not a staple of play in the NHL. Former veteran winger Rick Tocchet committed a spate of them a few years back, and they have been in the black bag of tricks of oft-suspended journeyman defenceman, Bryan Marchment. But at the next level, the NHL, it's just not considered professional.

One unlikely supporter of the "tough apprenticeship" approach to development was David Hemery. Hemery didn't know Sidney Crosby's story until it was outlined for him, so he certainly wasn't up to speed on the Cabana incident. But when I told Hemery what Crosby was up against and how he was targeted by Cabana or, say, the Swiss player at the under-18s, he suggested Crosby might in fact benefit from these tough situations—and others likely to come. Hemery said that a more protective, less daunting approach to player development might not prepare him so well as the existing, yet "flawed" major junior game with too many matches and too many knuckleheads.

"One personal feeling, rather than through research, is that for many, having it too easy takes away some of the motivation to strive," Hemery argued. "I had the option to (train) indoors in the winter at Harvard. I chose to train outside, running through the snow, because I believed that others might have taken the easy option and I wanted to have (a motivational) edge."

Perhaps the best reflection of Crosby's will and toughness was that, although he missed several games after the Halifax incident, he came out of the dressing room that night and finished the contest against the Mooseheads. Tougher stuff, Hemery would concede, than a run in the snow.

Kekalainen didn't mention Canadian Jason Spezza in the translated copy of the *Veikkaaja* story, and Spezza's name didn't come up when I asked the Senators' executive about his statements. But Kekalainen didn't have to. It was nothing to connect the dots between his reference to the star system in Canadian junior hockey and Spezza, Ottawa's first-round pick, second overall, in the 2001 draft.

Spezza had been in the media spotlight since age 14. He had played in the OHL All-Star game at age 15. Don Cherry pumped him up on "Coach's Corner" on *Hockey Night in Canada*. Playing in Brampton and Mississauga, on the outskirts of Toronto and within easy reach of the national media, he was at the time Canada's best known and most intensely covered major junior player. He had been tagged a star, the Next Big Thing—even though he hadn't played for a winning team in the OHL until he was traded to Windsor midway through his third season. The Senators had claimed Spezza with the draft selection that came over to the team along with towering defenceman Zdeno Chara and journeyman Bill Muckalt in the trade for Alexei Yashin.

The Senators brought Spezza to training camp in the fall of 2001 and dressed him for several exhibition games. One local hockey writer saw enough to tout him as the next pick for the Calder Trophy, ahead of Atlanta's gifted winger Ilya Kovalchuk. Ottawa's brass didn't like what they saw, however, and sent Spezza back down to Windsor in the Ontario league. If that wasn't tough enough for the 18-year-old to swallow, Senators' coach Jacques Martin piled on, dismissing Spezza as not even remotely ready for the big time, saying the NHL was "a men's league." Spezza's name was all over the media. He was under the spotlight. He struggled when he was sent back to junior. The rumour out of Windsor had been that his work habits weren't great. The rumour gained steam before the 2001 draft when he was nabbed for being underage in a Windsor casino. Good or bad, whatever he did fell under uncompromising scrutiny. What Kekalainen described as a star system was for Spezza and others a media fishbowl.

Kekalainen's Senators had suffered plenty because of the Canadian star system. In the franchise's early days, then general manager Randy Sexton had banked on Quebec league star Alexander Daigle as a future franchise player. That went terribly wrong—at times Daigle seemed barely interested in hockey, never mind making the sacrifices needed to win. But it was far more likely that Kekalainen had Spezza in mind when he made his case in the Finnish newspaper.

Spezza spent the 2001–02 season in the Ontario league.* The next year he divided time between Ottawa, where he received spot shifts or watched from the press box as a healthy scratch, and Binghamton, where he paid dues and the cost-conscious Senators could avoid paying his NHL salary. But in the 2003 NHL playoffs, Spezza gave hockey fans and the Senators' management a glimpse of the player he should become.

The Senators had opted not to dress Spezza for their opening series against the New York Islanders or for their second-round victory over Philadelphia. Instead the Senators filled out their roster by seniority— how else could you have explained playing journeyman Jody Hull or enforcer Chris Neil ahead of Spezza. Only when the Senators were facing elimination from the conference final against the New Jersey Devils did they put Spezza into the line-up. His play in Game 5 was a revelation. He scored a highlight-reel goal and was named first star in a dramatic win over the Devils. And on *Hockey Night in Canada* Don Cherry heralded the arrival of his former Mississauga IceDogs chattel.

It was all a little premature, though. Spezza spent most of the 2003–04 season with Ottawa but he took his place in line behind three veteran centres, Radek Bonk, Todd White and Bryan Smolinski. But by the fall of 2005, Spezza seemed finally ready to break out as a full-time NHL player. He had torn up the American Hockey League with Binghamton during the 2004–05 season. "A man among boys, completely dominant," one scout said of his performance in the NHL's lockout year, an unintended reworking of Jacques Martin's "men's league" knock. "The A was stronger that season than ever before, with all the young players who were available (because of the lockout). And he was clearly the best among a bunch of guys who will be all-stars or front-line NHLers for a generation."

Spezza's opinion about the star system in the Canadian junior game came with patient first-hand experience. "I never wished that I could be anyone else or just fade into the background," he said. "The attention really didn't bother me. My family kept me grounded, and we always

* The Windsor Spitfires traded Spezza to Belleville in midseason. His numbers for the season: 53 games, 42 goals, 63 assists for 105 points.

talked about things. The lesson I learned was to keep an even keel. I don't get too high in good times or too low when things aren't so good."

Spezza's father Rino was, like Troy Crosby, a goaltender as a young man. "What might have been toughest was reading in the newspapers that Jason wasn't working hard enough," Rino Spezza said. "That's hard not to take personally, especially when it's a teenager and when we knew it wasn't true. But really it was Jason who taught us a lesson on this one. He just said that sometimes they were going to write good things and sometimes it was going to be tougher. It's not always going to be easy."

These were the things that Jason Spezza passed on to Sidney Crosby at the world junior camp in Halifax, where the 14-year-old had worked as a stickboy to the junior stars. "I told Sid what it was like to be out there, with all the attention," Spezza said. "I told him that you have to look after your game and not let it get to you. Have fun, don't let the other stuff drag you down."

TWELVE

"I think he's a good player. But I don't play against Crosby."

Spezza's advice notwithstanding, the mounting pressures and constant media attention that Crosby faced would have tried a saint's patience. For a couple of years fans had heard about a looming lockout of NHL players. By the fall of 2004 their worst fears were coming to pass. Or, more precisely, impasse. Meetings between the league and the NHLPA were rare and unproductive. Increasingly, it looked like the NHL lockout was going to destroy the entire 2004–05 season. With no NHL, fans and sports media were starving for any hockey action they could get. And thus was Crosby the focus of more attention. The Crosby watch was a regular feature of nightly sportscasts. Nevertheless, Crosby was able to maintain his boyish charm, humility and composure—at least, that is, until his second trip to the world juniors.

Crosby had managed to get through the Cabana incident without permanent harm to either body or reputation. As the 2005 world junior camp drew near, Crosby was scoring at a three-point-a-game pace, better than his first season in Rimouski. The Oceanic occasionally struggled in the first three months of the 2004–05 season. And, what Donald Dufresne had said during the previous playoffs about playing like there was going to be a next season, well, this proved cruelly on point—he was demoted to assistant coach, and general manager Doris Labonté took charge on the Océanic bench. Yet no fingers were pointed at Crosby for the change. It wasn't a case of Crosby pushing for Dufresne's removal nor the coach failing to reach the star player. Labonté just believed that Dufresne, a nice guy, wasn't getting everything he could out of his players. There was history in play for the principals. The fiery Labonté had taken over bench duties when l'Océanic, with Brad Richards, won the Memorial Cup in 2000, so he had reason to believe his approach might work again. And for the people of Rimouski there was even more history in play; they remembered Dufresne as a happy-go-lucky kid in high school and Labonté as a driven young man who came back to Rimouski as a Phys. Ed. teacher, a pusher and shouter.

In fairness to Dufresne and l'Océanic, the Q had stuck them with a brutal early-season schedule. Rimouski was playing 11 games in 17 days in November because Crosby, the Q's best gate attraction, was going to be unavailable for a month starting in December and lasting to the conclusion of his stint at the world junior tournament. The league, in other words, drew up its schedule to sell the most tickets, even at the risk of skating its best player into the ice.

When the selection camp for the Canadian under-20 team opened, Crosby was the lead story. In every scrimmage and exhibition game, Crosby stepped up. And when the microphones were pointed in his direction and when the reporters gathered, it became a Canadian hockey love-in. The line-up featured 12 players back from the squad that had torn through the under-20 field the year before, only to lapse in the third period of the gold-medal game and gift a victory to the U.S. There was a sense that those covering the team wanted the best for the Canadian program, by this point without a world junior hockey gold since 1997. And they wanted the best for Crosby, who had been accommodating and accessible going back to his days as a tyke. By December of 2004, the Canadian hockey media had just about run out of ways to recast the impasse between the NHL and the Players' Association—they were covering a story that had no heroes, only villains. A story that featured no action to excite the masses, only myriad negotiating points that excited labour lawyers. By comparison *Waiting for Godot* was a thriller. The media and the fans hungered for a great game, a great player and good news. The Canadian juniors played a great game. Crosby was a great player, shoulder to shoulder with other great players. And there was good news, though that wasn't quite all the news.

Grand Forks, North Dakota
December 25, 2004

With the NHL in a deep labour freeze, it was fitting that the University of North Dakota was playing host to the 2005 world junior tournament. It wasn't just a frigid setting. It took the game well off the professional axis to a place where the love of the game could not be disputed. And the symbol of the local devotion to the game was the Ralph Engelstad Arena, a.k.a. the Ralph, home of the UND Fighting Sioux. The arena is named for the alumnus and former UND player who donated more than $100 million to the construction of what must be, with its 48 luxury boxes, 11,400 leather chairs and square miles of marble flooring, the plushest arena in the world. And, if you looked hard enough around the Ralph, you'd find not just team photos from several generations and portraits of stars from the old days right up to Zach Parise, you'd also find banners for every NHL team—in fact, you'd find banners for teams that have gone out of business: the Kansas City Scouts, the Winnipeg Jets, the Quebec Nordiques, the Colorado Rockies, the California Golden Seals and even the Cleveland Barons. Perhaps the intended message is that pro hockey is ephemeral, while the collegiate game, in North Dakota at least, will last as long as this arena stands. And it would seem the Ralph could survive everything short of an interplanetary collision with a comet.

If Sidney Crosby had opted to play U.S. college hockey instead of the Canadian junior game, he might well have landed at the Ralph. After all, Zach Parise had opted to Grand Forks and Jack Johnson was heading to UND as well. Maybe fans of the Fighting Sioux thought the tournament would in some way be a battle of merits between the respective systems—with the defending champion U.S. filling its roster with players who were going the collegiate route, taking on the best the Canadian juniors had to offer.

Unbeknownst to the North Dakota fans, however, was the fact that the Canadian juniors had more in common with the NHL teams whose banners were tucked away in the upper reaches of the arena. In lieu of the comet, nothing was likely to hit the Ralph with greater impact than Canada's complement of under-20 players for this 2005 world tournament.

The roll-out of Canadian fans, thousands of them driving 150 miles south from Winnipeg, were going to clog the border crossings for two hours every game day. The vast majority of fans in attendance at any game—not just Canadian contests but U.S. games as well—wore Team Canada sweaters or maybe the old Winnipeg Jets colours. The media contingent was not quite up there with what you'd expect for a Stanley Cup final, but it was close. Reporters from all the Canadian media outlets filled up press row. TSN—The Sports Network—had not just the usual camera positions for game coverage, but also a set for in-arena panel chat for pre- and post-game analysis. In other years, the world junior tournament was a niche attraction, a complement to NHL hockey. This year it was a substitute for the NHL, and the Canadian team passed for a reasonable facsimile of, say, the Detroit Red Wings.

Like a lot of great NHL teams, the Canadian juniors were only as good as they had to be as exemplified by their 7–3 victory over Slovakia in their opening game of the tournament. Crosby moved over to right wing so his tourney roommate, Patrice Bergeron, could play centre. Bergeron was the best example of the team's professionalism. As an 18-year-old second-round draft choice, a previously obscure junior out of the Quebec league, Bergeron had spent the entire 2003–04 season with the Boston Bruins, scoring 16 goals. He had also been the youngest member of the Canadian team that had won the men's world championship the previous spring. Corey Perry, a rangy winger who led the London Knights to the top of the Canadian junior rankings early in the season, filled out Canada's first line. With his two goals and his line's lordly control of the puck in this opening game, it was clear that Crosby was destined to play a much larger role than he had the year before.

"It's amazing to get a chance to play with Sidney," Bergeron said.

"He has such great vision. He sees things happening a second or two before they do—when he's crossing the blueline he has an idea of what's going to happen two passes ahead at the net."

Grand Forks, North Dakota
December 26, 2004

Crosby had a sense of what was going to happen on the ice, but didn't foresee trouble ahead with the media on Team Canada's off-day. That's how he ended up blind-sided. TSN on-air reporter Gino Reda asked Crosby if he would consider playing in the NHL the next fall if the league declared an impasse and opted to ice teams with replacement players. It wasn't a bait-and-switch, no ploy to get Crosby into a difficult position. After all, his agent Pat Brisson had been unambiguous about his player's position. He had told the *Ottawa Sun*: "There's no way he'll be a replacement player. That is not what Sidney is about. He's about playing with the best and that won't be the best."

But it wasn't a question that was put to other members of Team Canada, not even to Patrice Bergeron, who was in fact a member of the NHLPA, and as such, was apprised of the issues. No, it was a question that was put to the youngest and best-known player in the Team Canada line-up, the one who had yet to pass through the NHL draft. It was a question that was posed to Crosby because of his star status.

And, for once, Crosby stickhandled into trouble. "I haven't really given it a lot of thought but my dream is to play in the NHL," Crosby told Reda. "I think, if I do have an opportunity, I would probably go."

It was an "Oh Shit" moment on several fronts. Oh Shit, just the message we need out there, NHLPA executive director Bob Goodenow must have thought. Oh Shit, how are we going to put out this fire? Pat Brisson must have asked himself. Oh Shit, make room for this at the top of the sportscast, the producers at TSN told the crew in the truck.

Sidney Crosby had been dragged into a fight not of his own making. Or maybe he had fallen into it. He certainly had not jumped in. Ever careful to put team first, himself a distant second, he had suggested that his desire to play in the NHL was going to take priority over the interests of the biggest team of all, the players' collective.

In retrospect, it was unfair to expect a 17-year-old to have command of macro- or micro-economic issues—whether it was a cap on team payrolls or a revenue-sharing plan or variations on restructuring arbitration. And though he had lived a rich life with regard to the game of hockey, Crosby had no way of grasping the implications of scab labour. Nonetheless, some media outlets weighed in with accounts of major league ballplayers who served as replacement players back in 1995 and were forever shunned by teammates who had stayed out. This, their stories outlined, is what the future star of the game could expect when he crossed over as a replacement.

Grand Forks, North Dakota
December 27, 2004

Back on the ice, Canada thumped a weak Swedish team 8–1 with Crosby again scoring two goals. Again the game didn't get as many headlines as the musings of its star player. A visibly shaken Crosby asked TSN for the opportunity to explain it all away after the rout. He said that he thought Gino Reda was asking him "something about if NHL players came back."

"It was just a misunderstanding. I didn't understand the question. I responded by saying that I'd play and it was just a big mess-up. I'm kind of glad it's cleared up now. I wouldn't be there (as a replacement player). I want to play in the best league in the world and the NHL isn't the NHL if there aren't NHL players."

And then Crosby said something that, for all Jason Spezza's warnings, would give any fair-minded adult reason to wonder if there was something to Jarmo Kekalainen's criticisms of the star system. Crosby sounded very much like a young man equipped to play hockey, but not wholly prepared to handle a media onslaught that would leave Madonna trembling.

"It's a little confusing for someone growing up wanting to play in the NHL," he said, and then proceeded to demonstrate just how confusing it was to him. "I understand what's going on a little bit but not fully. I try to understand as much as I can. It is sometimes hard because you're growing up and want to be there, but at the same time, it's tough because you can't because of what's going on."

That hardly came off like a gifted young man who thought himself a privileged star. That sounded like a young man who had overheard but mostly tuned out people talking about the millions of dollars he'd make. That sounded like a young man who had heard the siren's call of the WHA and opted to stay another year in junior, learning his trade. And after his gaffe on TSN, he had stood up for the Players' Association, though he wasn't yet a member, though the NHLPA was negotiating much more enthusiastically for its veteran members than for the incoming class of players of which Crosby was the valedictorian. If you boiled down his statement about "what's going on" with regard to the NHL and the Players' Association, his message was simply: "What do I know? I'm just 17."

Grand Forks, North Dakota
January 2, 2005

Before the Canadians' semi-final game against the Czech Republic, Wayne Gretzky met with the press. He didn't attempt to qualify his endorsement of Crosby as the game's next star, but instead tried to explain it. "What separates the good players from an average player is what you do when you don't have the puck," Gretzky said. "Crosby seems to find openings and is in position to get in the play all the time."

But Gretzky made it sound like Crosby might not get to the NHL as soon as he hoped. He warned that the cancellation of the 2004–05 season—rumoured to be imminent—might set off a chain of events that would delay Crosby's NHL debut. "To wipe out and lose an entire season would definitely not be good for anyone," said Gretzky, the Phoenix Coyotes' managing partner and future coach. "I've said this since September, whether publicly I'm not sure, but privately to friends, that if the season does get cancelled we're looking at a year-and-a-half, maybe two years. That's what is even more alarming. The players don't get paid from April to October. So I can't see us coming to an agreement in August or September, and we're going to be back where we were."

Going into the world junior semi-final, a school of thought emerged whose adherents believed that an extended lockdown of the NHL might ultimately be in Crosby's best interests. Some even suggested that the heralded prospect was less ready for the NHL than originally presumed.

The media had billed the world junior tournament as Sidney Crosby's star vehicle, his personal showcase, his stage. But by the end of the semi-final, many were claiming that Crosby wasn't living up to the advance hype. Oh, Canada had been dominant. The Canadians had never trailed in a game. They hadn't given up an even-strength goal in a stretch of almost four full games. One member of the scouting fraternity offered a no-nonsense summary: "The other teams are beaten before the puck is dropped. They know it. The Canadians know it." Even before the medal round, debate had started about the 2005 team's place in world junior history: was this the best-ever Canadian squad? Or even the strongest side from any country, stronger than Soviet teams that tore up the world juniors in the '70s and '80s? The Canadians had made a compelling case that they were just that.

Yet Crosby was having less impact as the tournament wore on. He was becoming less the headliner than one very good component of an awesome whole. The forecast from the previous world junior tournament still seemed to apply: the youngster was finding tougher sledding—at least in the offensive zone—against the better teams. The semi-final was a case in point. Coach Brent Sutter matched his top line, Perry-Bergeron-Crosby, and his top blueline pairing, Dion Phaneuf and Shea Weber, against the Czechs' No. 1 line of Rostislav Olesz, Marek Kvapil and Petr Vrana of the Halifax Mooseheads. After scoring 12 times in their first five games, the Czechs' best managed only four shots on Canadian goaltender Jeff Glass. Crosby's commitment to backchecking was no doubt a factor in that. And though Crosby's willingness to hustle on defence was admirable, it wasn't the stuff that comparisons to Wayne Gretzky are made of.

The semi-final turned out to be the Canadians' closest game on the scoresheet, a 3–1 win. It was not even remotely competitive, though.

There had been no threat of a Breclav replay, with the Czechs partying and taunting Crosby. His nemesis from the under-18s, Marek Schwarz, had again shone under an onslaught of Canadian shots. Meanwhile, the Czechs had managed to muster only 11 shots. The Czechs' goal, by Rostislav Olesz, a Florida Panthers prospect, came on a short-handed two-on-one break with less than four minutes left in the third period.

Crosby picked up an assist on a Bergeron goal, but that and his blanket-coverage backchecking, wasn't enough for honours marks from NHL scouts. "He was okay," one said. "He was good. Just don't make it seem like he tore the place up. He didn't dominate."

Media reviews of Crosby's performance were also lukewarm. "Nobody wants to be the one who doesn't get it, the one who misses the meteor in the way some once argued Wayne Gretzky would never make it in the NHL," Damian Cox of the *Toronto Star* wrote. "Well, when it comes to Crosby, I don't get it." Although Cox noted that Crosby scored six goals in three games, he suggested that "hype-fatigue" might have been at the root of his disappointment with the phenom's performance.

Moreover, several players on the Canadian side had eclipsed Crosby's performance. At least four would have been playing in the NHL if not for the lockout.

Dion Phaneuf, the towering, hard-hitting defenceman and Calgary Flames' first-rounder, had almost single-handedly taken the will right out of the Czech forwards who, down a goal or two and fearing a bruising assault, pulled the chute at the Canadian blueline on every rush.

Centre Patrice Bergeron made all the right moves with and without the puck, and he certainly sounded professional. When asked about Wayne Gretzky coming into the Canadians' room, Bergeron said the gesture was "nice," but added that "we don't need too much of a pep talk to get motivated."

Two Philadelphia Flyers first-round draftees from 2003 had also stepped up with contrasting fashions—Jeff Carter, a big forward from the Soo Greyhounds, physically overpowered defencemen while Mike Richards of the Kitchener Rangers used guile, guts and keen hockey sense to get the job done, drawing comparisons to 1970s vintage Bobby Clarke. These players' performances reinforced the conventional wisdom that the world juniors is "the 19-year-olds' tournament," and 17-year-olds like Crosby, however gifted, will eventually struggle to keep up with the big boys.

Grand Forks, North Dakota
January 4, 2005

In the final, Crosby and the Canadians were in against one player who was regarded as the top 19-year-old in the world, Alexander Ovechkin. Grand Forks was Ovechkin's third world junior tournament. He had been arguably the best forward on a Russian team that had captured the 2003 world juniors in Halifax. Two years later he was able to combine surpassing skill with a degree of physical maturity that, it seemed, nobody in the Canadian line-up could match, least of all Crosby. Ovechkin, at 215 pounds and a legitimate six-foot-two, was an NHL-sized power forward. The Washington Capitals had snapped up Ovechkin with the first overall pick in the 2004 draft and he would have stepped directly into the NHL if the league hadn't shut down. Instead, Ovechkin represented Russia's best chance to knock off the powerful Canadian squad. In the semi-final victory over the host and defending champion U.S. team, the Russian had done as he pleased. And with the prospect of meeting Canada in the final, Ovechkin was certainly talking tough.

"Do you remember Halifax?" Ovechkin asked defiantly. "Everybody said that Team Canada would win the championship. We won. We proved that Russian hockey was better."

And while he didn't exactly talk trash when Crosby's name was raised, Ovechkin dismissed any personal matchup. "I've never seen him play," Ovechkin remarked. "I think he's a good player. But I don't play against Crosby. I play against Team Canada. Hockey is a team game."

It seemed that if Canada was going to subdue Ovechkin, it was going to take Phaneuf or one of the big bodies on the blueline to drop the hammer on him. Crosby? Maybe he could keep the puck away from the Russian, or hustle on the backcheck, but no more than that.

Face-off. Hockey's two top prospects skated into the frame. After a classic, thumping open-ice body check, one skated away. But not the one many would have expected.

From the start of the opening face-off, coach Sutter matched the Perry-Bergeron-Crosby line against Ovechkin's. Sutter also made a point of lining Dion Phaneuf up against Ovechkin. Midway through the first period, with Canada out to an early 2–0 lead, Ovechkin carried the puck down the left wing and pulled up at the Canadian blueline. He then cut toward the middle of the ice. He didn't want to challenge Phaneuf. He looked for his linemates to skate into the picture. But he didn't see Crosby coming at full speed on the backcheck. The safe play would have been to just lock up Ovechkin, a play that most two-way first-line forwards would have made—Steve Yzerman, say, or Mike Modano. Not Crosby. Though he was giving away four inches in height and at least 25 pounds, Crosby didn't hesitate to lay hip and shoulder into the big Russian forward.

It wasn't quite a knockout punch. A dazed Ovechkin did manage to get up and skate away, shaking his head in disbelief. And he did play a few more albeit ineffective shifts before pulling himself out of the game. He would show up at the press conference after the game with his right arm in a sling. Crosby had managed to separate Ovechkin's shoulder.

In the process Crosby had also managed to separate the Russians from the gold medal. Canada rolled to a 6–1 victory. Bergeron led the tournament in scoring and came away with the most valuable player honours. Phaneuf was named the tourney's top defenceman. Carter scored in the final. So did Richards.

Crosby didn't score in the final, but make no mistake—he made the most important play in the game. A gutty, reckless but completely legal open-ice bodycheck. Canadian fans had packed the Ralph for every game. And they came expecting to see some sleight of hand and flash from Crosby. Instead, they saw him make a play that didn't evoke Mario or 99 so much as Wendel Clark or Gordie Howe. Crosby didn't miss a shift, but the hit had taken something out of him. Like with the Cabana hit, though, he was determined not to have it knock him out of the game, especially for this golden moment.

Crosby admitted later it wasn't a coincidence he found Ovechkin in the crosshairs. "Yeah, I knew it was him," Crosby said. "And really, it was a situation that we knew to look for. We knew that nobody was challenging Dion (Phaneuf) in this tournament. No one beat him wide during the tournament and everybody had stopped trying. And from watching him and from the scouting reports we knew that Ovechkin liked to pull up at the blueline and skate toward the middle."

For the post-game celebrations a bunch of Canadian players came out for the press conference including Carter, Richards, Glass and Bergeron. Crosby took his place among them in front of about one hundred journalists and cameramen, mostly from the Canadian media. When the questions came from the floor, players took turns answering. When Glass took a shot at the once brash and now chastened Ovechkin, the Canadian players laughed. When Richards talked about how the team had built on the disappointments from the loss to the U.S. in the previous year's final, Crosby nodded and smiled. It seemed that Crosby, so used to being the centre of attention, took special pleasure from just being one of the boys. It wasn't his victory. It was *theirs*.

Nonetheless, the hold-over members of the Canadian team recognized a difference between Crosby, the player who had to wait his turn in Finland, and Crosby, the first-liner in North Dakota. "Sidney was so much stronger on the puck," Mike Richards said. "It was unbelievable the difference in his strength. And he was a lot more aware of what was happening on the ice. He had a better understanding of what it was going to take for us to win. It was strange. It was like a carry-over from Finland. We had a bunch of players that knew each other so well from over the years coming up, and in North Dakota Sidney was now one of those players. (Brent Sutter) didn't have to bother with the team-building exercises. On the ice and off the ice we picked up where we left off the year before."

The tournament was enough to make 19-year-olds sound positively wistful about the experience. Corey Perry, a gawky kid who wouldn't impress you as either introspective or even serious-minded, sounded overwhelmed when asked to describe how he was going to look back on the experience years later. "The whole way I had in my mind the idea that this was something special," Perry said. "A lot of guys don't get a chance in their whole career to play on a team that comes together so quickly (and that) plays so well. For me, Sidney and Patrice are such great players. You know, lots of guys don't get a chance to play with one guy with that type of skill—I got to play for my country with two guys who are just amazing talents. I don't know if I'll ever get a chance to be part of something like this. Our team (the London Knights) has been amazing this year—going practically three months without losing a game—but it's hard to compare one to the other."

Like Perry, veteran hockey men believed that this Canadian squad was special. "This was the best Canadian team that I ever saw in more than 20 world junior tournaments," said Lorne Davis, the *eminence grise* of the Edmonton Oilers' scouting staff. "They were so well coached by Brent Sutter, so ready to win, great talent, great character. It was probably the best team from anywhere. There were some great junior teams from the Soviet Union, ones that just dominated the competition. Still, I don't think that they were better than this Canadian team. The only question mark might have been in goal, just because there's no knowing how good the Canadian goaltending was. But I think we'll look back on this team and say, 'That team was so good that the kids all played up at Crosby's level.'"

Ted Hampson of the St. Louis Blues was another senior scout who had tracked the tournament since the '80s and couldn't name a better world junior team. "There've been some great junior teams that played in this tournament," Hampson said. "I look at the Swedish team that Peter Forsberg and Markus Naslund played for—just a great team and it didn't even win, getting stoned by Manny Legace. Well, there wasn't one minute in this tournament when there was any chance that was going to happen. I liked how our goaltender (Blues draft choice Marek Schwarz of the Czech Republic) played against Canada, but there was never any doubt about who was going to win that game. By the end of the tournament you had boys playing like men ... like veteran pros. I really think that the Canadians probably could have skated with some American Hockey League teams."*

Even the cautious scout who had initially rated Crosby's play as only "okay" came away from the final impressed with his performance: "I'm

* Hampson's estimation that the teens could have skated with the top minor league pros was borne out that spring. After their teams were eliminated from the OHL playoffs, Mike Richards and Jeff Carter joined the AHL Philadelphia Phantoms and led the squad to a Calder Cup championship.

sure that he was banged up during the tournament," the scout confessed. "So when he went into Ovechkin like he did (that) was pretty gutsy. And you got to give him marks for getting with Sutter's defensive program. Everybody knows that he's got the talent to look after defensive responsibilities—he showed that he's willing to do it and did it against the best 19-year-old out there."

— THIRTEEN —

"Je sais qu'il sera comme ça."

Just a couple of days after the Canadian juniors celebrated their first world championship in eight years, newspaper photos and video footage spread cross-country showing Crosby fighting back tears.

After the party, Crosby flew from Winnipeg to Montreal and then on to Mont-Joli, Quebec, near Rimouski. When he unpacked his hockey bag, his skates and pads were there but his red game sweater, No. 9, the one he had worn in the gold medal game, was gone. Crosby knew he hadn't misplaced it. He knew he had put it in there. He wanted it to take a treasured place alongside the trophies and banners and other sweaters from other tournaments. But the sweater was gone. It was one thing to lose a piece of luggage. It was an entirely different matter to lose something from inside the luggage.

Crosby cried. He phoned home in tears.

"It's hard to explain what he's feeling," Troy Crosby told the *Globe and Mail*. "It's just a sick, sick feeling. No one can understand just how important that jersey is. It can't be replaced. Winning that gold medal was so special and the jersey is the one he wore while they did it. To go from such a high feeling to such a low feeling so fast is hard."

Sidney spoke to reporters about the sweater before his Quebec league game between the Oceanic and Baie-Comeau. "Definitely I'm upset," he said. "It's tough. You play in the best series and win, and it's a symbol for sure. It's something you want to keep, something you want to have. Right now, it's pretty frustrating. I don't know what happened to it. It could have been taken or it could have gotten lost. All I know is, it's gone."

A week before, the 17-year-old was being asked his opinion about collective bargaining issues. Just days before, Wayne Gretzky was again anointing him his successor. And if you leafed through the most recent newspaper clippings, you would have found a mix of stories either pumping him up or criticizing his performances.

But when Crosby was red-eyed, talking about the lost sweater, it should have reminded everyone that this was still a boy in the centre of a man-sized world of money, expectations and responsibilities.

The sweater had been stolen. Air Canada immediately went into damage control. Officials said there was no evidence that the sweater had been lifted while Crosby's hockey bag was in the airline's possession. Of course, there was bound to be concern about liability here, given that it was an extraordinary item that had gone missing. Its estimated value? Well, off-the-rack sweaters might run a couple of hundred dollars. This, however, was not off the rack. It was a special issue sweater with a traceable label for authentication. The players' white sweaters were put up for auction on the internet to raise funds for a tsunami relief fund, and bidding ended at $22,000 for Crosby's. It's safe to say that his red sweater from the gold medal game would have had even greater value on the memorabilia market—except that as stolen property, it was virtually unfenceable.

"There's not any words to describe how disappointing and upsetting the whole thing is," Trina Crosby told reporters. "We're obviously very disappointed in this and we'd like to do our best to ensure that he gets it back. We're waiting patiently to see what Air Canada comes up with. We're just going to cross our fingers and hope that it all works out."

To some, Crosby's reaction was understandable. Denis Hainault of Hockey Canada described the jersey as "a momento of a lifetime." Others were less sympathetic. Columnist Gary Mason in the *Vancouver Sun* took

Crosby and "the ever-burgeoning group of adult sycophants advising him" to task. "(The) furor over his missing Team Canada jersey—the flames of which were partially fed by Crosby and his parents—was unseemly," Mason wrote.

Some might find it hard to believe that a 17-year-old would have been torn up over a lost hockey sweater. But I just thought back to the damp eyes and utter silence on the bus after the Canadian under-18s lost to the U.S. in Piestany, and Crosby's distress after the second loss to the Czechs at that tournament. Would those players on that bus have cried if they had lost their gold medals or their Canada sweaters? Maybe some would have sucked it up or sworn, but others would have broke down just like Crosby.

Police in Montreal recovered the sweater four days after it was reported missing. It turned up in a sidewalk mailbox with a related newspaper story attached to it. Police immediately suspected the sweater to be authentic in part because it had that unmistakable hockey-bag odour. An investigation led to the arrest of an Air Canada employee who was charged with theft of an item worth more than $5,000.

Sidney's mood lifted. "They said it smells pretty bad, so that's a good sign," a relieved Sidney said on a Halifax television broadcast.

"He was supposed to have a week off to rest because obviously he was at the world junior tournament and didn't have any time off during Christmas," agent Pat Brisson explained. "This sweater thing has made a mess of that. I guess now we all can move on."

There was just a small chorus of critics who took the Crosby group to task over the lost sweater. The number of critics grew, however, days later when Sidney became the centre of a controversy that caused him much more grief than his lacrosse-style goal against Quebec, his comments about being a replacement player, or the theft of his Team Canada jersey.

⊛

For years, the Canadian Hockey League has staged a midseason all-star game bringing together its best players, most of them already drafted by NHL clubs. The players are drawn from the CHL's three member leagues, the WHL, the OHL, and the QMJHL. In the mid-'90s, the CHL switched the format of the game, making it an exhibition featuring only the best prospects eligible for the NHL draft that summer. The CHL Top Prospects Game started out as a fixture at Maple Leaf Gardens. Eventually, the CHL started to move the game around Canada. The league awarded the 2005 edition to Vancouver. The host team was the Vancouver Giants of the WHL.

For months, the game was billed in Vancouver not as another date in the Sidney Crosby Show, but as a chance for fans to see the phenom against the Giants' own Gilbert Brule, to scouts and many western pundits the second-best draft-eligible junior in the CHL. And given some of the mixed reports on Crosby's performance at the world juniors, Vancouverites were looking to Brule to let the air out of the hype. The attitude in and across the WHL is well-entrenched: the western league is far superior to the other two junior loops. This is not a judgment call made season to season so much as a regionally undisputed truth, a matter of faith. And thus, in the Dub, Crosby wouldn't be regarded as the second coming of *anything* until he had leaned in against Brule and the best of the west's draft class.

And even for those who doubted the WHL's superiority, the game figured to fascinate because Crosby was going to be in close proximity to the man who had been his loudest critic, Don Cherry. Every year the CHL brought in Cherry to serve as an honorary coach and publicity magnet. Was there going to be a truce? Was Cherry going to embrace Crosby? Or was Cherry going to lay into Sidney and his family once more? It might not have had much to do with the game, but it was going to be impossible to ignore.

But four days before the Top Prospects Game, officials in Vancouver received word from Rimouski that Crosby was pulling out of the game because of a back injury. "The final decision was made by Sidney himself after this afternoon's game in Moncton," Oceanic GM and coach Doris Labonté stated. "Since he won the gold medal with Team Canada at the world juniors, he hasn't been in top shape. Emotionally, he is drained. Sidney's health comes first. The time has come for him to rehabilitate physically and mentally."

Ron Toigo, the Giants owner and the Top Prospects Game's promoter, lit into Crosby and Labonté. "For the guy who wants to be the next Wayne Gretzky ... the history of Wayne Gretzky is that he would be here with one leg if that's what it took because it's good for the game," Toigo exclaimed. "Somewhere this has lost focus. It's all about the game and the fans who want to see this guy. The direction from the GM is unfortunate, very small-market minded and a real disappointment to all of us here."

Toigo said he had offered Crosby and his family first-class airfare to come out to Vancouver, special accommodations and even a quick vacation on Vancouver Island just to attend and promote the game. But the teenager declined.

Toigo managed to drag out his righteous indignation over a couple of days of press coverage, and even managed to squeeze juice from the old political standby, western alienation. "I think he'd probably be there if it was in Montreal or Toronto," he told the *Vancouver Sun*. "Sure it's a long flight to Vancouver, but first-class accommodations are pretty comfortable and it's not that long of a flight. If you have a bit of a nap, you wake up in Vancouver and away you go."

For all the slashes and cross-checks and elbows and facewashes that Crosby ever played through, he had never taken cheaper shots than those dished out by Toigo. Crosby had never compared himself to Wayne Gretzky nor suggested he wanted to be "the next Wayne Gretzky." It was Wayne Gretzky who had tapped Sidney Crosby, not the other way around. To imply that Crosby was sandbagging or malingering is to ignore the fact that he had missed a game in Prince Edward Island the week before, citing a back injury. And though Toigo claimed "it's all about the game and the fans," it was also about his promotion. The one fellow who stood to do best out of the Top Prospects Game was neither Sidney Crosby nor Gilbert Brule, but Ron Toigo.

Toigo might have been feeling somewhat remorseful about raking a 17-year-old over the coals, because he did allow that Crosby seemed like a decent young man. "This is so out of his character you wonder where that advice came from," he said. But no matter. Toigo had painted a target on Crosby's back and handed the media a fistful of darts.

Gary Mason wasn't the most vicious of the Crosby baiters, but he bought Toigo's line. "He's old enough to know better ... " Mason wrote in the *Vancouver Sun*. "But the people who deserve most of the blame are those around Crosby ... People like his coach, his GM, his agent, his parents. Instead, they let him down."

Soon everybody was all over Crosby. Too predictably, Don Cherry weighed in after the Top Prospects Game. "Crosby said he was very tired, very fatigued and that he had a bad back," Cherry said on his syndicated radio show, *Grapeline*. "The thing that really gets me is the two games just before that he had eight points ... I see him knock down a defenceman, get the puck, put it in the top corner, I see him get a breakaway ... So much for a bad back and fatigue."

Brisson returned fire. "As far as Don Cherry is concerned, to me it's almost a disgrace to have the (Canadian Hockey League) endorsing someone who is constantly looking for attention (at the expense) of a young 17-year-old kid," Brisson argued. "The CHL obviously endorses it because they had him as a coach, they had him at the banquet. He's more an entertainer and a clown than someone whose opinion I would respect."

Perhaps the public bought Toigo's line. Perhaps some people went along with Mason's reasoning, that Crosby's withdrawal from the Top Prospects Game was a matter of selfishness. Or perhaps hockey fans thought Crosby was taking a bogus mental-health day.

Funny thing is, the contingent most important to Crosby not only understood his decision but also appreciated it, namely his Rimouski teammates. "We were happy that he did that," Rimouski winger Marc-Antoine Pouliot told me. "The easy thing would have been for him to go to the prospects game. Lots of guys like the attention. They would have gone to show what they can do against the top prospects. But Sidney didn't do it. He didn't think he was too good for (the prospects game). To be his best for our team, he needed some rest and he needed injuries to heal. By not going, he was telling us that Rimouski was more important to him than all that other stuff. It wasn't selfish. It was exactly the opposite. Sidney is always team-first."

Coach and general manager Doris Labonté maintained he didn't direct Crosby to pull out of the game. If you think it through, it's hard to imagine that a general manager would risk alienating the franchise player over something like this. "We wouldn't tell Sidney to go or not to go," Labonté said. "Sidney understands what it takes to get ready to play. He wasn't ready to play in the prospects game. If he went to Vancouver, he wouldn't be ready to play for us. This wasn't a 'star' decision. I respected that. His teammates respected that."

John MacKinnon of the *Edmonton Journal* was one of the few in the media to understand that Crosby's decision would play one way with his teammates, and another way with the critics. "(Crosby's) first responsibility is to the Oceanic and to the QMJHL, and he obviously does his best to meet those obligations," MacKinnon wrote. "(He) would have played if he was fit and healthy, which he is not."

And it wasn't a point lost on Crosby's peers, the prospects who went out to Vancouver for the game. "I know what type of guy that Sidney is," said Mike Blunden of the Erie Otters. "I played against him at the under-17s (the Canada Winter Games) and I played with him on the under-18 team. If he was healthy, he'd have gone to the prospects game. I don't think you could get anybody to say that Sidney thinks he's too good or too much of a star (to come out to the game). That's never been his attitude. He wanted to get out there and play for a Nova Scotia team that didn't look like it had a shot at the medals (at the Canada Winter Games). He's the most competitive guy you can find. The media didn't get that one right and the criticism Sidney took wasn't fair."

Quebec City
February 15, 2005

The scene should have warmed the heart of a hockey fan.

It was a night to celebrate grassroots hockey and the junior game: a junior player destined for great things was coming to a venue where so many great players had skated before.

Only at the Colisée in the provincial capital did you get a sense of the historical context of Sidney Crosby's stint with Rimouski. Since the Montreal Canadiens shut down the Forum, Le Colisée stands as the most historic rink in the province. It's home to the junior Remparts today, but the banners in the rafters recognize Quebec City's storied hockey history.

There are banners for the Quebec Bulldogs who won Stanley Cups in the old Colisée, back in 1912 and in 1913 before the NHL was founded. And there are banners for the Bulldogs' Joe Malone, professional hockey's first scoring star who once scored 44 goals in 20 games. After the original Colisée burned down in the late 1940s, it was replaced on the same site by the cinder block edifice that became the home rink of the Quebec Aces. The Quebec senior league team's "four-bullets" logo is emblazoned on other banners hanging high over the ice surface. So too is the No. 4, recognizing Jean Béliveau, who starred for the Aces before he moved on to the Canadiens. There's a Memorial Cup championship banner from Guy Lafleur's turn with the Remparts in the early '70s. Another honours the Quebec Nordiques who managed a championship in the old World Hockey Association before crossing over to the NHL and, later, moving on to Colorado. Malone. Béliveau. Lafleur. And now a Remparts team owned by Patrick Roy, who led Montreal and Colorado to Stanley Cup championships.

More than fifteen thousand fans packed the Colisée on a Tuesday night to get a glimpse of Sidney Crosby playing the hometown Remparts. Only about a thousand or so could have appreciated the arena's history. The rest were 12-year-old players in town for the Quebec peewee tournament. That Crosby, the biggest name playing hockey in NHL-less North America, was only five years removed from peewee-age hockey himself, was almost certainly a point lost on the crowd. That this audience was already aware and in the thrall of Sidney Crosby was not lost on those who would have him skate with their products into the marketplace. Twelve-year-old mallrats would know Britney Spears just as 12-year-old hockey players would know Sidney Crosby—an unfair analogy perhaps because the former possesses fame and limited talent and the latter burgeoning fame and boundless talent. Nonetheless, the turn-out indicated that the immediate future of the game was bright indeed. They were getting to see the star of the next generation of players—and, as he was only four or five years older than many here, they were getting to see the star of *their own* generation of players as well.

L'Océanic came to Quebec City the hottest team in hockey: 13 consecutive wins, 16 games without a loss. The one tie in that mix was, in fact, the game in Prince Edward Island that Crosby had missed with his back injury. You could cite a few factors in l'Océanic's spectacular run. Labonté's presence behind the bench clearly had the Rimouski players going about their business with greater resolve. Then there was Labonté's all-eggs-in-one-basket decision to load up his top line with his top three forwards, Crosby, Marc-Antoine Pouliot, and Dany Roussin, with Crosby reprising his role from the world juniors on the wing. Labonté also made one trade that changed the team dynamic, the acquisition of defenceman Mario Scalzo Jr., an undersized blueliner who had little hope of an NHL career. Scalzo Jr. was, however, an effective junior who seemed to get away with at least one outrageous gamble a shift, whose approach was pinch first and ask questions later. Labonté played Scalzo Jr. and his blueline partner Patrick Coulombe with the Crosby line to form a five-man unit that might see 25 minutes of ice time in a close contest.

And then there was the Crosby factor. First, he had delivered a message to his teammates by declining to go to the Top Prospects Game. Then he backed it up by raising his play to a new level. He had scored his 50th goal in his 50th game a couple of nights earlier, but his impact wasn't best measured by statistics—with the exception of wins and losses. No, there just seemed to be more of the stuff that doesn't show up on a scoresheet. Checks skated through. Checks levelled. Hustle on backchecking. Labonté described Crosby as "notre Mick Jagger"—meaning he was both the team's star attraction and the player who defined the group.

Perhaps the best indicator of Crosby's 2005 play came from the same NHL scout who had rated the teenager "okay" at the world juniors barely six weeks earlier. I spoke with him after he had made a sweep of the Quebec league, which included three Rimouski games. This time the scout was unequivocal in his assessment. "The best performances I've ever seen by a junior," the scout said. "He was always strong on his skates but now he's almost impossible to move off the puck." I threw out names of those he had eyeballed. Forsberg? Lindros? Thornton? Lecavalier? Kovalchuk? Ovechkin? "He was playing at a level higher than any of them," the scout said. He then added: "I never saw Gretzky as a junior and I was playing junior (not in Quebec) when Mario was in the Q, so I don't know where they were in terms of development. If Crosby isn't where they were, then he's closer than all those others. He might be getting knocked (by the media), but there isn't a scout who isn't thinking along the same lines."

Crosby told me that Rimouski's break-neck schedule prior to the world juniors and the run of practices, games and travel with the under-20 squad had taken a toll on him. His elevated play was a byproduct of a more relaxed Rimouski schedule and a few more pratice days. "In the last few weeks I've started to feel comfortable and rested again," Crosby said.

A party mood prevailed during the warm-up at le Colisée, something that owed to the presence of the peewees in for the tournament and to the appearance of the wunderkind. But because this was hockey circa 2005, when the NHL season teetered on the brink of collapse, you didn't have to be a fatalist to think that this feel-good story was too good to last. Sure, the arena lights were bright, but there was a shadow hanging over the QMJHL, over the hometown Remparts and Crosby's Oceanic.

Before the opening face-off, high expectations were tempered by anxiety along press row. No matter where you went, even to a scene like this at le Colisée, the business of hockey was bound to intrude on the game of hockey.

The NHL lockout was dragging on and on. Most days there was little promise of resolution. Most days there was either bad news or no news at all. The cancellation of the 2004–05 NHL season was looming. So too was the cancellation of the 2005 NHL entry draft, otherwise known as Sidney Crosby's draft. The possibility—or some, like Gretzky, would have said the likelihood—of the NHL remaining shut down in the fall of 2005 was prompting speculation about Crosby's plans. Would he be going to Europe if there wasn't going to be a relaunch of the NHL in the fall? To that point in the lockout, NHLers like Vincent Lecavalier and Brad Richards had made as much as $250,000 a month in the Russian league, while Joe Thornton and Rick Nash made somewhat less but lived a lot better in Switzerland. For Crosby, there'd be money in Europe and a higher level of competition than he'd face in a third season of junior. On the other hand, would he be opting to play closer to home, say in the American Hockey League? There he would face the likes of Jason Spezza or even Jeff Carter and Mike Richards, the best in class of young pros.

Pat Brisson wasn't tipping his hand. He said that no decision had been made. He claimed that options might have been explored but none had been discussed with Crosby. "Sidney just wants to play the game," Brisson said by phone from Montreal. "All the business decisions to be made off the ice will be made by Sidney and his family, and they'll face those issues when it's time. He doesn't want to be distracted by all these other things."

Brisson did seem to rule out one option, namely, a return to Rimouski. "Sidney is ready to move on to the next level," he concluded. "We just don't know where that might be right now."

Gilles Courteau, the commissioner of the QMJHL, begged to disagree. Courteau maintained that, in the event of an extended lockout, Europe was not an option for Crosby, at least if the owners of the Rimouski Oceanic still wanted him. The commissioner said it was a matter spelled out in the standard major junior player contract—that a player had to be released from his junior obligations if an NHL team wanted him, but otherwise he was bound to his major junior club. "The only thing I can say is that he's under contract with Rimouski and the (QMJHL) for another three years (through to the end of 2006–07 season)," he said. "If there's no NHL I don't know what Sidney is going to do, but I know on our side that, according to his contract, he has to come back. When you sign a major junior contract at our level, you sign for four years."

Some agents were predicting that the dispute between l'Océanic and *leur* Mick Jagger for next season was heading to court if the lockout stretched past summer. Said one agent: "It's likely that Crosby's side could argue that at age 18 he will have a right to work ... to seek employment as he sees fit." The agent suggested that Crosby could cite precedent in the case of John Tonelli, the player in the 1970s who successfully won the right to play professionally at age 18. But the agent didn't think that the legal route would put Crosby on the fast track to Europe or the AHL. "No matter which side wins, if it goes to court, it's almost a sure thing to be tied up there in appeal," he suggested.

Other agents weren't impressed. Said one: "Crosby has a contract with Rimouski and I don't see an out. The team has its side deal with Crosby. And that Crosby might be in Rimouski more than the two seasons going up to what should have been his draft year—well, that's what they see as part of (the team's) investment."

There was reason to believe that Courteau was less worried about Crosby going to Europe than the precedent it might set. Officials had to worry that other CHL players might seek to follow Crosby to European pro leagues and wind up diluting major junior competition. And some agents weren't looking forward to talking to junior clients who might want a taste of the European pros rather than another season of riding buses across the Canadian prairies for $60 to $100 in weekly pocket money.

When the game did start, you had to wonder if a court order was about the only way to tie up Crosby. Even though Rimouski was in the throes of a wearying stretch of road contests, and even though Crosby had been held pointless in a win over Gatineau a couple of nights earlier, it was clear Crosby had taken his play to a new, higher level. He was stronger than he had been with the under-18s in the summer of 2003 or against Shawinigan in the playoffs 10 months before. He had a comfort level playing with linemates whom he had grown to know over almost two full seasons. Sure, les Remparts weren't the toughest competition that Crosby and l'Océanic were going to face in the Q. Quebec was a middle-of-the-pack club. But Crosby was going about his business with a confidence bordering on impunity.

On one of his first shifts, Crosby took a pass on the right wing outside the Quebec blueline—he had at that moment peeled out of the offensive end when a dump-and-chase had been broken up. Crosby was thus at almost a dead standstill, a standing start with the puck. A Remparts defenceman had him one-on-one and was in good position for a basic lockup. But just from the defenceman's posture, you could tell there was nothing basic about this situation. Crosby burst out of the blocks with the puck and flashed out in front of him, tempting the blueliner to take the puck away from him. At the very moment the blueliner reached for it, Crosby was by him and in alone on goaltender Maxime Joyal.

It seemed Crosby did something like that on every shift, and he did pick up an assist on Rimouski's opening goal by Pouliot. But netminder Joyal was the story of the game. L'Océanic dominated play, outshooting Quebec by a two-to-one margin, but the visitors needed a late goal by

Francis Charette to beat les Remparts 2–1. Crosby was routinely mugged and drew five Quebec penalties. It wasn't one of his memorable performances but by the accounts of scouts, it was consistent with his level of play late in the season. In the last seconds, with thousands of young peewee fans rising to the occasion, Crosby sent a long shot clunking off the post of an empty net.

It was about this time that a buzz went down press row. RDS, the Quebec sports broadcast network, was carrying the game and its reporters had word that a settlement had been reached in the cold war between the NHL and the NHLPA. The print reporters were furiously trying to verify it.

At the end of the game, the scribes ran down from the press box to get Crosby's reaction to the rumoured settlement. He said he was "relieved"—if it was true—and he looked forward to the draft going ahead as scheduled and getting a chance to go to an NHL training camp in fall. At least in part, Crosby seemed relieved that, for a moment anyway, he wasn't being asked about going to Europe or to the AHL or having to take on the Q and Rimouski in a court battle. When these topics were finally broached, he stuck to his talking line—"I really haven't thought about it or talked about it," he said once again.

"I'm not thinking about (the NHL) at all right now," he continued. "I'm honestly not. I'm concentrating on playing for this team and playing for a championship." He then said that he'd sit down with his family and his agent "after the season, sometime during the summer, and look at the options."

When asked again if he'd go to the NHL as a replacement player, Crosby one-timed it. "That's not one of the options we'll talk about," he said.

One reporter asked Crosby in French if he ever got frustrated by the questions about his future. "*Je sais qu'il sera comme ça,*" he said. *I know it's going to be like that.* And right then, the only thing he knew for sure was there would be more questions before he had any of the answers.

When I was able to get Sidney to the side, I didn't ask him about the business of hockey. He seemed weary of the topic and, in truth, the stuff of business was not what anyone remembered of Joe Malone, Jean Béliveau, or Guy Lafleur. Business had been a factor in their careers, no less than Crosby's. But all their business concerns—Malone's contracts, Béliveau's strained negotiations with the Canadiens, Lafleur's talks with the WHA—were forgotten over time. What mattered more was the game. Victories. Championships. That's why the banners hang in the rafters. No, instead I asked Crosby how important it would be for him if Rimouski made the Memorial Cup, Canada's national junior hockey championship tournament. And I asked if somehow winning the world juniors was on its own enough to make his season a success. "The Memorial Cup is the goal, for sure," he said. "I was lucky to get a second chance to play for the world juniors. And in the NHL you get more than one chance to play for the Stanley Cup. But this is going to be the last chance for us at the Memorial Cup—guys I've played with for two seasons. We want to go as far as we can ... take it as far as we can."

A run to the Memorial Cup was a way to extend his hockey life as a young man not yet a professional. It was a way of postponing his immersion into a 24/7 world of celebrity, of promotional appearances, of media handlers. For as long as he could stretch Rimouski's season, Crosby could keep up a semblance of a life like hundreds of other Canadian teenage players, the junior everyboys. For as long as Rimouski lasted, life stayed a lot simpler. He was still one of the guys on the bus, the kid who shared a basement apartment with a teammate. He wasn't just playing for the Memorial Cup—he was playing to put off—for a couple of days, maybe a couple of weeks—his rush into the public domain.

The next day the NHL settlement rumour was shot down. Close, but no deal. NHL commissioner Gary Bettman would announce the cancellation of the 2004–05 season before the week was out. All last-ditch and last-last-ditch attempts to salvage the NHL season failed. Junior hockey was as good as a hockey fan could get. Sidney Crosby was as good as a hockey fan could hope for. In hockey's darkest hour, a chance to play in the NHL in the fall was seemingly more than Sidney Crosby could hope for.

— F O U R T E E N —

"Money is not going to change me."

Toronto, Ontario
March 8, 2005

The Crosbys had once delivered flyers door to door to pay for Sidney's equipment.

In Breclav I had suggested to him that those days were behind him. And he had countered that it was going to get "easier from here."

Though he wasn't yet old enough to toast the deal with champagne (that he could now certainly afford), Sidney Crosby was flown in from Rimouski to announce he had signed a deal worth $500,000 a year to promote Reebok's new line of hockey equipment. He made the trip on the Reebok company plane.

About a hundred people were gathered at the Toronto Raptors' practice gym where the Reebok folks hoisted their signage and set their video monitors to showcase the company's brand-new celebrity endorser.

It wasn't the first endorsement or merchandising deal Crosby had entered into. He was already making $150,000 Canadian to endorse Sherwood sticks and to put his name to a fine line of licensed merchandise sold by a memorabilia company. And even if the Oceanic was coming through with the going rate that other front-line junior players were getting—that is, if the Tanguays were getting him at the bargain price of $100,000 or $150,000 a season—Sidney Crosby was comfortable and his family was comfortable too. A lot more comfortable than Wayne Gretzky had been in the Soo.

"This is a big deal, but it's not going to change me as a person," Crosby vowed. "Money is not going to change me. I'm going to be the same person."

It was a big deal. Or it wasn't. It depends on how you look at it.

In terms of hockey, it was a big deal. Word was that Crosby stood to make significantly more on this deal than Reebok's other NHL endorsers, Norris and Hart Trophy winner Chris Pronger and Norris-decorated Scott Niedermayer among others. In fact, word was that Crosby would draw more than three times as much as these distinguished veterans. Crosby's deal also had big implications for Reebok, which had spent $329 million U.S. to acquire Montreal's The Hockey Co. and its CCM brand, the old gold standard in hockey equipment.

In terms of the sports world at large, it wasn't a big deal, even for a teenager. Crosby was frequently compared to basketball star LeBron James in terms of his potential impact as a player. And it might be a fair comparison in this limited context. As a marketing force, however, there is no comparison. When James turned pro at 18, the estimated value of endorsement contracts he had lined up was a staggering $100 million.

Spike Lee's character Mars Blackman used to say, "Gotta be the shoes." Shoes, not skates. But it was something more than merchandise that was driving the marketing phenomenon. James was laps ahead of Crosby in terms of adolescent fame. While Crosby had been profiled in *Sports Illustrated* when in Rimouski, James got the magazine's cover treatment. While ESPN had done pieces about Crosby, the network broadcast several of James's high school games.

And Reebok's recruitment of an athlete not yet a pro—not yet even out of high school—was hardly unprecedented. Basketball shoe companies had been chasing high school players for a couple of decades. Sebastian Telfair was less a point guard and more a brand unto himself while still a student at a Coney Island high school. Though he wasn't selected in the top ten of the NBA draft, the six-foot high schooler was able to convert his New York City profile into an Adidas contract that paid him $15 million across six years, with incentives that could amount to $42 million over the term.

Even late-arriving athletes tiers below LeBron James, and at some greater distance from Madison Avenue than Coney Island, were in a position to do better than Crosby. Consider the case of Ben Roethlisberger, the Pittsburgh Steelers' quarterback who was awarded the NFL Rookie of the Year Award just weeks before Crosby sealed his Reebok deal. His take from endorsements for the year after his breakthrough campaign was an estimated $4.5 million.

Maybe the sheer numbers shouldn't have mattered so much as the exposure Crosby was about to receive. Perhaps the key here was not so much the money as the company he was going to be keeping. A teenager plying his trade in Rimouski was being fast-tracked to the front of Reebok's hockey division and thus taking his place in the company's stable of high-profile endorsers. That stable included tennis star Andy Roddick, NBA All-Stars Allen Iverson and Yao Ming, and hip hop's 50 Cent and Jay Z. (Given Crosby's musical taste—strictly new country—he might not fully appreciate the cultural clout of the latter stars.) Not far down the line was a scheduled appearance beside Jay Leno on *The Tonight Show*. He was also skedded to appear in the pages of *Vanity Fair*.

And even before the Reebok deal was announced, Crosby had done a photo session for Gatorade at a rink just outside Rimouski. And again, the Gatorade deal, while not worth as much as the contract with Reebok, was supposedly fetching him more than any other hockey player's drink endorsement. Again this deal was going to put him in the company of some well-established athletes, including Pro Bowl quarterback Peyton Manning, the New York Yankees' Derek Jeter and Brazilian soccer star Ronaldinho.

At the Reebok presser, it was easy to see why Crosby appealed to corporate marketing departments. He betrayed little or no nervousness. He fielded questions in English and French. He was the epitome of wholesomeness, well-scrubbed, fresh-faced, self-effacing, painfully polite. Maybe he would have come off a little bland if he had been framed on stage by, say, Iverson and 50 Cent, but *vive la différence*. Maybe bland and wholesome was exactly the image that would work for Crosby. And looking at him at the press conference, it was easy to imagine that Crosby would have been exactly the personality that the NHL would want out front when it re-opened for business. Hockey fans were divided about the blame for the NHL lockout. Most blamed the millionaire players, but there was no love lost for the billionaire owners. Crosby, though, was untainted. He was outside and maybe even above the fray. The fans had no reason to resent him. Maybe some would complain he had been over-hyped, but no one could have accused him of being overpaid—the complaint lodged against so many pro athletes, NHL players included. To this point he had played the game for all the right reasons, and he said, almost always, all the right things.

Crosby remarked that he had first thought about signing on with Reebok at the world juniors—his roommate and linemate Patrice Bergeron had signed his own deal with the company and used their equipment. It was a perfect moment. Crosby's explanation had nothing to do with money and everything to do with a bond between a teammate.

Troy and Trina Crosby watched from the back of the room. Again, Trina looked amazed by the events as they unfolded, while Troy seemed matter of fact. They had raised their son "to be a good person and treat others like he wanted to be treated," and by any measure, they were successful. The unintended benefit, however, was that they raised a son who could pitch skates or sports drinks and who knows what else, and a young man who could knock on consumers' doors and be invited in.

Reebok executives beat the drum. "Sidney is the perfect athlete to represent not only Rbk Hockey, but also the Reebok brand," said the company's vice president, John Frascotti. "He is one of the rare athletes who comes along once in a generation, and we are very excited to have him as part of the Reebok team."

Some experts surmised that Reebok and Gatorade were playing something akin to a sports futures market—investing in an athlete when the buy-in was low and banking on a steep, upward curve in marketability. "The idea is you buy low and sell high," Ashwin Joshi, a marketing professor at York University's Schulich School of Business in

Toronto, told the Canadian Press. "Brands have been going after junior players for a number of years. The idea is that you catch them young. They're cheaper to buy at this point in time when they have tremendous upside potential to them."

The young, emerging athlete has upside potential, yes, but risk as well: that was the warning of David Dunne, professor of marketing at the Rotman School of Management at the University of Toronto. "It's not enough to be a good athlete or a star performer," Dunne said. "It comes down to an athlete's presence, his ability to connect with the public. For all the ability that an athlete has, he has to be liked. And then there's the matter of reputation. You only have to look at the Kobe Bryant story to see how companies can be hurt by adverse publicity. The due diligence before recruiting a celebrity endorser (in sports) isn't just how the athlete will perform in games, but also if there are risks in behaviour, something that could damage his reputation later on, whether it's drugs, drunk driving or something along those lines. Suffice it to say that Reebok would have done an extensive background check on (Crosby). Likewise the companies that recruited LeBron James did the same."

Perhaps. But the flip side for Crosby was at least as risky: by taking on these endorsement deals Crosby was, in fact, *creating* a profile rather than exploiting an established one.

"Reebok is a much stronger brand than the NHL," argued David Dunne. He suggested that Reebok's recruitment of Crosby would validate his stardom far more than an NHL advertising campaign—or maybe even more than his own performance in the league. "Many more people might see Crosby in Reebok ads than see him (in junior hockey or) in an NHL arena. He'll be riding a wave of publicity. Both sides—the company and the endorser—benefit. One hand washing the other. And just as Michael Jordan's ads for Nike benefited Jordan, Nike and less directly the NBA, so is Reebok signing Sidney Crosby good news for the NHL."

Professor Joshi was a little more cautious. While he described Reebok's signing of Crosby as "a good strategic decision overall," he said it was far too early to put it in the W column for the NHL. "It all depends on how his career unfolds," he told me. "If he is in fact the Next One, then it will turn out to be a deal of immense significance to the NHL. Career performance holds the key."

Performance in the NHL was going to be crucial, but before he had a chance to make his debut in the pros, Crosby would invariably generate more heat in the media, just by getting out into the marketplace. Here, in Toronto, it was still a matter of baby steps, no matter how glitzy the show and slick the presentation. He wasn't going to jump directly to Times Square—in fact, his Gatorade deal was announced at a supermarket in Cole Harbour a few weeks later.

When he would get back to Rimouski it was going to be Christmas in March for his Oceanic teammates. Ever the team player, Crosby had made sure that Reebok outfitted all of them, along with the coaching staff.

Almost lost in all the thunder about the Reebok deal was the fact that l'Océanic was undefeated in 23 games (21 wins and two ties). Rimouski had climbed to No. 2 in the CHL's national rankings, behind only the London Knights, who had their own run of historic proportions. Led by Corey Perry, Crosby's linemate from the world juniors, the Knights had set a CHL record with a 31-game undefeated streak to open the season. And they weren't looking back.

Sidney Crosby was doing his part to keep hockey in the news, but the NHL seemed bent on nullifying any momentum he gained. Within two weeks of Crosby gaining attention for the game's future through his Reebok deal, the NHL announced the cancellation of its 2005 entry draft, originally scheduled for Ottawa in June. Fair to say that the draft was an inevitable casualty of the lockout and cancelled season. (But off the record, some executives thought the league could have gone ahead with the draft even without a collective agreement in place.)

For many, the idea of a lost NHL season had been unthinkable. Now a lockout stretching into a second season seemed all too possible. So the rumours continued to fly. Crosby to Europe in the fall of 2005. Crosby to the American Hockey League. Crosby undrafted to declare NHL free agency. Some of the rumours were pure fancy, among them the idea that

Crosby would suit up for the Toronto Maple Leafs' AHL affiliate, which was going to be relocated from St. John's, Newfoundland to Toronto. Others, though, seemed to have a bit more to back them up. At the forefront was a highly improbable but not quite unbelievable notion that Crosby was going to be chased by the Chicago Wolves, an independent AHL team with a deep-pocketed, eccentric owner.

In all the rumour-mongering, some complicating issues were underplayed. The CHL's deal with the NHL had lapsed, but the junior league did have an agreement in place with the International Ice Hockey Federation. Thus European leagues with ties to the IIHF would have to answer to the federation if they pursued any deal with a player under obligation to the CHL. Likewise, the CHL had a deal in place with the AHL. It therefore looked like the CHL could stymie Crosby.

Many speculated that a European team would actually pay Rimouski for Crosby's services if the lockout wore on. Effectively, the payment would amount to a de facto transfer fee. It didn't quite add up, though. Nowhere was Crosby worth more than to teams in the Q—it might have made sense if one of the QMJHL teams with a larger arena, either Quebec or Halifax, made a bid. But would Crosby have been as much of a gate attraction in Russia or Switzerland? Possibly. Still, Russian teams were able to get Brad Richards and Vincent Lecavalier from the Stanley Cup champion Tampa Bay Lightning, and the Swiss league signed Joe Thornton of the Boston Bruins and NHL leading goal scorer Rick Nash. For these proven NHL stars, their respective European teams didn't have to pay one ruble or franc beyond the players' salary.

Crosby did nothing to advance the story about playing in Europe in the fall of 2005, or any of the other stories for that matter. His line remained that he wanted to concentrate on playing for Rimouski and look at his options only at the end of the season. Pat Brisson echoed the sentiment, though he did suggest that fans in Rimouski "shouldn't buy their tickets yet"—an indirect way of saying that Crosby's return to l'Océanic was less than a sure thing.

Fact was, he and his family wanted to avoid the same PR stumbles that plagued the Lindroses. As Crosby told me, he didn't want "special treatment." More to the point, he just didn't want to appear to want spe-

SIDNEY CROSBY

187

cial treatment. In fact, the only time he ever sought any consideration was when he asked Rimouski to make sure that free tickets for his games be set aside for underprivileged kids.

Nonetheless, Crosby was still taking some hard hits in the media. He was being labelled a mercenary or worse. He was certainly getting a rougher ride than Gretzky had when he allegedly showed an interest in going to Europe back in his days with the Soo, or even for signing on with Nelson Skalbania's Indianapolis team in the old WHA.

Again, like Crosby's decision to forego the Top Prospects Game, his rumoured interest in Europe was not criticized by his fellow junior players. They, better than the pundits, understood why Crosby might have been looking for bigger challenges.

Ryan O'Marra of the OHL's Erie Otters, a forward projected as a first-round pick in the 2005 draft, had no problems with Crosby wanting to leave Rimouski if the NHL remained locked-out. "There just isn't anything left for him to learn or prove in junior," O'Marra said. "It's not that he thinks he's too good. At this point, he's *proven* he's too good. He's just in a different class from the rest of us. They're saying that if he went to Europe he'd be setting a precedent for other juniors to go over there. I know it's not something that would work for me. I'm pretty sure that most guys—even the guys rated in the top five (prospects by the NHL's Central Scouting Bureau)—wouldn't be looking to try to play in the top European pro leagues. Those guys would hear from their agents that they're better off here."

O'Marra compared Crosby's situation to that of Jeff Carter and Mike Richards, two NHL-ready forwards who were back in junior for the 2004–05 season because of the lockout. "Maybe they could have played in Europe this season and got something out of it," O'Marra said. "The way it stands right now they had to be sent back to junior. If Sidney Crosby wanted to go to Europe it wouldn't be for the money. It would be for his development. And he would know best what's best for him. Players know where they fit in and where they don't."

Often Wayne Gretzky and Mario Lemieux appeared out of play or out of position during the course of a game. But for Mario, and especially Gretzky, positioning was all about anticipation of play; eventually the puck caught up with them. So it was for Sidney Crosby on the ice and off. He had put himself in the best possible position to realize the business benefits of his genius. IMG rather than an independent agent; Rimouski rather than U.S. college; a modest media image rather than a star attitude: all of these and every other career move put him in the position to be front and centre with Reebok, to be the image of the NHL when it would re-open and relaunch.

"Junior hockey prepares you not just for the pros but for life."

Halifax, Nova Scotia
May 9, 2005

During the summer Sidney Crosby was going to rent some ice time to scrimmage with his friends. When he had some spare time he would even play street hockey with some kids from the neighbourhood. Old habits die hard. But Games 3 and 4 (and 6 if necessary) of the Q league final against the Halifax Mooseheads were going to be the last meaningful games that Sidney Crosby would ever play in his hometown—the last ones to show up in the record books. These games against the Mooseheads weren't a homecoming. He had been back since going off to Shattuck. No, these were his chances to say farewell, before going off to more famous arenas, bigger cities, brighter lights.

Sure, local fans and the media were holding out hope that they'd get games when the world championships came to Canada. Or that Crosby would someday be able to exercise superstar clout and bring a Team Canada exhibition to the Halifax Metro Centre. If those events ever unfolded, though, they'd occur in the far-off future. And thus Haligonians were lining up outside the Metro Centre and buying scalpers tickets on Sackville Street. They wanted a last look at the boy wonder they had always called their own.

It was storybook stuff. It was a conclusion to Sidney Crosby's Quebec league career that couldn't have been scripted better. With no NHL playoff games to top the bill, Canadian sports broadcasts were giving big play to the CHL post-season. Rimouski was the hottest team in hockey but l'Océanic had actually been chasing the Mooseheads in the standings almost all season. Rimouski's last regular-season loss occurred, incredibly, way back before New Year's, yet Crosby's team didn't catch up to Halifax until mid-March. In the end, l'Océanic finished only two points ahead of the Mooseheads. The difference was, of course, Crosby, who was named the QMJHL player of the week the last four weeks of the regular season.

Prior to this matchup, both Rimouski and Halifax had steamrolled opponents in the playoffs. Each had lost only once in nine games.

After a first-round bye and a four-game sweep of Lewiston in the league quarter-finals, Rimouski won the first three games of its series against the Chicoutimi Sagueneens. In those three games, Crosby had 10 points. It looked like business as usual. But then Chicoutimi, playing at home, knocked off Rimouski 5–0, forcing a fifth game. The loss was Rimouski's first in 35 games dating back to December 29th. For Crosby it had been even longer. His last defeat, including those world junior games that took him out of Rimouski, had come on December 6th—nearly five full months before. The loss against Chicoutimi clearly had a sobering effect on Crosby. Back in Rimouski, he scored four goals and Dany Roussin added a short-handed goal in a series-clinching 5–1 win. In nine playoff games leading to the Quebec league final, Crosby had nine goals and 22 points.

Rimouski was getting national headlines, but there wasn't much doubt that Halifax was the Q's second best team. The Mooseheads followed a route to the final almost identical to the Oceanic's—a first-round bye, a quarter-final victory (over Gatineau) in five games and a four-game sweep (over the Rouyn-Noranda Huskies). The Mooseheads didn't have an offensive star on the scale of Marc-Antoine Pouliot or Roussin, never mind Crosby. But Halifax's blueline was big and mobile with pro prospect

Alexandre Picard leading the way. And the team's fortunes were riding on netminder Jeremy Duchesne. The Mooseheads had picked up Duchesne in a trade from Victioriaville in January and he lost just once during the regular season thereafter. Duchesne was even better in nine playoff games, posting a 1.85 goals-against average and a .934 save percentage.

Not surprising, Rimouski and Halifax had split four regular-season games. All this made for a promising matchup. Plus there was the bad blood between the teams—most of it tracing back to Frederik Cabana's knee-on-knee hit on Crosby back in the fall. That raised the emotional stakes.

It was high drama. Or at least, a Halifax win in the third game of the series would make it high drama.

L'Océanic had won their opening two games against Halifax in Rimouski. Game 1 was a 9–4 blowout, with Crosby scoring the first goal three minutes in and picking up two assists as l'Océanic ran out to a 4–0 lead in less than eight minutes. It was as close to a perfect period as the home team could hope for. Three of the first five shots found the back of the net. Three power plays, three goals. Before the second intermission, Rimouski led 8–0.

In stark contrast, Game 2 in Rimouski was a roller coaster ride. Rimouski 2–0, after a Crosby goal midway through the first. Halifax 3–2, after Mooseheads goals on consecutive shifts early in the second. Rimouski 5–3, after a three-goal explosion in less than five minutes, also in the middle frame. And 5-all, after two goals by the Mooseheads' Czech import Petr Vrana just before the second intermission. The winner was scored by Rimouski's own Czech recruit, Zbynek Hrdel, midway through the period and Roussin added an empty-net goal in the dying seconds— but up until then the game was still in doubt. Said former MP Suzanne Tremblay, who took in the game from her seat in Section 9: "At the end of the game Sidney took time going off the ice. He just skated around. Not a victory lap, just looking out at the crowd. And when we started to cheer, he waved. It's like he has an appreciation not just for his gift (for the game), but for the way he's seen by people. Some people would say he has a great politician's sense of the moment—a flair for the right gesture. We thanked him and he thanked us. He knew that this was his last game in Rimouski, and we knew too. He was respected here—he was a star, but it was never claustrophobic for him. I don't know if it will ever be that way for him again."

It wasn't as sentimental for the Mooseheads, though. They thought l'Océanic players were diving and the refs were buying more often than not. They were convinced that the league was directing the officials to see things Rimouski's—and Crosby's—way. They were convinced that the Q and just maybe the CHL wanted their most famous name at the Memorial Cup. And it was clear that the business of the Memorial Cup would benefit from Crosby's presence.

Though he had put Cole Harbour in the national sports pages, though he had played for Nova Scotia teams and Canadian teams, Halifax fans didn't come to the Metro Centre for Game 3 of the series to praise Crosby; they came to see the Mooseheads bury him. To do anything different would have been a disservice to the home team. When Rimouski skated onto the ice, the fans booed. When Crosby's name went out over the PA system, they booed. One enterprising fan even waved a 20-foot-high inflatable baby pacifier.

The scout who graded Crosby "okay" in Grand Forks and then "the best junior I've ever seen" two months later had made his way to Halifax. He didn't equivocate about his expectations. "I can't see Rimouski losing," he said. "Crosby is on a mission. He'll do whatever it takes."

Phoenix Coyotes' coach Rick Bowness had good reason to want to fly under the radar and stay away from the arena. Just when Rimouski arrived in Halifax, the rumour of Wayne Gretzky becoming the Coyotes coach reached critical mass. Every reporter in town was chasing Bowness for his reaction to the possibility of being waved aside by the legend and part-owner of the Coyotes' franchise. But Bowness, who keeps an off-season home near Halifax, had followed Crosby's career with interest going back to age-group hockey. And so he took a seat on press row even though he was peppered with uncomforting questions. "I wasn't going to miss this," he said. "I could tell you that I'm coming out scouting or something like that, but I'm a fan too. It's once in a lifetime stuff. Such a great player, such a great kid and here, playing at home."

Also taking in the game was Brad Crossley, Crosby's old coach with the Dartmouth Subways. "Sidney called when he came in with the team," Crossley said. "He stays with his folks, not with the team when he plays here, but I can't imagine that it makes it easier for him. He calls every time he's in town and checks in—wants to know how the Subways are doing, what's going on in the local leagues. But it's not just me. I know that there are dozens of people, coaches, players, friends from school, that he catches up with. You could never accuse him of forgetting where he came from. It's clearly real important to him."

At home the Mooseheads had to think that owning the last shift favoured them. Coach Al MacAdam could therefore match Francois-Pierre Guenette and Frederik Cabana, the peskier checkers, against Crosby and get the most physical defencemen, Picard and Franklin MacDonald out against the phenom. Cabana would hassle him and get in his head, while MacDonald would wear him down physically. The plan also called for Halifax's tough guys to goad Crosby's protector, Eric Neilson, into cheap penalties and a fight or two, which they figured would be good for a couple of extra power plays, and force Rimouski to go deeper into their bench. They also were hoping that the refereeing would turn in their favour. Jeremy Duchesne had picked the worst time to go south, so coach MacAdam made the change in goal, opting to go with erstwhile back-up Jason Churchill. It was the standard ploy to get his team's attention, something pulled straight out of the coaching manual.

And none of this mattered in the least.

MacDonald and Picard could barely get Crosby's attention, never mind knock him off the puck. And going with Churchill was, for Hailfax coach Al MacAdam, simply sending a different lamb to slaughter.

Once again l'Océanic ran out to a 4–0 lead in the first period. Crosby scored twice in the opening six minutes. The first goal came on a power play, with the first unit buzzing all around the net. Crosby picked up the puck as he came steaming through the slot and waited, waited, and waited still, until Churchill went down. It was an absolutely nerveless display, a ridiculously artful move at a critical juncture. On his next shift

Crosby notched his second goal, a more conventional one, a sure-handed put-away on Churchill's doorstep. In the second frame, Mario Scalzo Jr. scored his second goal to give Rimouski a 5–1 lead. That one especially stung the Mooseheads and their fans. Scalzo Jr. had been down before the goal and, if he was to be believed, needed help getting off the ice. The more skeptical fans were sure he was just playing the ref for a patsy, trying to draw a penalty for the home team.

Scalzo Jr.'s wounds or theatrics notwithstanding, it was easy to see that, for Crosby, the game had taken on special meaning. Though he had been playing on Pouliot's wing, he moved in to take the face-offs, winning 17 of 29 and all the important ones.

Again, the Mooseheads mounted a comeback in the late going. Too late as it turned out. And though Rimouski goaltender Cédrick Desjardins looked at times loose and flustered, flopping anxiously, swatting at rather than scooping up the puck, he stopped just enough rubber to secure l'Océanic's 5–4 victory.

After the game, reporters crowded Crosby. "I got a couple of chances and I just took advantage of them," he said over the scrum. "Anytime, you want to start well; but on the road, that's important."

This series was not all Crosby, but each game seemed to start that way. In fact, a template for Rimouski games was emerging. In Games 1 and 3 against Halifax (and in other games along the way), the team was overpowering in the early going, when Crosby's unit was its freshest. The first five would draw a penalty on a shift and then stay on for the first minute or more if necessary. It was something Rimouski could get away with early, but something that tended to catch up with them as the game wore on. Think of a boxer who banks on an early knockout only to punch himself out. That seemed the course Rimouski was taking.

But unlike the fight game, there's more than one to a corner. Thus in the later stages of games, coach Doris Labonté used his second and third lines for longer stretches. These lines had some useful players. A crash-and-bang winger from Newfoundland, Mark Tobin, was a decent enough player to be a second-round pick of Tampa Bay. Undersized centres Francis Charette and Danny Stewart might not have had NHL potential, but they were effective juniors. Even Neilson had developed from a one-dimensional enforcer to a two-dimensional force, a decent checker. L'Océanic was more than a one-man or even one-unit team.*

Halifax, Nova Scotia
May 10, 2005

Bobby Smith was taking the loss in Game 3 as well as could be expected. Smith had been the Ottawa 67's centre who had squared off against Wayne Gretzky and the Soo Greyhounds back in spring 1978—a series the 67's barely survived. Now he was owner of the Halifax Mooseheads, the team Sidney Crosby had taken to the brink. In between and along the way Smith had picked up a Stanley Cup ring in Montreal and an MBA. He had done a stint as general manager of the Phoenix Coyotes, and he had been away from the game long enough to see it with a fresh set of eyes when he bought the Mooseheads. Smith grew up in Ottawa but he had been born in Nova Scotia, so his purchase of the team was a homecoming in that sense.

Other members of the Mooseheads' organization hadn't been happy with the refereeing in the series. And they hadn't been happy with what they thought was Rimouski's diving. They'd seen too much of Scalzo Jr.'s writhing on the ice after clean checks. They said nothing about Crosby on that count, but winked. Smith, though, had nothing but kind words for No. 87.

"How he's handled everything is a real credit to him," Smith said. "You can tell how much he loves the game—just how he plays and prac-

---

* Rimouski wasn't the deepest team in hockey. Consensus among the scouts was that the OHL London Knights were. A problem for Rimouski was its back-up goaltender, Jean-Michel Filiatrault. CHL teams are ostensibly under-20 squads but they are each allowed to carry three 20-year-olds, players known as overagers or OAs. Though the top 20-year-olds are already playing in the NHL, and real talents pay their dues for decent minor-league salaries in the American Hockey League, junior teams value the overagers who are willing to put in an extra year in major junior. Usually OAs fill key roles on teams, such as starting goaltenders or other spots on the first two lines or in blueline pairings. The cage became a soft spot for Rimouski when the team failed to convince Cory Schnieder, the U.S. goaltender from the under-18s, to come north. L'Océanic acquired Filiatrault assuming he would win the No. 1 goaltending spot. But this OA disappointed and, worse, by the time the decision was made to go with Cédrick Desjardins as a starter, Rimouski's roster was locked in for the season. So Rimouski was playing teams with three OAs, while it had only two of its own actually playing. The other OA on the bench represented an overly expensive insurance policy and a wasted opportunity.

tices. And off the ice he's been all you could ask for as an ambassador for the league."

Smith saw common threads that ran through Crosby's skills and Gretzky's, but also aspects of the phenom's game that stood alone. "Like Wayne, Sidney combines intelligence—an awareness of game situations, an ability to make decisions on the fly—with a vision that so few players have. But his strength and balance are what makes him so tough to defend (against). Wayne was more elusive, but also the game was different back in the '70s. Good players then would of course be good players now, but it was much more freewheeling back then. There was a lot more open ice. Now there's much tighter checking. Even though the Quebec league is the most wide open of the major junior leagues, it's less (freewheeling) than it used be."

Smith refuted the idea that business has squeezed the fun out of the game for players—but he made his argument not in the expected way. I had talked to him many times about his experiences with the Ottawa 67's—about growing up in Ottawa, playing with Doug Wilson and a couple of others from atom and peewee right through to major juniors, about playing for Hall of Fame coach Brian Kilrea, the very embodiment of Old-Time Hockey. Trading stories about 67's coach Kilrea, Smith made junior hockey sound like, as Gretzky had suggested, a great time for players too young to be too concerned with money or their futures.

"People will talk about the good old days and romanticize things but we weren't exactly innocents back in the '70s," Smith began. "There was a business side to the game even back then. I had an agent and I'm sure that Wayne did. The top players were going to need that—particularly at that time with the WHA (the World Hockey Association) in play and throwing money around. There are other things that the top players have to deal with today, but even back in the '70s the stakes were pretty high.

"I deal with the players. I know them pretty well. I don't think that the players are really any different today than they were back when I was playing with the 67's. The times are different—instead of playing cards on trips they're playing Nintendo or something like that. But what motivates these young men, what they think in certain situations, that hasn't changed and I don't know if it will ever change. Most players get it—

SIDNEY CROSBY

197

some kids don't. As an owner I can give them a chance to make the most of a great opportunity."

I asked Smith if he thought junior hockey provided a real service to its best players, the one percent, Sidney Crosby today and Smith himself back in the day. Smith admitted that the game isn't perfect, but came up with a variation on Winston Churchill's famous line about democracy—that it's the worst form of system except for all those other forms that have been tried from time to time.

"If I didn't believe in the junior game, then I wouldn't have invested in this team," Smith said. "And if I didn't believe in junior hockey I wouldn't be telling my son that he should play junior rather than going to a U.S. college on a scholarship. I found out after my playing just how important education is—and that's why my son will play junior. He'll play and get his education paid for … it's right there in the junior contract.*

"I don't buy the idea that junior hockey uses its players. Junior hockey prepares you not just for the pros but for life. I think that Sidney Crosby will look back someday and think the same thing."

At the team hotel I spotted Donald Dufresne in the lobby. I re-introduced myself to the assistant coach, noted that we had talked last year during the playoffs (back when he was the head man in Rimouski) and tried to make small talk. Standard stuff. Out of it, maybe I could warm him up to an interview, to hear about how Crosby's game had changed from season one to season two. "Everyone being a year older makes a big difference with this team … better for the experience last year," I said. It didn't break the ice. It didn't even crack it.

"You'd have to ask the coach that," he said.

A couple of other attempts—just some small talk again—got the same result. A shrug. A wave of the hand. No small talk.

Dufresne looked like someone had shot his dog. To lose a job coaching a major junior team is one thing. To lose it in your hometown

* The Mooseheads selected Bobby Smith's son, Daniel in the third round of the 2005 draft.

must be even harder. But to lose the job of coaching Sidney Crosby is, well, a real blow. Rimouski was on the verge of winning a Quebec league title and going to the Memorial Cup championship. It would have been tough for Dufresne to be on the outside watching that happen. Yet it had to have been gut-wrenching to remain on the inside and in Doris Labonté's shadow.

Talking with a couple of reporters who covered the Q regularly, they said that Dufresne's good-guy approach had hurt him. They also noted that Rimouski's great regular-season run traced back to when Labonté took over the show. They also told me that Labonté had made it clear he wasn't coming back next season—no surprise, because not only was Crosby destined to move on, but the core of the team was going to be gone also. The four others in the five-man Crosby first unit were at the end of their junior eligibility. Making it even tougher was the fact that the Q had awarded expansion teams to St. John's, Newfoundland and Saint John, New Brunswick. The way the draft rules were set up gave l'Océanic little hope of retaining even a semblance of the 2004–2005 team. And according to the reporters who covered Rimouski, Labonté favoured promoting another assistant coach, a young guy named Guy Boucher, a new-school analyzer of game tapes, into the top job next season. Dufresne would be out, again.

A little later Crosby came into the lobby. His teammates were wandering around in sweats and t-shirts and, with their weeks-old playoff beards, looking not altogether unlike teens brought in off the street. Crosby, though, was freshly pressed in a suit jacket, his open collar the only concession to the casual occasion. His attempt at a playoff beard had produced only a few small wisps at the corner of his mouth and made him the butt of much good-natured joke-telling.* Though he was staying at his folks, he had come in for a team meeting and a meal. The security at the hotel—a theme place that had its male staff walking around in kilts—was chasing away dozens of autograph seekers, not child fans but those entrepreneurs who sell autographed cards at mall

---

* In one magazine story, I wrote that Crosby could "shave with a face cloth." He evidently took issue with the fact-checker on the piece, saying he did use a razor. Much later, in August 2005, on *The Tonight Show*, Crosby admitted to Jay Leno that he "touched up" his attempt at a moustache with an eyebrow pencil.

shops and on the internet. Crosby looked exasperated as security showed the door to the card traders, all of them fortyish, in hockey sweaters and seemingly in search of their first dates. All of them looking to make a buck at the end of a Crosby-held felt pen—it was pretty unseemly. It made me think that Crosby in Halifax would soon be something akin to the Beatles in Liverpool—it was his hometown and maybe it would remain his home, but it could no longer be *home*, no longer that place where he could seek refuge.

Crosby was somewhat more expansive than Dufresne. Again, he chose his words carefully. "It's always nice to play here. It's important to get a win here if we can. If we can close this series out, it can mean a lot later on. I can't wait to get on the ice." Nothing presumptive. Nothing personal. Though I'd met him two years earlier, though we had played table tennis and pool, he seemed wary. He also seemed a little weary of it all, like he was suffering through the early onset of celebrity fatigue. Bobby Smith can say that the business of hockey has always been part of the game for junior players, but he and Gretzky weren't chased for autographs like Crosby. They certainly weren't concerned about their image as it played with corporations looking to bring them aboard as endorsers. No surprise that in his hometown Crosby wanted to get back on the ice— it was the one place where he had some peace, where what was familiar to him as a kid hadn't changed that much.

☺

The fans went to Game 3 at the Metro Centre looking for a turning point in a classic series. They came to Game 4 hoping just for a decent contest. They got something more than that: not a Moosehead victory, just a memorable performance by Sidney Crosby in his last game in hometown Halifax. And somehow it seemed fitting that one of the people who approached me to see if I had a ticket to sell was, yes, a locked-out NHLer. Aaron Johnson, a defenceman with the Columbus Blue Jackets, had been a member of the Rimouski team that won the Memorial Cup in 2000 when Halifax hosted the tourney. He had driven in from Cape Breton with the hopes of landing a game-day ducat. "You know, I play the game, but I'm a fan of it too," said Johnson, who, if you didn't know what he did for a living, would have blended right in with the city's college crowd. "Sidney's last game here and that he has a chance to lead a team to the Memorial Cup, that's huge." So huge in fact that Johnson's NHL cred and Rimouski connections couldn't get him into the arena. He would have to deal with a scalper, like others who wanted to catch a piece of history.

The Mooseheads' simmering anxiety and frustration showed from the opening shift. Out against Rimouski's first unit, the big defenceman Franklin MacDonald was squared off against Crosby on the cycle in the Halifax end. Crosby had his back to MacDonald in the corner and controlled the puck in his skates. MacDonald hit him with a cross-check to the lower back, knocking him down. Not enough to knock Crosby off the puck—he fell but with the puck still in front of him. He got back on his skates in a split second and MacDonald did it again. Same result. When MacDonald did it a third time, the ref at last raised his arm and whistled down the penalty. The boos rained from the stands and the giant inflatable baby pacifier was waved tauntingly down at rinkside when Crosby lined up for the face-off on the power play.

The scout who declared that "Crosby was on a mission" was up on press row taking notes. "I read what Scotty Bowman said about Crosby— all about his strength," he told me. "The way that he's able to keep his balance and keep control of the puck on the cycle while bigger guys are draped all over him. He's so strong on the puck that some people will think he's diving anytime he does go down. It's just a game of keep-away that he plays and two things make it effective. One, he draws penalties from it. Two, when you're not expecting it, he can pass out of it, pick up players that leave you wondering, 'How'd he ever see that guy?' The one downside is that he'll take a lot more punishment playing his game than Gretzky or Mario ever did—and if you say he's like Peter Forsberg skill-wise and game-wise, you know that's part of the bargain." The scout was referring to the litany of injuries that have compromised the career of Colorado Avalanche centre Peter Forsberg, widely if not universally regarded as the best player for at least stretches of the new millennium.*

* Forsberg signed as a free agent with Philadelphia in the summer of 2005.

Rimouski didn't capitalize on the man advantage, but continued to put pressure on the home team. Halifax, however, opened the scoring on a power play goal by Rane Carnegie six minutes in. Jeremy Duchesne, back between the pipes and with every reason to have his confidence in shreds, gamely protected the Mooseheads' lead, shutting out l'Océanic with several big stops. The biggest of them was a glove save on Mark Tobin at the 13-minute mark, a one-timer that looked like it was heading for the top shelf.

But on the very next shift, Crosby put on a display. He looked like he had tired of Duchesne's delay of the inevitable, like he wanted to let the air out of the giant pacifier, like he had things to do and places to go.

Again, the unfortunate MacDonald was Crosby's foil. This time Crosby was a one-man cycle, starting in the corner and along the boards, heading toward the net, reversing direction, reversing again, going from one corner to the other, cutting to the middle of the ice while his teammates peeled off into open ice looking for a pass. It was an epic display of puck control—if you actually mapped it out it would have looked something like the travels of Marco Polo. But at the very end of it all, MacDonald unleashed a frustrated slash to Crosby's left arm; and Crosby fell to the ice clutching his wrist. A hush fell over the crowd. The fans wanted a good game and even a Halifax win, but evidently not at the cost of their local hero being knocked out of the game. They knew that this wasn't one of Scalzo Jr.'s Actors' Studio moments.

When Crosby came out for the next shift, the only audible sigh of collective relief came from those who didn't boo him.

Crosby had a couple of other good moments that period. Near the end of the first, he worked a no-look, purely intuitive drop pass at the Halifax blueline to Pouliot, and then on the return fired a laser-like pass through three sets of skates and sticks that landed on the tape of Roussin's stick. Another play that drew gasps but didn't result in a goal.

At the end of the first period I spotted Coyotes' coach Rick Bowness again. He was shaking his head in disbelief at Crosby's performance. "It's the mistake that people make about Sidney," Bowness said. "They think that he's small. He's not. He was shorter but now he's around five-foot-eleven, big enough. But when you see him during the summer, walking around in shorts, his legs are huge. He has glutes like Ray Bourque had.* People who don't know about him would wonder if he'd be able to stand up to the punishment. But he'll be dealing out punishment, not taking it. If he were any taller, he'd be the most (physically) dangerous player in hockey."

Crosby was still the most dangerous offensive player and he tied the game 1-all early in the second period, finishing off a pass from Mario Scalzo Jr. But on this night it wasn't the five-man first unit that troubled Halifax, so much as the second line, with Mark Tobin and Zbynek Hrdel on the wings of Francis Charette, a tiny blond-haired centreman who looked all of 13 when he took off his helmet. The Charette line accounted for three goals in a four-minute stretch of the second, giving Rimouski a 4–2 lead to carry into the final frame. And though Halifax rallied in the third period and drew within a goal, the Mooseheads once again fell one goal short with Rimouski goaltender Cédrick Desjardins being just good enough again, despite nervous moments.

The post-game optics weren't entirely great, however—what can you say about the Q when its championship trophy falls into two pieces as the victorious team passes it around? That, however, was just comic relief. Most of the fans stayed or warmed up to the moment, politely applauding as the teams traded handshakes. But when Crosby lifted the championship trophy, the crowd cheered him as loudly as they had booed him after each Oceanic goal. And when he skated with the trophy, the inflatable pacifier was nowhere to be seen. Nothing the ref did hinted that the fix was in—four penalties to Rimouski, three to Halifax. Nothing suggested that the league conspired to deliver Rimouski to the Memorial Cup. It was a victory for Rimouski, and for the league just as much, because in this final game, Rimouski proved to be something more than a one-man or one-line team. In fact, Rimouski looked to have some promise for the Memorial Cup.

Despite the "disappointing" one-goal performance in the final game,

---

* Hockey players are renowned for being hard to fit in dress pants, such is the over-development of the hindquarters and quads. Bourque, however, was legendary in this respect. I once asked a Hall of Famer what was the most amazing thing he ever saw in hockey. "Ray Bourque's ass," he dead-panned.

Crosby was tapped as the Q's playoff MVP and his name was inscribed on the Trophée Guy Lafleur. The playoffs were supposed to feature tighter checking, but there was no evidence of that in Crosby's gaudy statistics. He rang up 31 points in 13 games, winning the post-season scoring race by 11 points. The players stayed on the ice for half an hour after the game. Players who hadn't dressed for the game, the scrubs who would be in the line-up next year—all of them dressed to take their turn with the trophy, the cup in one hand, the base in the other. Even here Crosby made a point of staying on message, of hitting the team theme. "It's nice," he said. "We came here to win this and we did it, but at the same time I just tried to contribute as much as I could. To come away with that (MVP) trophy is just a bonus."

Troy and Trina and Pat Brisson were waiting for Sidney outside Rimouski's dressing room. The team bus had pulled right inside the bowels of the arena and the training staff loaded equipment into its hold. L'Océanic had to make the trip to London for the Memorial Cup in 10 days. In the interim, the team would have three days off. Most players and coaches were heading directly back to Rimouski overnight, an eight-hour drive. Management let Sidney Crosby stay with his parents in Cole Harbour for a couple of days, a chance to heal up and make a few dozen more phone calls to friends.

"It's great to do it in front of my family and friends," Crosby said. "They've given me support my whole life and to do it here, the place where I grew up watching junior, is a great feeling. I think the fans back home would have liked to see us do it there but we got it and we're bringing it home."

Crosby's former minor hockey coach Brad Crossley summed it up the next day. "The hockey gods must have had something to do with it. Rimouski played here during the season, but really Halifax had to get one last look at Sidney before he went off to bigger things. But I'm pretty sure that it's our last look at him as a player, not his last look at this city. He'll always come back."

"Freeze Corey Perry for two years and then unfreeze him and then compare."

London, Ontario
May 21, 2005

Start not with the Memorial Cup games but with the interest the tournament generated. The Memorial Cup is by definition a national competition and as such, annually attracts a media contingent representing the whole country. The 2005 tournament, however, was something altogether more impressive: there were more than three hundred requests for media credentials. You couldn't turn around without bumping into a guy wielding a television camera or some semi-famous name in make-up ready to sit on a rigged up "Mem Cup Central" set.

The Memorial Cup is staged every year. This, however, was another event entirely, a blockbuster, one that featured attractions that played above the title. This was *Sidney Crosby vs the Greatest Junior Hockey Team Ever*™. It was the opening game of the tournament, the Rimouski Oceanic versus the host London Knights. This matchup was the tournament's true essence, with the Western Hockey League champion Kelowna Rockets and the Ontario league runners-up Ottawa 67's relegated to supporting roles, minor ones. And, if anything, the buzz around Sidney Crosby and the crush of media brought to mind another instance not long ago when another individual eclipsed the game in this most team-oriented of major sports—namely, Wayne Gretzky's very brief farewell tour.

The exact circumstances differed. In 1999 there was despair about the state of the Canadian game. Here, in 2005, there was complete exasperation with the National Hockey League. In 1999 it was farewell to a beloved icon whose talents were fading; in 2005 it was the debut of an until-recently-obscure teenager whose talents were blossoming. In 1999 the star was playing out the string with a team long eliminated from the playoffs; in 2005 the *vedette* was competing for a national championship and what could be the crowning achievement in the most spectacular junior hockey career in history. And the most important difference: the 1999 featured attraction could not fail; but in 2005 anything less than transcendence would be regarded as failure.

Yet there are common threads in these two most uncommon stories, foremost among them the matter of celebrity. Sure, Gretzky was taking a bow in 1999 and six years later Crosby was attempting to make a grand entrance. But just as Gretzky was on one side of a hundred mikes and bright lights in that last week of his career, so too was Crosby in London, more so than at the world juniors, more so than in Halifax the previous week. And like Gretzky had for two decades, Crosby sought out relief and refuge. Call it a bubble or a cocoon. At the end of his career, Gretzky was well practised in the art of ducking in and out of view. Crosby was surely shrewd enough to have an idea about what lay ahead for him, and he benefited from his time talking to Gretzky and Lemieux and others who had to accommodate fame. When IMG put Crosby into a media-training program at age 15, he might not have understood then why it would be so necessary to know the rules about how to speak, what to say and to whom. A couple years later, he put it all together. He knew how to lay low.

"I understand it's part of it," Crosby said at one session. "It's part of being a hockey player and I do what I have to."

He also understood that his name played above the event. He skated around a London press opinion that the tournament boiled down to a matchup between Crosby and the Knights' Corey Perry, Crosby's linemate from the world juniors in Grand Forks and the Ontario league's leading scorer and player of the year. For his part, Perry seemed uncomfortable with the comparisons, saying in interviews that, for all his silverware and for all the Knights' successes, he considered Crosby a "better player." He also said this of their former Canadian under-20 teammates, Jeff Carter and Mike Richards.

"I don't come here looking for that," he said of the Crosby vs Perry storyline. "If that's the way it's billed, it's not going to change the way I play. These teams got here not based on me, or him (Crosby), but the way the teams played. I'm here to play hockey. I take this when it comes, but I can't worry about this so much. This is a once-in-a-lifetime opportunity."

As for Crosby, it wasn't that he completely went underground, but Oceanic management wasn't about to allow the demands of publicity distract him and his teammates from the task at hand. Coach Labonté thumbed his nose at event organizers and the Canadian Hockey League brass when he bussed the Oceanic to the town of Aylmer, a half hour away, for a practice on the eve of the tournament. Rimouski had been scheduled to skate at the arena in London in front of a legion of reporters and assorted other rubberneckers. The CHL was more interested in the promotion and publicity possibilities (albeit, for a long-sold-out event) than the Oceanic's game readiness—which is to say that the officials' interests were at odds with Labonté's. So the general manager organized this stealth practice, knowing that the team would be fined for the transgression.* Though he made a show of apologizing, Labonté regarded the fine simply as the price of doing business. And without prompting he connected the dots—the switcheroo was not so much for the benefit of the team than for the protection of Crosby.

As Labonté told reporters: "The basic thing is, first, to respect all the engagements and duties we have to do as an organization, as players. But otherwise, we have to take him as much as possible away from all the attention. It's everywhere. Last night, at the restaurant, we have to sit

---

* The CHL fined Labonté $1,000 for taking the practice out to Aylmer.

in a special spot because people are coming up to him and grabbing napkins and asking him to sign them. He would sign (autographs) for everybody, because he feels like he has to be a Béliveau for the people. He feels that. He understands it incredibly for that age. He wants to give the best of him, but there are times when he needs privacy, and as a team now, our game plan coming in here was to take him out of the attention when it's possible."

One of Labonté's statements was especially telling. He said that Crosby was accompanied off the ice by "someone ... not a policeman, but (someone) who is always near him to keep him moving, because there are people who are respectful, but others who are not."

On one more count this was Gretzky redux, if not in fact then at least in lore. Back in the mid-'80s word was that an off-ice security detail was routinely assigned to Gretzky. But at this point in his career, Gretzky was already a professional, already a million-dollar player. Crosby needing some sort of bodyguard at age 17 defines just how much more difficult it is to manage stardom in 2005 than it was a quarter-century ago.

It was now harder than ever on the ice. And it was now harder than ever off it. Though Labonté was saying things about Crosby's readiness to move on to the pro ranks, QMJHL executives hadn't officially stepped back from the claim that Rimouski and the league controlled Crosby's fortunes in the event of an extended NHL lockout. Nor had they stepped back from QMJHL Commissioner Gilles Courteau's vow to take the matter to court to protect the Q's interests.

All this would have been enough to break a seasoned professional, and it seemed like nothing could have prepared a 17-year-old for such a pressure cooker. Gretzky, the veteran so accustomed to the spotlight, seemed thrown for a loop by all the attention in those farewell games. It took a lot of faith in Crosby's skill and character to believe that he could skate out of this vortex against superior competition—and thrive.

Maybe his coach in Dartmouth, Brad Crossley, or Tom Ward, the man behind Shattuck's bench, could claim to know Sidney Crosby better than Doris Labonté. Maybe even his assistant, Donald Dufresne, could claim the same. Still, Labonté's reading of Crosby was instructive. He had other great players in Vincent Lecavalier and Brad Richards. And he had a good idea about the character of players at the next level. "He was made to play hockey," Labonté said of Crosby. "Not just his legs, his skill, his vision of the play, but his mind. He was born for it. He knows the surroundings of hockey. He has known it forever. But he's not cocky, and he's not shy. He's just right, and he wants to be right for all the people."

And though QMJHL officials had made a lot of noise about taking Crosby to court if he tried to play in any league other than the Q (or the NHL) next season, Labonté sounded resigned to losing Crosby after the Memorial Cup. Labonté wasn't on message but he saw there was no use writing a sorry ending to what had been a good news story. "I'm sure (he's moving on)," Labonté said at a press session. "He has proven everything he has to prove in junior. The Memorial Cup would be the top, but it's a team trophy, not an individual achievement. All the individual trophies—he's got them. So it's time for him to go to a higher level ... for his own good."

Labonté, as always, read from a script he wrote on the fly. The official line didn't interest him.

☉

Appropriately, the Memorial Cup's opening game was its marquee matchup, Crosby and Rimouski versus the host Knights on the Saturday night of the Victoria Day weekend. Just a week earlier, the world championships in Austria wrapped up. After capacity crowds and large television audiences for Canada's victorious run at the World Cup of Hockey the previous fall, broadcasters believed that the Canadian hockey audience would invest a passion in the Worlds that was usually reserved for the Stanley Cup. It didn't play out that way. Interest seemed comparable to those years when the world championships were televised in the mornings following late-night Stanley Cup thrillers. NHLers Rick Nash and Joe Thornton, former first overall picks, raised their games in Austria, but the fits and starts, the falsely raised hopes and the crashing disappointments of the NHL's collective bargaining fiasco had pushed pro hockey's fan base beyond the limits of its patience.

No, the Memorial Cup was the real article, the best a hockey fan could get.

From the moment the Oceanic took the ice, it looked like Crosby was anxious to just get on with it. After all, it had been 10 days since the team had last seen game action. Of course, with it being the first game, the opening ceremonies were near interminable: a procession of dignitaries, an army band, introductions of every player on the rosters. (Rimouski brought along four goaltenders in all.) As the highest number on the visiting squad, No. 87 was the last player introduced, and he nervously shifted side-to-side on the blueline as the mix of cheers and boos welled up.

Crosby's start could not have been more breathtaking. Right off the opening face-off he bolted down the ice on the right wing and for a second the London defencemen looked like log-rolling lumberjacks that split second before falling into the water. Despite the thousands of words written about Crosby, despite seeing him in world junior contests, despite the videotape screenings of recent games and all the scouting reports, the Knights D-men looked thoroughly unprepared for the pace that Crosby brought to the game. He threw a backhand pass to Pouliot who whistled just wide of the London net. A collective gasp went up in the arena. Not even 10 seconds into the game and Crosby had not only created a scoring chance, he also seemed to be toying with his opponents in the process.

Marc Methot, a low-scoring defenceman for London, notched the first goal in the third minute. But then Crosby and Rimouski's five-man unit took over. Crosby tied the game at the six-minute mark on a power play goal off a London skate. Then he made a glorious pass through traffic to Pouliot for the go-ahead goal, one that Crosby's linemate roofed. And then, with about five minutes left in the period, Crosby drew a London penalty that led to a goal by Rimouski's Dany Roussin. Three-one Rimouski and Crosby had been on the ice for all three, effectively making every one. The capacity crowd included a few hundred Rimouski supporters, the remaining nine thousand in London Knights green who sat in stony silence. Their team had lost seven games all year. They were having their helmets and hearts handed to them.

It only threatened to get worse. On consecutive shifts, London took penalties. Rimouski had a five-on-three power play for a full minute to close out the period. The Greatest Junior Hockey Team Ever™ and the home crowd notwithstanding, 4–1 would have represented too deep a hole to crawl out of, 5–1 would have been game over. But the Rimouski first unit looked a little weary from all the shifts logged. They made a couple of sloppy passes back to the blueline. Then a couple of workaday saves by London's Adam Dennis. The Knights killed the penalty and skated into the dressing room taking some solace in the fact that they were down only 3–1.

Again, this was the Rimouski fast-start template. As it turned out, it was not quite fast enough.

Rimouski seemed to be in command of the game, poised to turn this marquee matchup into a rout. But over the course of the next couple of dozen shifts, the Oceanic's weaknesses would be exposed and the Knights' strengths would become apparent. And so too would this night's matchup make obvious the flaws in the game of hockey, at the junior level circa 2005, and in the NHL.

In the second period, the Knights closed to within a goal when Dan Fritsche beat Desjardins in the third minute.* Thereafter the referee, drawn from the Western Hockey League, started whistling everything in sight. Now this is not to lay blame entirely at his skates. According to those on the benches, tempers were over-heating. Both teams had reputations in their respective leagues for being a little less than Boy Scouts, but even by their standards the jawing and trash-talking was moving in a dangerous direction. The ref gamely tried to head off an ugly incident at the CHL's showcase event, but as a result, all flow was sucked out of the second period by the continuous procession of players heading to the penalty box. Rimouski had to kill off penalty after penalty. Crosby's influence on the proceedings was therefore diminished.

That said, the Knights did a better job blanketing Crosby in the few five-on-five situations they encountered. The fellow who best understood the challenge of shadowing a star player was behind the London bench, coach Dale Hunter, who, during his long NHL career, often had drawn

---

* A measure of London's depth: though not a first-liner with the Knights, Fritsche had played in 19 games with the Columbus Blue Jackets in the 2003–04 NHL season and was back in junior because of the lockout.

such assignments. Hunter wasn't necessarily considering the genetic component when he matched his son, centre Dylan Hunter, against Crosby. Nevertheless, Dylan fit the profile of the solid checker. But the best work against Crosby was done by Brandon Prust, a Calgary Flames draft choice, but perhaps no better than the 10th best prospect in the London line-up. Prust shadowed Crosby all over the ice. The plan was clear: wear him down by finishing every check; wrap him up at the end of every play; pin him or knock him down; turn this from short-track speed skating into a wrestling match.

Not surprisingly, the ref seemed prepared to let London do exactly that. Again, in fairness to the ref, this wasn't just the turn of one game, but the overall state of junior hockey these days. Even the state of hockey in all venues. More than ever, referees tolerate clutching and grabbing. Moreover, junior hockey is encouraging it and even effectively sanctioning it by adhering to a one-referee, two-linesman system. There is just too much on a referee's plate—and the players know it. The Knights could put Crosby in a figure-four leg-lock behind the play and do it with impunity, knowing the ref was following the puck. The Knights and the Oceanic also knew they could take their shots at drawing a penalty with a well-placed dive in front of the referee. Mario Scalzo Jr.'s reputation as the Alexandre Despatie of the Q caught up with him when he was whistled for a dive in the second period, but it was but one call when a dozen more were just as worthy. Most dives weren't called, but neither were a lot of penalty-worthy infractions, leaving players, Crosby in particular, vulnerable. Just at the horn to end the period, Crosby was slammed into the boards behind the London net, with a glove in the back of the helmet smearing into the glass the face that will soon be on cereal boxes and collectors' cards everywhere. When he skated off the ice, Crosby looked exasperated and disgusted. He had a few words for the ref—not that he chased him or made a show of it—just to inquire, you have to suppose, about what, short of death or bodily harm, would constitute a penalty.

One OHL coach later remarked: "It was brutal reffing from the first period on. Not to take anything away from their talent, but the Knights are just about the worst in the Ontario league for diving."

By the third period the home team had everything going its way and l'Océanic was trying to hang on to the slimmest of leads. The ref's run of calls in the previous frames had made the Rimouski players gun-shy about laying the body and stick on the Knights. That and the obvious fatigue of Rimouski's first unit made the game an inevitability. Crosby became less effective as the game wore on. The hopes for a Rimouski win stood in the crease. Cédrick Desjardins was nobody's idea of a great junior goaltender—no NHL team called his name on draft day. Yet in the most important game of his life, he stole the show from all the future NHL stars. London was blitzing Desjardins who looked a lot more composed than he had against Halifax. Corey Perry, the most persistent threat all night long, tied the game in the fifth minute of the third. It was a long way from the end of regulation, but no one doubted it would take overtime to settle the contest. And it did.

With every passing shift, through to the end of the third period and into overtime, Crosby fought harder but seemed to have a diminishing impact, generating few chances. He would show a flash of skill here and there but he left a lot of his game in the first two periods. It also seemed that the second- and third-liners who had been key contributors against Halifax in the Q final—Mark Tobin, Francis Charette and Danny Stewart, among others—just didn't have the game to compete on even terms with their counterparts on the Knights.

It was a classic game you didn't want to end, and thankfully the denouement was unlikely but not a fluke. A turn-over in the neutral zone led to a long two-on-one, Perry carrying the puck the length of the ice. The Knights' top scorer, the OHL's most valuable player, a true sniper—everyone, Cédrick Desjardins included, looked for Perry to shoot. He passed instead, snapping off a perfect dart to the least-likely player in the London line-up, Marc Methot, a four-goal scorer during the regular season. The Knights' 48th shot was the fourth to beat Desjardins and gave London a critical victory.

After the game Crosby did his best to hold it together. He emphasized that it was just one game in a tournament, that there was lots of hockey left to play. He stood crowded by dozens of members of the media, crowded more effectively in the press tent than he was for half the game against London. "They're everything that everyone said they were," he said of the

Knights. "Our goalie really helped us tonight and really kept us in the game. They had a lot of momentum coming through the second and the third and we just didn't get a lot going in those two periods."

Only when Crosby walked away with a few of his teammates did he betray any real distress. By all accounts, he has never been a phlegmatic loser, not someone who gets over his defeat easily or quickly. Neither is he a bad loser, someone who whines and points fingers. But here, Crosby looked like he had just come back from the dentist and the freezing was coming out. He was wincing when talking to Desjardins and Scalzo. It wasn't just anguish. It looked like physical pain.

Shortly thereafter, Oceanic coach Labonté took stage in the press tent beside the Knights' Dale Hunter. Labonté was a little more forthright in his assessment of the game than Crosby was. He sounded a gracious note to start, saying that his team wasn't "used to that kind of opposition." Thereafter he torqued up the rhetoric. When quizzed about the refereeing, about London getting four consecutive power plays in the pivotal second period, he ducked and dodged, saying that the Oceanic had already been fined at the tournament and he wasn't dipping any deeper into owner Monsieur Tanguay's petty cash. But then a reporter asked Labonté about what was clearly a sore point, namely the Knights going to the net and running Desjardins. London defenceman Bryan Rodney had creamed the goalie twice. Fritsche also went into the goaltender like he had been fired out of a cannon. Labonté looked ready to blow a head gasket. "When you break the law, the policeman is there to stop you," he said. "(The referees) have the authority to stop things if they think there is something to stop. If not and it's legal, we have to accept the verdict."

When I eventually peeled the coach away from the microphones (he did seem to be enjoying taking the heat off his star player), I asked him about the decision to go with his five best players as one unit. A master of the non sequitur, Labonté offered: "We have skills too. What we saw in the third I've seen too many times. We have systems. I have a system. The players have a system. It's not always the coach's system that they play. Maybe that's what makes (the first unit) tough sometimes—nobody knows what they are going to do. They create ... and have fun. It's great to have skill (in players) to coach, but does that make it easy? No."

Doris Labonté was only enhancing his instant legend status as a colourful, comical and controversial coach, but at least one NHL scout thought he had arrived in London with a solid, well-calculated plan. "Rimouski came up short but had a real chance to win the game," he said. "Doris didn't use Crosby on his first penalty-killing unit even though he's great in that role—a team has to respect what a threat he is even when it's on the power play. But Doris knows that this can be a long tournament. He played Crosby a lot but wasn't going to risk burning him out or getting him so tired that he risked getting hurt. And he's doing things that make you think that he wants to get some of the attention off Crosby—to take some of the heat or criticism himself."

The setup to the four-team Memorial Cup tournament favours the team that comes out of the round robin in first place. That team gets a bye directly into the final, while the two teams finishing next best square off in a semi-final. This year, like most other years, the semi-final was to be played less than 24 hours before the final.* Not surprisingly, in the last 10 years, only once has the winning semi-finalist managed to knock off the rested finalist. If Rimouski was going to be that team, they were going to need a lot of help. The other teams, Western league and defending Memorial Cup champion Kelowna, and Ontario league runner-up Ottawa, would have to knock off London. It started out as a far-fetched prospect—the Kelowna Rockets figured to be tough but the Ottawa 67's had finished sixth in the OHL's Eastern Conference during the regular season. It entered the realm of pure fantasy when, on the second night of the tournament, Ottawa and Kelowna staged an overtime classic of their own, a game that stretched past midnight, into a second extra period. Kelowna had applied pressure all night long, but Danny Battochio, an undersized netminder, stopped 62 shots, a tournament record. Battochio,

---

* In some years a third-place tie forces a tie-breaking game on the Friday of the tournament, the scheduled off day, thus leaving a team with the prospect of playing a round robin game, tie-breaker and semi-final in three consecutive days, only to face a rested squad in the final. The CHL is currently looking at having an off-day between its semi-final and final.

who like Cédrick Desjardins was passed over in the NHL draft, bought his team time and Brad Staubitz scored in the fifth minute of double OT to give Ottawa an improbable 3–2 victory.

Sunday night had given way to Monday morning, thrilling hockey fans but disheartening l'Océanic. Kelowna had a date with the Knights just 18 hours after the marathon loss to the 67's. Even for the defending champions, it proved too tough an order.

With two goals from Corey Perry the Knights beat Kelowna 4–2 in clinical and routine fashion. The die for the tournament was cast. Rimouski needed a couple of wins to safely advance to the semi-final, but had no little chance of coming away with the bye. That looked to be London's.

London, Ontario
May 24, 2005

Sidney Crosby was honoured and inconvenienced.

Oh, he'd never say that, not after attending the Canadian Hockey League's award luncheon and walking away with his second consecutive player-of-the-year award. But the fact was, an award luncheon is just no way to prepare for a crucial game just hours ahead. Rimouski's management hadn't been happy when the luncheon date was set. But Doris Labonté wouldn't have stood in Crosby's way had he begged off the event. Given the fall-out from the Top Prospects Game, though, Crosby just had to attend. He smiled for the cameras but didn't stick around to make an acceptance speech or take questions from the media. No matter. All the while, the Ottawa 67's were resting up and getting their heads around the task at hand, that night's game against Crosby and l'Océanic.

The luncheon was an unwanted distraction, but not enough of one to get Crosby off his game. He wasn't in his best form against the 67's but Rimouski came away with a necessary 4–3 victory, a score that was much closer than the play itself, and once again a testament to Danny Battochio's gutty goaltending. In the second period alone, Battochio stopped Crosby on three clean breakaways, including one rush where there was nothing but clear ice between Battochio and Roussin, Pouliot *and* Crosby who was carrying the puck. Rimouski led 2–1 after one period and 3–1 after two. A late Ottawa rally fell short. Like the London game, the first unit accounted for all of Rimouski's scoring—Crosby and Pouliot each scored a goal and Roussin two, including the winner in the third period.

The 67's had opted for the often-tried and usually-failed approach of physically intimidating Crosby. Will Colbert, the Ottawa captain, put stick and elbow to Crosby's grill in the third period. It wasn't enough to knock the head off the headliner, but it did get Crosby squawking at the 67's defenceman.

The shots continued after the game. Ottawa coach Brian Kilrea, an old master at head games, feigned ignorance if not innocence. "To be honest, I didn't think we hit anybody," Kilrea said. "If Crosby got hit somewhere, we must have bounced off their man. If there were players who hit, then I'll have to see the replay to see who got them."

Labonté said he didn't think that the physical play was taking anything out of Crosby's game. He suggested it was just a matter of expectations. "He could be more spectacular, but we shouldn't forget all the pressure that's been on him since the first day he was here. It's not the best that we have seen before, but under the circumstances, I think he deserves a lot of congratulations."

The Rimouski coach said that in post-season, Crosby and the team just had to roll with the punches. "If (the referees) see it and they don't think there's a penalty, I just can yell and influence them for the next shot. I'm not the one who's making the decision on that. We're used to that during the season and during the season we put a bodyguard around him, but this is not the time of the season to retaliate and get bad penalties."

All said, the game against Ottawa highlighted both the good and the bad in the state of Rimouski's game—the good was that the first unit was firing on all cylinders, the bad was that the second and third lines were having no impact comparable to, say, Game 4 of the Halifax series. Maybe it was the step-up in class or simply the pressure cooker of an event where a bad shift or two can send a team home, but Rimouski's support players were in the weeds.

London, Ontario
May 25, 2005

Wayne Gretzky had come into London for the Rimouski-Kelowna game. Like he had at the world juniors, Gretzky wasn't in attendance to mentor the prospect so much as to keep tabs on him in his two capacities as a hockey executive: as general manager of the Phoenix Coyotes who, he hoped, would have a chance to draft Crosby; and as the chief executive of the Canadian Olympic team that might prevail on Crosby to play, if not in Turin in 2006, then in Vancouver in 2010.

Rimouski needed a win over Kelowna to advance to the semi-finals of the Memorial Cup. L'Océanic managed that, though narrowly, beating the Kelowna Rockets 4–3, a result that sent the defending champions home without a win in three games. Finally, Rimouski's second and third lines checked in with Zbynek Hrdel and Francois Bolduc getting goals. For the third straight game Crosby picked up a goal and an assist, with Mario Scalzo Jr. scoring a short-handed goal to round out the totals.

Crosby was testy at times on the ice. Late in the first he slammed his stick into the glass after the ref missed a high stick that caught him in the face. The fans rained boos down on Crosby, who must have felt that the no-calls were just inviting more egregious stuff. By the end of the game, though, he seemed happier in his press session than he had at any other time throughout the week.

He expressed relief that the team had avoided a tie-breaking game, saying that a tie-break, semi and final in three days "would be pretty crazy." He acknowledged that there was a fair bit of physical stuff in Rimouski's round-robin wins over Ottawa and Kelowna, but claimed to be no worse for wear. "I feel good," he said. "Definitely the last two games were intense but it's nothing I haven't felt before."

And Crosby was also asked about his time away from the games. "We hang out around the pool at the hotel in London," he said. "It's our last few days together ... our last days of junior hockey. Lot of times we talk about things that have gone on. There are mixed feelings ... but I'm not thinking about the end (of junior hockey)."

It was the game that everyone, fans and NHL hockey executives alike, had waited for, Sidney Crosby's break-out on the national stage. In his second game against the Ottawa 67's in four days, Crosby scored a hat trick and added a couple of assists in a 7–4 pasting of the OHL runners-up. Instead of worrying about a reprise to his previous 67's round-robin rough up, Crosby left Ottawa in his wake. His was an offensive perform-ance you wouldn't see in a full season of going to any NHL arena.

Just like he did against the Knights, Crosby conjured up a scoring chance while the fans were settling into their seats, 10 seconds or so after the opening face-off. He then scored less than two minutes into the game. He then scored again. It was one of those nights when Doris Labonté sat back and worried not about his system, or his star players' system, or the absence of any system at all—for out of a chaotic run-and-gun pace, Crosby and the others on his unit made something beautiful.

With his third goal, Crosby dispelled any doubt that he was not just gifted, but blessed with something out of the ordinary. Crosby drifted a high-arcing lob from the left wing outside the blueline, a trick shot worthy of a pool hustler. The puck floated over Danny Battochio, who was about 10 feet out of his crease looking to chase down a dump. The puck caught the top corner of the net. A fluke? Maybe. Was he aiming? Few doubted it.

Battochio was pulled off the ice in the last game of his junior career, but what should not be forgotten is the fact that he kept the 67's in the game far longer than they deserved. He was arguably the best Ottawa player in the loss.

Ottawa 67's coach Brian Kilrea, the principal of hockey's old school, the leading advocate for under-talented over-achievers, hadn't bought into the Crosby-as-the-next-one hype all week long. He was, after all, the coach of the Canadian under-20 team who threatened to put Mario Lemieux on the fourth line.* But, after the second loss to l'Océanic,

---

* In 1984 when Kilrea coached the Canadian under-20 team, Lemieux declined an invitation. Canada finished 4th without Lemieux.

Kilrea's players didn't hesitate to laud Crosby. "You have to give him all the credit," said 67's forward Brad Bonello. "His line did all the scoring. There's a reason he's called the next Gretzky."

"We really put it on ourselves to step up and give the team an emotional lift," Crosby noted. And he said he wasn't rattled by the 67's rough play in the round robin. "I'm always prepared for the worst. I go in there expecting to be checked. It wasn't as much as I thought it was going to be. I'm not complaining by any means. I didn't spend a lot of energy going through that."

The players downplayed the quick turn-around to the final—l'Océanic would be playing on about 16 hours rest before they met London in the final. They claimed, rightly, that they had to do this several times on road trips during the QMJHL regular season. For his part, Labonté issued what should have been a warning to the London Knights. "(Crosby) can do more. Oh, he can do more. He has not played his best. He was very good (against Ottawa), but I have seen him better during the season and (in the final) he is going to be better. I'm not talking about points, but you're going to see all he has got in his body."

And when Labonté was asked to compare Crosby with London's own heralded prospect, he responded dismissively. "Corey Perry is 19 (20 actually) and Sidney is only 17. Freeze Corey Perry for two years and then unfreeze him and then compare. There will be no comparison."

London, Ontario
May 29, 2005

Sidney Crosby's junior career and the Rimouski season should have wound down when the clock at London's John Labatt Centre ticked down the final seconds. 0:04 0:03 0:02 0:01. But instead it was effectively all over less than three minutes into the first period of the Memorial Cup final.

It was going to take a near-perfect game from l'Océanic to beat London—from the five-man unit, a quick start, and from the rest of the team, no harm. There's no knowing if the stars were disappointed; the role players didn't give them a chance. Just a few shifts into the game, the ref, an Ontario leaguer, sent Rimouski's Jean-Sebastien Côte to the penalty box for cross-checking.* At the whistle, Rimouski's enforcer, Eric Neilson, punched Perry in the chin and the London star went down like he had been shot. He did everything but grab his chest and kick his feet. Neilson's brain-lock and Perry's piece of high-school theatre were good for a five-on-three power play. (Perry recovered sufficiently to take part in the two-man advantage.) Crosby was out for the first minute of the penalty kill and managed to keep the puck on the perimeter before clearing the zone. But seconds after Crosby skated off on the change, Dan Fritsche squeezed a puck through the pads of Cédrick Desjardins and sucked the air out of the Rimouski bench in the process.

The shot from Neilson, Perry said later, "stung for a while, but that was the play that got us going."

Through the rest of the first period, Crosby exchanged unpleasantries with Marc Methot, the defenceman who was the unlikely offensive star of Game 1. Methot roughed up Crosby when play was stopped. In turn, Crosby tried to provoke him into drawing a penalty—in one instance Crosby whacked the pads of London goaltender Adam Dennis when play was whistled down, setting off a mini-melee. It ended up just being an exercise in frustration for l'Océanic overall, and for Rimouski's star in particular.

London defenceman Bryan Rodney made the score 2–0 before the first intermission and the Knights just remorselessly pulled away. L'Océanic had no gas in the tank. It was 3–0 in the third, more than enough for the best team in junior hockey this year, and the best junior team in a long time.

During the third period I went up into a section in the upper bowl that had been assigned to Rimouski fans. I sat with Michel Roussin, Dany's father. As Rimouski played out the string and London went for what was a 20-minute victory lap—adding one goal—I asked père Roussin what Crosby had meant to the franchise.

* Although the CHL brings in on-ice officials from all three leagues for the Memorial Cup, it hands the jobs for the final to those who have received the highest grades from the officiating supervisor. Thus can a team play in a national championship game with a ref who had worked its games all year long.

"It was a very hard season for Dany (in 2002–03)," his father said. "He never had played on a team that lost so much. It was hard being away from home. All we heard was that Sidney was coming. I wanted to believe that one player could make that much of a difference—the truth is, I didn't. No one player can help a team that wins 11 games all winter. But Dany told me after skating with him, he can. I still didn't believe it. But when I saw him play the first time, I knew that it could be all different for this team. They will lose today, I know. But they played with a real joy. They had fun on the ice and you never see that. And they brought joy to a lot of people in Rimouski and all over the place."

I caught up with one of the fans I had met at a morning practice in Rimouski the year before, Pierre Blier. He and his wife had driven down for the week and were sticking the game out to the end, long after the outcome was decided.

"We made the trip because it's the last time for this team together. The team is like a family to the town of Rimouski and this is like that time when one of your sons moves away from home—when he goes off to college or to the city for a job. It's sad that they won't be together, because Sidney will move on, because the 19-year-olds will move on and some other players will go in the (junior) expansion draft. It was an amazing time but it's junior hockey. It's not supposed to last forever. We hope one day that there will be another team like this one and another player like Sidney. But we know that we've been very lucky to have Sidney a short time. A lot of teams go 10 or 20 years without a chance like that—and for a young (franchise) to already have had three players like Sidney, Lecavalier, and Richards, you can hope for that but not expect it."

Against a backdrop of cheers for the Knights and drunken locals heckling the Rimouski fans, Blier tried to put Crosby's time in Rimouski into a larger perspective. "Sidney was always respected and he was respected because he showed respect," he said. "He made an effort to learn the language. He did incredibly well. And the people in the press challenged him with questions and made him work hard—and in a way that's a way of showing their respect, not (patronizing) him. I don't know if he changed anything politically for anyone. There are people who believe in an independent Quebec and they can still like and respect

GARE JOYCE

222

Sidney as a player and as a person. (Sidney) is away from politics. Maybe he shows some people that there's decency and respect in many places, not just in our town—but I think that most people already knew that."

The game was 4–0 in the end. Desjardins was pulled in favour of the over-ager Filiatrault, who hadn't played in weeks. The waving of the white flag.

Labonté had complaints about the refereeing during the tournament but he chose the high road after the final. "They were the best team," acknowledged the Rimouski coach. "We were trying to beat them, but it was kind of a mission impossible. Their machine was almost perfect. They didn't have any injuries, they didn't make any mistakes and they were doing everything well so that really becomes a mission impossible."

It was a motion seconded by the Rimouski players. "They played better than we did," said Marc-Antoine Pouliot. "They were in our face all night. That's the best team we've played this year."

Crosby was slow to emerge from the dressing room. When he did, he was surrounded by a throng of reporters. "The bottom line is we played a better hockey team," said Crosby. Then the questions were fired at him from all directions. What about Europe? What about the AHL? Did he think there was a chance at a settlement? Each question represented a chance to misstep once again, like he had in Grand Forks. He now handled each with his standard response—he hadn't thought about it or discussed it with his family because he didn't want to be distracted during the season. The time would come, now that l'Océanic's season was over—now that his time in Rimouski had drawn to a close.

I asked Pat Brisson, who was standing by watching Crosby field questions, if this was really true. No one could not give *any* thought to all this, could he? "I'm telling you, it's true," Brisson said. "That's how he wanted it."

He wouldn't be staying at his billets' home anymore. He would never play at le Colisée in Rimouski again. If he went back, it would be just to visit, maybe to see his No. 87 retired.

Until then there was one last thing left for Rimouski's management. Team president Andre Jolicoeur stood outside the dressing room, watching Crosby take questions and accepting handshakes from executives of other major junior clubs. Early in the week, following the Memorial Cup, Rimouski was going to have to submit its list of protected players for the QMJHL's expansion draft. On that list would be the name of Sidney Crosby. It was effectively a waste of a slot on that list—and Rimouski could use every slot it had because the roster would be decimated by players like Pouliot and Roussin who were going to be moving on, and Mario Scalzo Jr. who had used up his eligibility. It was a gesture, akin to lighting a candle and putting it in the window of the dressing room. Jolicoeur explained why he felt the team had to do it—in a cold-hearted business that chews up and spits out coaches, that trades high-schoolers hundreds of miles away in the middle of a season, Jolicoeur put it down to sentiment.

"We'll protect Sidney in the expansion draft because nobody knows what the future brings," he said. "We hope that he'll be playing in the NHL. He has done everything that he can do (in junior). We don't expect him back. We will retire his number I'm sure one day. But so long as there is a chance that he'll play junior—even one in a thousand—we have to know that he'll play junior for Rimouski. It wouldn't be right any other way. It will be very tough for our team next year. Teams have to protect 16-year-olds in this draft unlike other (expansion) drafts. And we have to protect players who haven't signed contracts with NHL teams. This was the last game for this team as you see it, but not for the franchise. If he had to come back to junior, it would not be the best thing for him. But if he had to—for whatever reason, I don't know—then going somewhere else to play, to an expansion team even, would be a much worse thing for him than coming back to Rimouski. We owe this to him for all he has done for us."

Toronto, Ontario
June 2005

Pessimism about the NHL's prospects for the coming season seemed to lift the week after the Memorial Cup. Meetings between the league and the Players' Association came more frequently, sessions lasted longer and statements to the press were less gloomy. If you had put your ear to the broken telephone—what someone heard from a team player rep, what someone else overheard from a well-placed league executive—the 2005–06 NHL season was there to be saved and the announcement was imminent. Just a few details remained. Among those details, though, was the order of selection for the draft. If the word over the broken telephone was to be believed, then the league was looking at a lottery that granted every team at least one ping-pong ball in the bingo tumbler. Sure, the draft would be weighted in favour of teams that had finished out of the playoffs over the previous four or five seasons; and the formula for calculating a team's chances of landing the top pick would be a matter best trusted to an MIT grad. But when the NHL's general managers and scouts gathered at a hotel out at the Toronto airport for the league's draft combine, everybody had an interest in Sidney Crosby. It was more than a rooting interest for the good of a league in need of healing. Everybody thought that his team had a real chance at coming away with Crosby.

The combine is the oddest event—or non-event—in the NHL. One hundred or so draft-eligible prospects from around the world first undergo basic physicals and measurements. Then they submit to strength tests, everything from the basic push-up and sit-up calisthenics, to vertical and standing broad jumps, and ultimately to VO2 tests on stationary bikes. (The VO2 is a rigorous physical test to calculate the amount of oxygen consumed during exercise, but the prospects likely conclude that VO2 stands for Vomit Twice.) And finally there are interviews with clubs, private audiences that take place in suites reserved by the teams and in the absence of agents, family members and anyone else who might try to filter the messages. And so, over the course of days, you see players in shorts and t-shirts and running shoes being put through their exertions while a bunch of league executives and scouts eyeball them like so many hungry hobos staring at the blue-plate special through the window of a restaurant.

It was something of a surprise when Crosby put out word that he would attend the combine. He was going to give the lower-body testing a pass because of injuries that carried over from a long season—which was tantamount to Michael Jordan passing up vertical-jump tests at the Dream Team's training camp. Never has anybody arrived at the combine with so little to prove. It was like having Dale Earnhardt Jr. renew his driver's licence before the Daytona 500.

The battery of physical tests isn't really an indicator of whether a player can play. In fact, there are all kinds of stories about teenage prospects who were barely able to budge the minimum bench press of 150 pounds and then went on to be major NHL players. What the physical tests do tell the teams is a little about a player's history or character. If he has achieved a level of elite play despite minimal time spent in the gym, then it's a little easier to project growth in his game. But there are a lot of athletes who'd score high marks in these tests but can't skate and would never be able to play no matter how much coaching they received. If Crosby couldn't do a push-up or last 30 seconds on the stationary bike, it wasn't going to matter. He had already demonstrated what he could do on the ice. Every scout in the room had seen him logging 30-plus minutes a game, finishing the last shift as hard as he began the first.

And then there's the combine interview. I had joked with Pat Brisson in Halifax that the combine was going to be "a good opportunity for Sidney to interview teams." With his dedication to working out, his strivings toward personal improvement, and his reputation as a decent and mature young man, Crosby was the stuff coaches, general managers and scouts dream of. And they knew it. The consensus was that Crosby was above reproach and beyond comparison.

No hockey man could have held it against Crosby if he gave the combine, and especially the physical testing, a pass. Not after the months of hard work and physical pounding. Everyone was prepared to give him a bye.

The combine is an annual weird scene, but never had it been this weird. When Crosby's appointed time came—1:30 p.m. on Saturday, the second day of testing—it seemed like every scout and general manager in the league was in attendance. The phenom's arrival at the combine set off a commotion not seen since Elvis Presley reported for military duty. And while the scouts and general managers usually feign indifference about the proceedings, all the hockey men were straining, up on their tip-toes, watching Crosby walk in. Just their numbers would have constituted a fire-code violation. But it was altogether even more of a mob scene because another 30 or 40 prospects packed the room. At least half of them were Europeans who wanted to get their first look at the boy wonder. A bunch of Russian players—in finger-thick gold chains, high-tops and baggy shorts, straight out of *Slam* magazine and looking for the world like the kid in the "Pretty Fly for A White Guy" video—blocked Crosby's route to the sign-in area. They stepped back. Some tried to look unimpressed. Others looked on with gaping mouths.

The first part of the testing was the most closely watched part of Crosby's combine experience. Coincidentally, the technology quotient here was the lowest—a simple measurement of Crosby's height and weight. Hockey's greatest lie is told in every program: six feet. There isn't a player who is actually six feet tall as advertised. Rather, it's the number, the slot where players who are five-foot-eleven or five-ten-and-a-half congregate. (Any self-respecting six-footer will claim to be six-foot-one or six-foot-one-and-a-half on his hockey card.) Crosby's listed height this season—five-foot-eleven—always seemed a trifle generous. And it proved to be just that. Crosby stood with his back to a height chart on the wall, with its numbers plain to everyone standing within 20 feet. There was no danger of him obscuring the five-eleven mark. No, he was five-foot-ten. The number listed in the official Central Scouting results was 5'10.3", which was exactly the same as Gilbert Brule, the Western Hockey League's rival talent and the No. 4 ranked North American prospect according to NHL Central Scouting.

And what of it? Will it be something that limits Crosby at the next level? There wasn't anybody in that room that thought along these lines—or at least who'd admit to it. No, there was something reassuring in the fact that this exceptional talent should stand no higher than the everyman. Crosby wasn't Eric Lindros, who won battles on the ice by virtue of just being bigger than everybody else. Lindros's career was a hockey reworking of Wilt Chamberlain's old line: nobody cheers for Golaith. At his best, Lindros was effective but unloved. He captured trophies but never anybody's imagination. Maybe Crosby's lack of height might play against him when he tries to cycle the puck against Ottawa's Brobdingnagian blueliner Zdeno Chara—or maybe not. But one thing is for sure: no one will ever root against him because he possesses brute physical advantages. He can be the opponent, but not the villain.

In the testing that Crosby did undertake, he proved to be average among the crowd of prospects at the draft. His teammate from the under-18s two years earlier, Mike Blunden of Erie, posted big numbers in the upper-body strength tests: 134 pounds and 139 pounds in the right-hand and left-hand grip-strength tests, 13 reps in the 150-pound bench press and a combine-best 58 reps in ab-crunching curl-ups. Dan Bertram, a forward from Boston College, was even more impressive: 40 push-ups in his timed set, 140/136 pounds in the right-hand/left-hand grip strength, 14 reps on the bench. For his part, Crosby was five pounds less than average in right-hand grip strength at 123, and right on the average mark for the left hand with 125. He managed six reps on the bench, two less than the forwards' average, and 23 push-ups, three less than the average. Gilbert Brule of the WHL was a rep or a couple of pounds ahead of him at most of the testing stations. Crosby did stand out in one aspect, but there wouldn't have been one scout in the room who could have seen it coming. Among forwards at the combine, he posted the highest mark in a test labelled "sit and reach," a test of flexibility through the trunk of the body. His reach was 54 centimetres—the average was 38 and only one other forward reached beyond 43 centimetres. Fact is, Crosby's number for sit and reach would have stood him in good stead among the combine's goaltenders, a bunch of stringy, muscle-bereft kids who looked like they were bound for a Yoga for Teens class.

Said one scout: "I was surprised that he was as cut as he is in the upper-body. Not big or bulky, but he seems pretty well put together. Everybody knows he has the lower-body strength. You can see that when he's on the ice or even when he's walking around in his sweats—big thighs, big glutes. But he has upper-body strength as well and as he gets older he'll fill out and be able to pack muscle on better."

As far as the interview portion of the combine went, Tim Murray, a scout with the Mighty Ducks of Anaheim, was effusive in his praise. "We tried to wind him up in our interview, just to see if we could unnerve him. He was supposed to come see us yesterday but (the appointment) was listed as today (Saturday) on his schedule. It wasn't his mistake but he still apologized. But I needled him a bit. He handled everything just right—he knew when we were kidding and he knew when we were serious. He was exactly what we expected. He said all the right things. He knows the drill. The one thing that I came away with, though, was that he takes losing hard. He's still upset about the Memorial—still thinks he should have been better and that Rimouski should have won."

Another scout for an Eastern Conference club continued the theme. "You could see his mood change when we went there (discussing the Memorial Cup). It was nothing we had to push him on. You know, he's all sunshine 99 percent of the time but that other 1 percent is important—there's no danger that he'll become complacent. A lot of things might happen that might get in the way of him being a great player, but the idea that he'd ever become satisfied or that he'd accept losing is a non-starter. He has the perfect make-up. I look at Benoit Pouliot (the Sudbury Wolves forward ranked No. 2 behind Crosby by the NHL's Central Scouting Bureau) and think, 'This guy can be as good a player as he wants to be,' which says a lot about his skills and the questions about his character. I look at Crosby, though, and it's another thing entirely. I think, 'He's going to get everything he can out of himself and try to make everyone around him better.' That's not the difference between No. 1 and No. 2 in the draft. That's the difference between No. 1 and everybody else here and 99 percent of players in the league."

Tim Murray's Ducks figured to have a good shot at drafting Crosby—but for one appearance in the final two springs ago, Anaheim was a fixture in the bottom third of the league. When I asked Murray what getting Crosby would mean to his club, he stuck to the first person off the hop. "Look, my contract is up in weeks," he said. "If we get Crosby I can sit back and for 10 years look like a genius to my bosses. But seriously, we're a club that has questions about ownership and right now we don't have a general manager. The whole franchise would change overnight."*

It might have seemed like hyperbole. Murray was hinting that the most valuable player in hockey was a 17-year-old who had yet to play an NHL game. At the very least it seemed like irrational exuberance. But the

---

* A few weeks later Murray was hired by the New York Rangers.

more I thought about it on the drive home from the combine, the more it seemed to echo what Tim Burke had told me en route to Breclav—that this teenager was going to be so good, not just for a team, but for the entire league. His scouting report and Murray's turned out to be prescient.

And, what's more, Sidney Crosby had understood all these things to be true. In his best moments he had been just a modest teenager who'd be a fit escort to the prom for your daughter. In the face of brutal and unfair criticism, he never allowed himself to be dragged into a fight. He had always been able to anticipate play a split second ahead of everyone on the ice. And he seemed to have anticipated his place in the game too. "Perfect pass. Perfect play," read Daniel Doré's scouting report. "I just make the most of whatever situation it is," Crosby himself said. He would have his perfect draft. He would make the best of his opportunities on *The Tonight Show* or in the pages of *Vanity Fair*. But was he more talented than Gretzky or Lemieux? That was a point open for debate. But there is no debating the fact that, of the geniuses of hockey, he was and likely will forever be the one most self-possessed, the one best emotionally equipped to turn genius into stardom.

"Hopefully if I have a chance ... "

Ottawa, Ontario

July 30, 2005

The morning of the 2005 NHL entry draft, Sidney Crosby and Jack Johnson went for a workout in the gym at the Westin Hotel. Johnson had been out to Cole Harbour to practice and hang out with Crosby for the week prior to the draft, and here, in Ottawa, they were rooming together for the weekend. A lot of the draft forecasts indicated that the two friends from Shattuck-St. Mary's would be the first two players selected at the 2005 NHL entry draft, by Pittsburgh and Anaheim respectively. By the time they made their way to the restaurant in the hotel and joined Crosby's family and agent, Pat Brisson, it was clear they weren't going 1-2. No, to get to their table—tucked off to the side, away from the view of most of the patrons—the two teenagers had to walk past a table where Anaheim general manager Brian Burke was breaking bread with Bobby Ryan and his family. Ryan, a big winger from New Jersey, had torn up the Ontario Hockey League with the Owen Sound Attack. It was clear that

Burke's mind was made up—and that Johnson would fall to the No. 3 slot, owned by the Carolina Hurricanes.

From their table, Crosby and Johnson could see, but not quite hear, dozens of fans who had assembled, behind a fence in front of the hotel, a full three hours before the draft was scheduled to begin. By the time the players made it to breakfast, security guards at the Westin had chased off autograph seekers and other rubberneckers. Though the NHL was in desperate need of some good publicity in the wake of the season-long lockout, the outreach to fans wasn't about to begin at the draft.

Only reluctantly had the NHL agreed to broadcast the lottery that determined the order of team draft selections. And though the "host" Ottawa Senators lobbied to have the draft at their home arena, the Corel Centre (as originally planned), the league opted for a much smaller setting: a hotel conference room. Other years the draft selections were made in front of thousands of fans, hundreds of players and their families. It made for an electric atmosphere and high drama, not to mention a lot of tears when players' stock dipped and they went unselected. There was going to be nothing like that this year. The Westin was in a virtual lockdown. It wasn't just that the fans were barred at the door. By the time executives, general managers and scouts started to file into the conference room, a league official went to the stage and advised them over the PA system that "security would remove" any personnel above the specified number allowed on the floor.

From breakfast on, agents, players and executives milled around the lobby of the Westin, which was practically humming with rumours of trades and imminent signings. The NHL was back in business, but its team executives were guarded, almost skittish. They had but a few days not only to digest a 600-page collective agreement, the most complicated in sports, but also to implement it. The first order of business: the general managers had a brief window to buy out veteran stars whose contracts just didn't fit in with the new team payroll cap. Next on the list: the general managers also had to move quickly to sign juniors from the 2003 draft before they became eligible to re-enter the draft in Ottawa. Almost every significant re-entry-eligible junior was locked by the deadline of five p.m. on the 28th. The most prominent player not to get signed turned out to be Crosby's linemate, Dany Roussin, who was prepared to accept an offer right on the deadline but for a problem with a fax machine. Looming after the draft: the signing period for free agents was set to open—big names such as Peter Forsberg and Scott Niedermayer were at large, but teams had to figure how to fit the deals under the cap. The market would be adjusting and new values were being set minute by minute during the week. Factor in the draft itself and there was a year's worth of business to catch up on—and it had to be handled over the course of days. It was like the NHL was handed a Rubik's Cube for the first time and immediately put on the clock.

In all this there was only one certainty: the Penguins taking Crosby with the first pick in the draft. Ken Sawyer made that clear in New York when Pittsburgh won the lottery. He then laughed when asked if the team was going to listen to offers for the pick. If he had said yes, he would have been gang-tackled by general managers. Any team would have taken Crosby and none would have listened to trade offers.

At the stroke of noon the lights went up and the voices of the broadcast team working the event carried to the back reaches of the conference room. The recognizable components of the draft seemed to be in place: the big board listing the draft order of teams, the commissioner in his power suit and even a mayor equipped with a speech rife with lame jokes. But the draft as an event fell as flat as the mayor's welcoming monologue. There was little doubt about the league's reasoning for having the draft on such a small stage. It wasn't a matter of optics so much as *sonics*—the league couldn't bear the thought of the commissioner getting booed in an arena full of hockey fans. Maybe the commissioner expected to be applauded by those at the team tables here in the conference room, but it was strictly one hand clapping when he walked up to the podium. His words were clearly heard without a filter on the broadcast to Canadian fans, but it was strictly what you'd expect— good to have the great game back, doing it for the fans and all the rest. Only when Bettman announced that Pittsburgh was on the clock with the first pick, and called for general manager Craig Patrick, did you get a sense that something historic was about to take place.

"On behalf of Mario Lemieux and the entire ownership group, the

Pittsburgh Penguins select, from Rimouski of the Quebec junior league, Sidney Crosby," Patrick said.

Crosby stood up in the green room where the other players waited. Unlike Mario Lemieux, he was going to walk up on stage and put on the Pittsburgh sweater. There had been no strain in his contract talks with the Penguins. In fact, a documentary crew had followed Crosby going out to dinner with his future linemate, landlord and owner.

Ever since Commissioner Bettman announced that Pittsburgh had won the lottery, the Penguins had been counting down to this moment. Yet, in the interim, the franchise's fortunes had already started to turn around.

All of Craig Patrick's peers on the floor of the conference room knew about moves that he had made and moves that were imminent. During the week, Patrick had locked up the Penguins' unsigned 2003 draftees, including Stephen Dixon, Crosby's fellow Nova Scotian, fellow Quebec league all-star and fellow member of the 2005 world junior champions. Patrick was able to sign his draftees, mostly for a fraction of what had been the standard seasons before. That was the new market talking, to be sure, but all the players had visions of playing beside Sidney Crosby and Mario Lemieux. In past seasons, Patrick had lacked the wherewithal to sign high-profile free agents. He had been compelled to trade away top veteran players such as Alexei Kovalev and Martin Straka because the franchise could no longer afford them. Now, though, the new economics of the National Hockey League was giving the Penguins a fighting chance in a league that had long given little hope to teams in small markets. Pittsburgh would soon be a desired destination for free agents. And a surge in revenue was giving Patrick the ability to give chase to those free agents.*

At 29 tables on the floor of the conference room you could have found team executives concerned about winning back their fan bases.

---

* The biggest names to sign as free agents with Pittsburgh in August were: all-star defenceman Sergei Gonchar, formerly of Boston and Washington; forward Ziggy Palffy, late of Los Angeles; and John LeClair, a former 50-goal power forward in his heyday with Philadelphia. Prior to the lockout, the Penguins had signed winger Mark Recchi, a veteran who had played on Pittsburgh's Stanley Cup winners back in 1991 and 1992.

Not at the Penguins table. Within minutes of the announcement that Pittsburgh had won the 2005 draft lottery and secured the right to draft Crosby, phones in the Penguins' season-ticket sales office were ringing off the hook. Within an hour callers trying to snap up season tickets had to wait 40 minutes or more to talk to a salesperson. Within a day there were reports of season-ticket purchases by fans hundreds of miles away—and in one case, from Australia. By Sawyers' reckoning the regular season was going to be sold out before September.

It's hard to estimate how dark the picture would have been without Crosby—the Penguins had finished last in league attendance in 2003—04, drawing 11,877 fans per game on average, about 5,000 below the league average. In their best seasons, the team had drawn just under 17,000 to the Igloo. That the team had a chance to set new marks had everything to do with the bounce that Crosby was giving them.

So too did the expression on Lemieux's face. The staff could have turned out the lights in the conference room and lit the scene with his broad smile. Sure, there were other factors, among them his apparent return to health and the rule changes designed to eliminate clutching and grabbing. Only weeks before he had been negotiating a sale of his controlling interest in the franchise to his friend, San Jose—based businessman William (Boots) Del Biaggio. And a relocation of the franchise under Del Biaggio's ownership seemed either a likelihood or certainty. Now Lemieux was re-examining his options—he was prepared to sell a piece to Del Biaggio but he wanted to hold on to control of the club. His franchise was worth a heck of a lot more with its recent surge in popularity and, yes, with Crosby. He was now talking about the possibilities of his team, its chance to win right away, maybe even come away with a Stanley Cup that would cap his career and serve as his legacy. The unspoken subtext was that this team now had a chance to be a money-maker for its owner well past his playing days.

There was applause. Not an ovation, like there would have been in an arena of hockey fans. There was a round of hugs from his father, mother, sister and grandmother. Not in the stands, in view of thousands, but in front of a cameraman set up backstage in the players' green room. It felt less like an event in a young man's life than a reality-TV show. And it felt even more like reality TV when, just seconds after he donned his Penguins sweater and posed for photographs on stage with Lemieux and Patrick, Crosby was waved over to a TSN camera for an interview. Then and at a press conference later, he spoke of "sacrifices"—not his own but his family's, his parents'. It was a great message for the occasion. He struck just the right note. No braggadocio, just thanks. No talk about what the team or the city of Pittsburgh owed him, just what he owed the people who helped him get to this point. Crosby was being hailed as the player who could save the franchise in Pittsburgh—check that, as the player *who was already saving* the franchise in Pittsburgh, even though his first NHL game was a little more than two months off.

League officials led Crosby from the draft floor to a smaller confer- ence room where a podium and microphone were set up. Twenty-four television cameras were trained on Crosby when he entered. His media training served him well. He spoke again of the sacrifices his family made—"the early morning" practices that his parents took him to and "the extra job," the delivering of flyers door to door, that helped pay for equipment.

There had been word circulating that he had plans to take his family on a vacation to the Dominican Republic, but when asked about his immediate plans, he mentioned only hockey. He said he was going to train in L.A. and then he was going to Whistler for the Canadian junior team's summer camp (even though it would be unlikely that Pittsburgh would make him available for the world under-20s in the middle of the NHL season). No, he had no plans for a holiday from the game. In fact, he made it seem that his holiday was somewhere *within* the game.

One reporter asked him about being touted as not just the best young player coming into the league, but rather the player "the NHL needs." He was also asked about what kind of player he would like to be, on and off the ice? The answer was as close to a mission statement as you could get from Sidney Crosby on the cusp of much bigger things.

"On the ice, I think I'd want to be someone who makes things happen offensively—definitely have to be a well-rounded player to play in the NHL today. That's something I've got to make sure I am.

"Off the ice, just, you know, someone who is respected. Obviously I'm going to be young, I'm going to be a rookie. I'm going to try to learn as much as I can and just be someone who is open-minded and be a student."

When he spoke of playing in Pittsburgh, it was a conditional thing: "Hopefully if I have a chance ... "

It was, to his mind anyway, no sure thing: "I look at it as a challenge ... "

He said all the right things. And yet there was an apprehension in his bearing. Almost certainly it had nothing to do with hockey and everything to do with everything else—not the player he wanted to be on the ice, but the person away from the game.

This was a young man who not even two years before had told me that he was disappointed he had to give up playing baseball with his friends. That his Little League team had a chance to be a dynasty. Now he was the image of the team that was squeezing a storied Major League Baseball franchise into the back pages of the Pittsburgh sports sections.

This was a young man who not even two years before had told me that he liked the idea of kids in the neighbourhood asking for him when they went out trick-or-treating on Halloween. That they'd even knock on the door to see if Sidney could come out and play. Now others were knocking on his door, those who wanted to use his name and image to sell their products.

This was a young man who for the last two years had taken delight in sneaking out to neighbourhood rinks in Rimouski to play shinny with teammates and some of the local kids. Who still liked to take shots on a net in his basement. Who still liked to hang out with his lifelong friends and skate with old teammates from Cole Harbour and the Dartmouth Subways. It was hard to imagine that he could ever do these things quite so easily and freely again, as much as he might want to.

And in eight days, on August 7, 2005, he was going to turn 18.